THE
AUTOBIOGRAPHY
OF A MAVERICK
CHRISTIAN

DAVION MAURICE WOODMAN, SR.

ISBN 978-1-0980-6529-4 (paperback)
ISBN 978-1-0980-6530-0 (digital)

Christian Faith Publishing, Inc.
832 Park Avenue
Meadville, PA 16335
www.christianfaithpublishing.com

Printed in the United States of America

Forsake All I Take Him

I can do all things through Christ who strength-
ens me.

—Philippians 4:13 NKJV

CONTENTS

INTRODUCTION

The essence of myself is that I am a maverick (a maverick is an unorthodox or independent-minded person) and I've been one most of my human life. Though recently, and appropriately, I've come to the realization I am a maverick Christian as well; that is to say, I had an epiphany moment of faith which significantly changed my religious life. For I now live as a maverick Christian which doesn't come from my Roman Catholic heritage nor by virtue of choice; however, it is incidentally attributed to my ever-increasing faith in *Jesus Christ* alone. As I have at all times believed in *God's* awesome *Word* and all that *he* has taught because he has said it, and his Word is absolutely true. In addition, just as with my fellow Christian, friend, or adversary throughout this humanistic and materialistic world, I too have suffered all types of persecutions and I'm still going through tough times, difficult circumstances, harsh life experiences, and life's bitter disappointments.

For these reasons and more, I am a maverick Christian needing to become fully equipped by the power of the *Holy Spirit*, who resides in my heart to help me overcome the pressures and trials of this present life, thus putting "on the whole armor of God" that I "may be able to stand against the wiles of the devil" (Ephesians 6:11 NKJV), and become more and more *Christlike*; "Let this mind be in you which was also in Christ Jesus" (Philippians 2:5 NKJV). I believe in *Jesus's* love for me, hoping in *his* promise of eternal life, and I ask *him* for *his* mercy and strength daily. And each day that I grow in trust and belief in *his* love for me, I believe I am blessed because "Blessed is the man who trusts in the LORD and whose hope is the LORD." (Jeremiah 17:7 NKJV). My good intention is to focus and refocus, as I need to do, on the Spirit World of the one and only *God* our *holy heavenly Father*, and my aim is to achieve perfect humility, unconditional love, and willing service to *him*. I also implore each day that I may ever love the sacred heart of *Jesus* more and more. And I aspire to value the virtues valued by *him*; in this way, *he* can make my heart like *his* heart which is meek and humble.

Simply put, my epiphany moment of faith is likened to *faith* in the acrostic:

FAITH = Forsake All I Take Him (Him is the Lord Jesus Christ)

A Prayer of Self-Dedication

Lord Jesus Christ,
take all my freedom,
my memory, my understanding, and my will.
All that I have and cherish
You have given me.
I surrender it all to be guided by Your will.
Your grace and your love
are wealth enough for me.
Give me these, Lord Jesus,
and I ask for nothing more.

Whole Heart

I was once captive by the enemy
He had me thinking I was out of reach
O Jesus, mercy shut his mouth.
I once was crippled by the weight of shame
Embarrassed, I couldn't even show my face
O Jesus, then I heard You speak.
Your love it comes with no conditions
You give us Your whole heart
My hope is in the blood of Jesus
I know who I am
Because of who You are.
I hear you calling me beyond my sin
You tell me that grace has taken care of it
O Jesus, You're my victory
O Jesus, You're my victory.
Your love it comes with no conditions
You give us Your whole heart
My hope is in the blood of Jesus
I know who I am
Because of who You are.
I serve a King with good intentions
God, You will never
Turn Your back on me
How could a wretch become Your treasure?
The love of God
Has changed my destiny.
Your love it comes with no conditions
You give us your whole heart

My hope is in the blood of Jesus
I know who I am
Because of who you are.
Your love it comes with no conditions
You give us your whole heart
My hope is in the blood of Jesus
I know who I am
Because of who you are.
—"Whole Heart" by Passion in
Popular Christian Song

ABOUT MAVERICK CHRISTIANS

We fellowship amongst local bodies of believers and are not bound by legalism, man-made rules, nor denominationalism. Sometimes we gather in homes or other places. We maintain the right, as believers in Jesus, to freely understand the Holy Bible for ourselves. Maverick Christians are not a denomination. We are an unbranded movement of believers in Jesus Christ led by the Holy Bible as God's Word and led by the Holy Spirit. We follow the Lord not bound by creed and have the tendency to resist the controls of religious institutions.

You may have noticed us already. Some of us visit often to your local church and view us as church mavericks. Some of us regularly attend your local fellowship and have a seemingly unique understanding regarding what is considered the norm. There are those of us who do not feel bound to worship together on particular days. It might not be easy for us to feel settled or at home in many churches. Nonetheless, we are all maverick Christians and have learned to recognize each other in our love and zeal for God wherever we go. As Christians, we have various levels of commitment to Christ and with other believers as we grow in the faith, grace, and knowledge of our Lord. Those who lead among us do so by their example, not by lordship as the Bible shows ought to be.

Historically, we have not been well-understood, not been well-spoken of, and even persecuted throughout the ages. We have been known as counter-culturists, reformers, even movement starters, having an understanding different from the mainstream and challenging what is esteemed as to be taken for granted. Some of us have some simple expectations in what we seek for church fellowship, which we might not easily find. Perhaps we feel that we are not getting spiritually fed well in some churches.

Other churches might exhibit more of the presence of God noticeably. It may be that we have bloomed where we were planted to only find ourselves needing a bigger pot. We know we will not find the perfect church, so a combination of various fellowships may seem to work better. Still yet, some of us are members in churches (I myself am a member in the Catholic Church and a frequent visitor or guest in other Christian non-denominational churches) and are quite active in recognized positions but still possessing a certain maverick mentality which has us at variance in some ways from what is regularly done in church denominations we are members of.

Despite what you may think of us, since we have placed our faith solely in God's Son Jesus Christ for our salvation and abide by the basic tenets of Christian faith, we are Christians and part of the universal body of Christ. We are not maverick heretics, although some may wish to brand us as that. However, we are not branded;

we are free maverick Christians. We think freely as individuals in the mind of Christ. Mavericks are not loners but come together in herds. We gather in homes, church buildings, or other locations when and where we do as we follow our great Shepherd, the Lord Jesus Christ.

—MaverickChristians.com

"Pray to God right now and ask Jesus to be your Savior!"

1

MY ANCESTRY AND FAMILY HISTORY

Honor your father and your mother, so that you
may live long in the land the LORD your God is
giving you. (Exodus 20:12)

My ancestry and family history began with my father's side of our family: the patriarch and my great-grandfather, William Baron Woodman, an African American whom I never knew, fathered my grandfather, William Baron Woodman II (my grandfather's brothers were Coney Woodman, Britt Woodman, and George Woodman); my grandfather, William Baron Woodman II (his wife was Jean Woodman, my grandmother) fathered my father, William Baron Woodman III, whose nickname is "Billy" (his sister was Beverly Woodman, my aunt), husband of my mother, Marlene Delores Landry, of whom I was born Davion Maurice Woodman. All of the generations from my great-grandfather, William Baron Woodman, until my birth were four generations.

Most significantly, my ancestry and family history also began with my mother's side of our family, the influence of three strong-willed women in my life. It is these three beautiful women whose love and spirits still guide me as their word said to me became my guiding source: the matriarch and my great-grandmother, Mary Alice Guillebeau, an African American (her husband was my great-grandfather, Paul Carrington, an Irish American whom I never knew) gave birth to my grandmother, Maurice Danice (her husband was my grandfather, Robert Landry, a Creole) who gave birth to my mother, Marlene Delores Landry (her brother was Vernon Landry, my uncle), wife of my father, William Baron Woodman III of whom I was born Davion Maurice Woodman. All of the generations from my great-grandmother, Mary Alice Guillebeau, until my birth were also four generations.

Early Origins of the Woodman family (www.houseofnames. come/woodman-family-crest)

The surname Woodman, which comes from my father's lineage (William Woodman, his grandfather), was first found in Yorkshire (abbreviated Yorks, formally known as the County of York; is a historic county of Northern England and the largest in the United Kingdom) where they held a family seat (A family seat or simply a seat was the principal manor of a medieval lord, which was normally an elegant country mansion and usually denoted that the family held political and economic influences in the area. In some cases, the family seat was a manor house. Dynasty names were sometimes derived from the name of a family seat. An example of this would be the House of Windsor, the royal family of the United Kingdom and the Commonwealth realms.) as Lords of the manor of Woodmansey.

Later, another branch of the family was found at Fenrother in Northumberland (Northumberland is a unitary authority and historic county in North East England).

> This place was an early period held under the barons of Bothal, by the family of Fenrother. In the reign of Henry III, and subsequently, the Herons had possessions here; and among other owners have been the priors Tynemouth, and the family of Woodman: it is now the property of Mr. Woodman, and the Duke of Portland.

An interesting entry was found:

> In a proclamation by Edith od Wessex, Queen of Edward the Confessor, judgment is asked for on a certain undesirable tenant named Wudemann,

to whom the queen had lent a horse and who had
not paid rent for two years.

Further to the north in Scotland, it was "an old surname in
the parish of Strichen. William Wode was juror on an inquest made
in St. Katherine's Chapel, Bave, ley, in 1280. Nicholas Wodman
became burgess of Aberdeen in 1400, Thomas Wodeman attained the
same distinction in 1486, and is mentioned again in 1493. Andrew
Wodman was a forestaller in Aberdeen in 1402. The surname is also
common in Northumberland."

There are two distinct possible origins for this name. The first,
having derived from Old English personal name Wudernann (in
1070 Wudeman) and secondly, for the occupation a woodcutter:

> A Wodeman occurs in Domesday, and at an ear-
> lier period, individuals so designed gave names to
> Woodmancote, co. Sussex; Woodmanstone, co.
> Surrey; Woodmansey, co. York.

Distinguished members of the Woodman family include
Richard Woodman (1524?–1557) English Protestant martyr born in
Buxted and lived in nearby Warbleton in East Sussex. He was burnt
during the Marian Persecutions in 1557 in Lewes. Traditions of
Woodman linger in Sussex. The site of the house is still pointed out.

The Woodman family migrated to and settled in several different countries throughout the seventeenth, eighteenth, and nine-
teenth centuries including Ireland, the United States, Canada,
Australia (emigration to Australia followed the First Fleets of con-
victs, tradespeople and early settlers), and New Zealand (emigration
to New Zealand followed in the footsteps of the European explorers,
such as Captain Cook [1769–70]: first came sealers, whalers, mis-
sionaries, and traders. By 1838, the British New Zealand Company
had begun buying land from the Maori tribes and selling it to settlers, and after the Treaty of Waitangi in 1840, many British families
set out on the arduous six-month journey from Britain to Aotearoa
to start a new life.

Born on November 22, 1955

> Behold, I was brought forth in iniquity, and in
> sin my mother conceived me. (Psalm 51:5)

I was the firstborn child and the first son of Marlene Delores Landry and William Baron Woodman III. My mother gave birth to me on Tuesday, November 22, 1955, at 9:21 p.m., at Los Angeles, California, in University Hospital, and she named me Davion Maurice Woodman. Davion in French means beloved. She gave me the French middle name, Maurice, after my grandmother whose first name was Maurice. Occasionally, my grandmother would make light of her French boy's name, Maurice. When I was a small child, my mother nicknamed me "O'Toole," after Peter O'Toole, a British stage and world-renowned film actor. She called me "O'Toole" throughout my childhood.

> Los Angeles, officially the City of Los Angeles and often known by its initials LA, is the most populous city in California; the second most populous city in the United States, after New York City; and the third-most populous city in North America after Mexico City and New York City. With an estimated population of nearly four million people, Los Angeles is the cultural, financial, and commercial center of Southern California. The city is known for its Mediterranean climate, ethnic diversity, Hollywood, the entertainment industry, and its sprawling metropolis.

Now after I was born at Los Angeles, California, in 1955, Dwight D. Eisenhower was the President of the United States. Furthermore, Walt Disney moves to Los Angeles, then considered the ritzy Bel Air district. He proclaims his new Disneyland Park in nearby Anaheim as the "Happiest Place on Earth." Walt Disney soon after gave birth to Disneyland when he officially opened it to the public on July 17,

1955. After Walt Disney gave birth to his Disneyland, four months later in that same year, my mother gave birth to me. As a child growing up in Los Angeles, I enjoyed many years of entertainment, fun, and excitement with my family and friends at Disneyland, the Happiest Place on Earth.

In addition to my birth on November 22, 1955, approximately one week later, on December 1, 1955, Rosa Parks was arrested in Montgomery, Alabama, for refusing to surrender her seat on a bus to a white person. Then four days later on December 5, 1955, the Montgomery Improvement Association was formed in Montgomery, Alabama, by Dr. Martin Luther King Jr. and other black ministers to coordinate a black boycott of city buses. Those events that occurred in Montgomery, Alabama, also gave birth in 1955 to what became known as the Civil Rights Movement. When I learned in US History that the Civil Rights Movement was given birth in the same year as my birth, and it was as old as myself; I have to say, this was somewhat flattering. The movement began largely with civil disobedience and acts of nonviolent protests. This caused many crisis situations between activists and government authorities both on the Federal and local levels (1955—Wikipedia; stageoflife.com)

2

NONRELIGIOUS CIRCUMCISION

While the Roman Catholic Church had condemned religious circumcision for its members and maintained a neutral position on the practice of nonreligious circumcision, immediately following my mother's delivery of me and my subsequent birth, she chose to have me circumcised on a nonreligious basis for health and cosmetic reasons. Many years later, when I reached puberty, Mom explained to me that she had me circumcised at birth for two reasons: First, for health benefits, such as decreased risk of urinary tract infection during my first year of life and decreased risk of sexually transmitted diseases (STDs) later in my life. Second, for cosmetic reasons, Mom explained to me that she preferred the look of a circumcised male organ as the exposed glans in her opinion made the organ look more normal, and aesthetically, she did not like the anteater or aardvark look of a covered glans.

Moreover, the male organ is far lower in maintenance. It never smells or accumulates smegma under a foreskin—trapped urine there. And most discerning women don't want a smelly organ near them during intimacy or lovemaking. In general, it is my understanding that women prefer men who have been circumcised, while there are women who will *only* be intimate with a man who has been circumcised. My mother's decision to have me circumcised at birth was certainly a good choice for both myself and my future bride. Consequently, circumcision did not limit my lovemaking opportunities by leaving me with a foreskin.

3

CIRCUMCISION
IN THE BIBLE

Circumcision was enjoined upon the biblical patriarch, Abraham, his descendants, and their slaves as "a token of the covenant" concluded with him by God for all generations, an "everlasting covenant" (Genesis 17:13). Religious circumcision generally occurs shortly after birth, during childhood or around puberty as part of a rite of passage. Circumcision is most prevalent in religions of Judaism, Islam, the Coptic Orthodox Church, the Ethiopian Church, and the Eritrean Orthodox Church.

> This is My covenant, which you shall keep, between Me and you and your descendants after you: every male among you shall be circumcised. "And you shall be circumcised in the flesh of your foreskin, and it shall be the sign of the covenant between Me and you. "And every male among you who is eight days old shall be circumcised throughout your generations, a servant who is born in the house or who is bought with money from any foreigner, who is not of your descendants. "A servant who is born in your house or who is bought with your money shall surely be circumcised; thus, shall my covenant be in your

flesh for an everlasting covenant. "But an uncircumcised male who is not circumcised in the flesh of his foreskin, that person shall be cut off from his people; he has broken my covenant. (Genesis 17:10–14)

4

A MUSICAL FAMILY

As a musical family with a rich heritage of jazz musicians from my father's side, my roots began in the Watts section of Los Angeles, California, which was then a harmoniously interracial village. My great-grandfather, William Woodman I, a trombonist, was part of the West Coast jazz scene since the 1920s. He would encourage his three sons—my uncle Britt, (a trombonist who was an important member of Duke Ellington's band during the 1950s and early associate of Charles Mingus) who learned trombone, saxophone and clarinet; my grandfather, William II, a saxophonist; and my Uncle Coney, who played piano and guitar—to learn music as a means of earning a living. He believed that as the country entered the Depression, the best financial opportunities for his sons would come from making music.

My great-grandfather opened the Woodman Brothers Studio on Wilmington Avenue in Los Angeles, California, offering music lessons and playing at local dances. Under the management of my great-grandfather, The Woodman Brothers Biggest Little Big Band in the World became well-known among musicians. They were so versatile and proficient as musicians that they often traded instruments in the middle of a set. It was not uncommon, for instance, for them to begin a set playing alto saxophone and then switch to trombone and finally to clarinet. My grandfather, William II—who had a professional career as a tenor saxophonist—also played clarinet and trumpet. My Uncle Coney played piano and banjo. My great-grandfather managed the group, handled the bookings, and arranged the music.

In the book *Central Avenue Sounds*, a history of the flourishing jazz scene near Central Avenue around World War II, my grandfather, William Woodman Jr., recalled that he and my uncles were well-known among local musicians.

"We were recognized because we were the only musicians who doubled on three instruments," he said. "You didn't hear of anybody doubling on brass."

After their band split up about five years later, uncle Britt played in a variety of clubs on Central Avenue, including the legendary Club Alabam.

One of the clubs he worked in, he recalled in *Central Avenue Sounds*, was owned by the gangster Mickey Cohen. "Our payroll checks were signed by him," he said (New York Times, October 17, 2000).

"Needie" and "The Great Migration"

My grandmother, Maurice Danice Sutton, more affectionately known to me as Needie, came to Los Angeles, California, from Houston, Texas, during the "The Great Migration: The First Wave" (1910–1940). It was during the 1930s that black migration changed in character when nearly 25,000 blacks, which included my grandmother, arrived in Los Angeles, California. Many black migrants were from poorer backgrounds, hailing mostly from Dallas, Texas; Houston, Texas; and New Orleans, Louisiana. This change represented the largest internal movement of any group in American history.

Like so many before her, my grandmother, who was part of the Great Migration, felt compelled to migrate, not to escape persecution like many blacks but, like many blacks, searched out economic opportunity for the future of her family and for herself in Los Angeles, "City of Angels." After her arrival at Los Angeles, she soon became employed for many years with the United States Postal Service. During her later years as a resident in Los Angeles, my grandmother was a secretary and office manager for Mr. Patterson's State Farm Insurance Agency.

After my grandmother had settled in Los Angeles, she invested in a two-story duplex on Hobart and West Adams Boulevard where she raised my mother and her brother, my Uncle Vernon whom they called Junior. But on "Good Friday," April 7, 1950, while my mother and her brother were at a friend's house party, at sixteen years of age, he was accidentally shot and fatally wounded by a kid goofing around with the owner's loaded hunting rifle.

Moments before this tragic incident had occurred, my mother, who was fourteen years old, was standing in front of her older brother as they both loved each other very much and never went anywhere without one another. When I was twelve years old, my mom told me if she had been two inches taller, it's possible she would have been accidentally shot instead of her brother, Vernon Jr. My grandmother and my mother never fully recovered from their tragic loss; sadly enough, they both shared in their grief, and it affected them emotionally and psychologically for the remainder of their lives.

My grandmother was mixed race, whose father was an Irishman named Paul Carrington, whom I never knew. Her mother, my great-grandmother, was an African American woman named Mary Alice. She was affectionately known to me as "Mama Dear." I called my grandmother Needie, meaning, "Gift of God." The following is an alternative meaning of Needie in the acrostic:

N is for narrator, tell many stories.
E is for enrich, a quality you share.
E is for encouraging, thanks for the motivation!
D is for dazzle, the sparkle of you.
I for independent, a balance between being overly reliant and alone.
E is for expressive, not one to hold within.

Relatives and friends compared my grandmother to the American singer, Lena Horne, in both glamour and beauty. She was adored and admired by both genders. Men desired her, and women courted her friendship. My grandmother dated men from all walks of life such as Emmett Ashford, nicknamed Ash, who was the first

African American umpire in Major League Baseball. After Emmett, my young grandmother, befriended a young Puerta Rican American man named Ernie Cruz, whom we simply called, "Ernie," who was from New York City. Ernie was a jovial man, a carpenter by trade and a good friend of our family.

When I was born, my grandmother was thirty-nine years old. I remember thinking that in my view, she was not old compared to other grandmothers, but she was younger, smarter, and prettier than they were. I saw in my grandmother beauty, maturity, and wisdom blended together. Her voice was soothing when she talked, and her presence meant the world to me. I cannot imagine my early life without my grandmother; my mother's role was closer to that of a big sister.

My grandmother's greatest contribution to my life was her genuine faith in me. She single-handedly boosted my sense of self-worth more than any other. She expressed her love in a thousand different ways. She helped me learn to read; she explained the facts of life; she predicted a wonderful future for me, which included becoming the president of the United States! My grandmother talked proudly about me, sometimes referring to me as her "beloved doll baby." I loved "Needie," but she loved me more!

Mama Dear

The grandest of the ladies was my great-grandmother and our family matriarch, Mary Alice, whom we affectionately called Mama Dear. She was the most loving and kindhearted woman I had ever known. My great-grandmother migrated to Los Angeles from Houston approximately two years after my grandmother's arrival. She was a talented freelance seamstress who sewed and made many clothes for a variety of people from all walks of life, including Vaino Hassan Spencer, who was an American judge, the first African-American woman appointed to a judgeship in California. I still remember how happy and excited I was when she made me beautiful shirts to wear. When I wore them, I could feel her love and comforting touch on me! Wearing her shirts also gave me a sense of pride.

My mother and grandmother once told me a story about a "pimp" who had lived next door to Mama Dear when she lived on the eastside of Los Angeles; they said she used to make clothes for him too, and he handsomely rewarded her with cash gratuities.

After her arrival from Houston, my great-grandmother settled at Los Angeles on 58th Street and Ascot, and many years later, she and her husband, John Guillebeau, whom was a dark-skinned Creole man from Louisiana, moved west to South Thurman Avenue and Smiley Drive at Mid-City, Los Angeles. My great-grandmother was a classic brown beauty—strong in character, fun-loving personality, tall and robust, who by today's standards could be seen as "old-fashioned." But by her standards, and based on her understanding of the Bible, she followed God's Word and didn't care what anyone thought.

As a little boy growing up in Los Angeles, I remember how she liked watering her garden in the summer, cooking, baking, sewing, and cleaning. My great-grandmother was a compassionate and kindhearted woman. If anyone needed anything—shelter, food, or clothing, and if it were possible—she'd make provisions for them. If you were visiting Mama Dear at her house for the holidays, you'd be blessed with a piece of her delicious See's Candy; she always kept a box in her living room on top of the coffee table or she'd spoil you with a slice of her baked sweet potato pie, peach cobbler, devil's food cake, or homemade cornbread.

Mama Dear was also firm in what she believed was right or wrong, and she knew when to say no. My great-grandmother would not be taken advantage of. She was a strict disciplinarian; my mother and grandmother attested to this. When I disobeyed her or got into mischief or became unruly, correction was swift! She believed in Proverbs 23:13, which says, "Do not withhold discipline from a child, if you punish him with the rod, he will not die." Therefore, I knew what was coming when I disobeyed her or became a defiant great grandchild.

Mama Dear would spank me with what she called "My switch." When I occasionally became unruly, she'd make me fetch a small thin branch from her apricot tree. What a frightening task that was! Fetching the rod to discipline me! Then she'd carve the small thin branch smooth with her pocket knife and proceeded to give me an old classic southern style spanking, or better known to me, "getting a whooping!" While she was spanking me on the back of my legs and behind, I remember hearing her say to me in a strong emotional voice, "Davion! I'm going to spank your behind until times get better!" When she had finished spanking me, Mama Dear would hug me and tell me how much she loved me. All in all, and you better believe it, I never questioned my great-grandmother's love for me nor rarely disobeyed her authority!

Another time when my great-grandmother's wrath was tested involved my sister, Leslie, who was two years old, and my brother, Vernon, who was four years old. While we were spending the night at her house, Vernon got into mischief, thinking that cutting Leslie's hair was fun. It wasn't. Mama Dear was furious and began yelling at him for cutting my sister's hair. Vernon pleaded with her for forgiveness, but Mama Dear had already made up her mind. She yanked him by the arm to her living room and she then sat on the sofa and pulled his pants down along with his undies and threw him across her lap.

She spanked Vernon with only her hand, but it hurt him beyond belief and it made him cry after about a minute. He screamed and kicked as she spanked his backside red. Afterward, Vernon was placed into the corner. This was not a fun time for him after all. But Vernon was only spanked by my great-grandmother once, and it was the most memorable spanking he had ever received.

When sunset drew near, my great-grandmother would always give me a warm bath. Whenever she gave me a bath, Mama Dear would use her deep sink instead of her bathtub because it was easier for her to wash me in it. When I grew taller, she would bathe me while I stood up in her bathtub. After Mama Dear finished washing me with the hot soapy wash rag, I would sit down in the hot bath and rinse myself off. It was refreshing indeed. From time to time, Mama Dear would also let me take a warm shower with her. Although taking a shower was always fun and exciting for a small fella like myself, sometimes it scared me when I stood under the spray of water. While moved with compassion on those occasions, my great-grandmother would take my hand and hold it as we washed.

Whenever Mama Dear called me from her back door to come in from playing outdoors, I'd hear her soft and soothing "love call:" "Yoo-hoo! Davion!" And I'd come running as fast as I could! To this day, I still hear her comforting "love call." Interestingly, it was her bed that I would fall fast asleep on for my afternoon nap whenever I visited her. When I spent the night after a day of play or school, and when I was tired, it was she who sang me to sleep and who would whisper long forgotten Negro spirituals to me. I loved Mama Dear, but she loved me more!

The Sacrament of Baptism

> I baptize you with water for repentance. But after me comes one who is more powerful than I, whose sandals I am not worthy to carry. He will baptize you with the Holy Spirit and fire. (Matthew 3:11)

After my birth and our discharge from University Hospital, my mother and I went home to live in a two-unit duplex (top unit) at Los Angeles, California, on 7th Avenue and West Adams Boulevard in Mid-City. My mother was a devout Catholic, and she fulfilled the

Sacrament of Baptism after she was baptized in the Roman Catholic Church. As a girl growing up in Los Angeles, my mother attended only Catholic schools. She attended Holy Name of Jesus (first grade to eighth grade) and Bishop Conaty High School (ninth grade to twelfth grade) where she graduated and earned a basketball athletic scholarship to the University of New Mexico. Both Holy Name of Jesus and Bishop Conaty High School are located in the Roman Catholic Archdiocese of Los Angeles, California.

According to my mother's Christian faith, she believed that the "Sacrament of Baptism" was essential to being saved from "original sin." In the Bible, this "original sin," also called ancestral "sin," is a Christian belief of the state of "sin" in which humanity existed since the fall of man, stemming from Adam and Eve's rebellion in Eden, namely the "sin" of disobedience in consuming the forbidden fruit from the tree of the knowledge of good and evil. For that reason, most Roman "Catholics" like to "baptize" their babies in the first few months after they are born. Additionally, my mother's Catholic religion required her to uphold the obligation to preserve and ensure the baptism of her children in Catholic Church.

Baptism is an important event in the believer's walk with Jesus Christ. The Bible talks about water immersion baptism in which a believer makes a public confession of their faith. Jesus led the way in example of water baptism! Within two months after my birth, I was taken to Holy Name Church located on Jefferson Boulevard between Arlington and Western Avenue at Los Angeles, California, and on the fifteenth day of January 1956, according to the "Rite of the Roman Catholic Church," I was baptized with water in fulfillment of the Sacrament of Baptism by the Reverend Father M. J. Condon, the sponsors being my grandfather, Robert Landry, and my mother's childhood friend, Elenora Anderson (Original sin—Wikipedia).

My Godfather/Grandfather: Robert Landry

My godfather, Robert Landry, who sponsored me at my baptism was also my grandfather, father of my mother. However, I never knew him because he had passed away when I was still an infant. Although my mother shared one photograph memory of him among a few other photographs, it showed my young grandfather with my young grandmother, "Needie," and my teenaged mother and her teenaged older brother, Vernon. They were standing next to their camper underneath a huge tree, in view of the freshwater lake at Lake Elsinore, California. Besides the photographs, all that I knew about my grandfather is what my mother had told me. She once described him as being a high-spirited, tall, dark, and handsome Creole man from New Orleans, Louisiana.

My grandfather met my grandmother in Houston, Texas. They later were married and moved to Los Angeles during the "Great Migration" of the 1930s. My grandfather and my grandmother's son, Vernon Landry, was their firstborn child whom I also never knew. My mother and her older brother were my grandfather and grandmother's only two children. How tragic a loss to never get to know my own flesh and blood. One day, I hope we will pass each other on eternity's great path with Christ and continue our walk together into heaven.

My Godmother: Elenora Anderson

Elenora Anderson was a Creole woman who was born in New Orleans, Louisiana. When Elenora was a young girl, her parents moved to Los Angeles, California, where they raised her. After arriving in Los Angeles, she soon met my mother, and they both became close childhood friends. When I was born many years later, my mother asked Elenora to become my godmother. Considering it to be an honor, she sponsored me at my baptism. Elenora, a Roman Catholic herself, promised to see that I was raised to be a Christian and follow the Catholic religion. She had an outgoing good personality and loved to dance and finger-pop.

When I was about seven years old, and during the early 1960s, Elenora taught me how to dance, and she showed me several popular dances including the "Mashed Potato Dance," the "Twist" and the "Watusi." Elenora was an attractive woman who was tall and thin with a copper tone complexion, and she liked chewing Wrigley's Spearmint Gum. I remember her happy smile lighting up the room, and she liked laughing and having fun. She also had a daughter named Linda who was the same age as my little sister, Leslie. Linda was almost a spitting image of her mother.

Since she was my godmother, Elenora mentored me for several years as I grew up. I remember seeing her for the last time in the summer of 1965 when I was nine years old. After that summer, my mother told me Elenora and Linda had to move back to New Orleans to help take care of her ailing mother. My mother received a couple of letters and a few long-distance calls from her within one year after she had left Los Angeles; but after receiving the letters and telephone calls, we never saw or heard from Elenora again. Since then, I still wonder from time to time how they are doing and whether or not they are still alive.

Child of God

After I was baptized from that moment on, I became a child of God. It is only in Baptism that one becomes a child of God. Becoming a child of God requires faith in Jesus Christ.

> To all who did receive Him, to those who believed in His Name, He gave the right to become children of God. (John 1:12)

Mom and Dad's Mixed Marriage

My dad was a non-Catholic Christian, but the Catholic Church did not forbid him from marrying my mom. It had been the practice of the Church to marry non-Catholics and Catholics for quite some time. The Church referred to these types of marriages as "mixed marriages." My dad, who loved my mom, desired her to become his wife, and for this reason, he acted according to requirements of the Catholic Church's instruction process for marrying my mom. Mom and Dad also found it necessary to obtain the expressed permission of the local Catholic bishop in the Roman Catholic Archdiocese of Los Angeles to get married in the Catholic Church. Accordingly, they both were granted the rite of marriage at Holy Name Catholic Church (same church where I was baptized) by the Reverend Father M. J. Condon, Roman Catholic Priest, who officiated and solemnized their marriage in fulfillment of the Sacrament of Holy Matrimony.

African American Catholic History

The emergence of black Catholics started with the arrival of Africans who made their journey with the Spanish settlers in Florida in 1556, some as slaves and others who were free. Claiming Catholic belief became a card to play for slaves in Florida; Spanish rulers were found to free any slaves who practiced Catholicism throughout the 1700s. Along with the Spanish, slaves coming from a Creole society (a mix of African and French culture) brought Catholicism to America as well. When I think of religious African Americans living in 1964, I don't always think of them as being Catholic. The majority of religious African Americans were Baptist and Protestant (and have been for many years) while a small denomination of Catholics being black. Today, many blacks are nondenominational Christians, meaning they are not self-affiliated with a traditional denomination and often separate themselves from the strict doctrine and customs of other Christian fellowships.

5

AFRICAN AMERICAN CATHOLIC CULTURE

While we live in a world today that has made huge strides toward equality between races, the Catholic Church is still lagging behind. After many years since the Civil Rights Movement, there is still large segregation between the races in the Catholic faith. For the reason that the races were separated for such a long time, the methods of worship between African American Catholics and predominantly white Catholics from Europe significantly differed and still differs to this day. Despite the fact that all Catholics worldwide share the same beliefs, celebrate the same mass, and practice religion according to the authority of the Vatican, divisions still exist, especially here in the United States.

"Sugar Hill"

My family's first home was a two-story duplex on 7th Avenue and West Adams Boulevard located in the midst of the West Adams historical neighborhood known as "Sugar Hill" in the Mid-City, South Los Angeles region of Los Angeles, California.

> The area is mostly known for its large number of historic buildings, structures and notable houses and mansions throughout Los Angeles. West Adams is one of the oldest neighborhoods

in the city of Los Angeles, with most of its buildings constructed between 1880 and 1925. It was
once the wealthiest district in the city, with its
Victorian mansions and sturdy Craftsman bun-
galows, and a home to Downtown businessmen
and professors and academicians at USC.

The development of the West Side, Beverly
Hills and Hollywood, beginning in the 1910s,
siphoned away much of West Adams' upper-
class white population; upper-class blacks began
to move in around this time, although the district was off limits to all but the very wealthiest African Americans. One symbol of the area's
emergence as a center of black wealth at this
time is the landmark 1949 headquarters building of the Golden State Mutual Life Insurance
Company, a late-period Modern structure at
Adams and Western designed by renowned black
architect Paul Williams. It housed what was once
one of the nation's largest black-owned insurers.

West Adams' transformation into an affluent
black area was sped by the Supreme Court's 1948
invalidation of segregationist covenants on property ownership. The area was a favorite among
black celebrities in the 1940s and 1950s; notable
residents included Hattie McDaniel, Tim Moore,
Joe Louis, Sweet Daddy Grace, Little Richard,
Lionel Hampton and Ray Charles. Now, it is a
youthful, densely populated area with a high percentage of African American and Latino residents.

Many African-American gays have moved
into the neighborhood, and it has become the
center of black gay life in Los Angeles, even earning the nickname of "the black West Hollywood"
or "the black Silver Lake." Many of the neighborhoods are experiencing a renaissance of sorts with

their historic houses being restored to their previous elegance. In total, more than 70 sites in West Adams have received recognition as a Los Angeles Historic Cultural Monument, a California Historical Landmark, or listing on the National Register of Historical Places. (Wikipedia)

"The Twins"

Eleven months later after my birth, my mother gave birth to fraternal twins, my brothers: Rene Eugene Woodman, nicknamed "Rene the Baby" because of his occasional childish outbursts; and Andree Kevin Woodman who was regarded as the "sweet child" because of his pleasant ways. "Fraternal twins" in contrast to "identical twins" are developed from two different eggs fertilized by two different sperm cells." They both were born on October 30, 1956, in Los Angeles, California, and came home to be my little brothers. At that moment, I had become a big brother of two baby brothers. Hooray! I felt that I had been a little baby too. But now I was big!

It was amazing to me at the things that I thought I could do! Like pushing the twins in the baby stroller, helping with baby feeds, and other baby needs. Dirty diapers, yuck! Then I'd find clean ones! My mom and my dad used to say I was smart and that I was the best big brother ever! I showed love and affection toward them when we cuddled, and they'd kick and they would wriggle! When they slept, I made no noise. But I quietly played with all my toys. If they woke with cranky cries, my mom and me softly sang sweet lullabies.

Rene was the oldest twin being born moments before Andree. Three months later, they both were baptized according to the "Rite of the Roman Catholic Church." My mother cared for them as she cared for me with feeding, bathing, and nurturing. She was comforting, and they would smile and show pleasure in their responses. The twins brought me companionship and fun! And as they grew, we played together as toddlers do. I enjoyed entertaining them, giving them a tickle, and they would giggle! Because I wanted to be the best brother in the world! And I was their big brother forever! My mother, my father, the twins, and me. We loved each other. We were a family!

Traumatized

When I was more than one year old in 1957, I had to have my stomach pumped due to an overdose of my mother's iron pills. I watched her take one iron pill every morning, which was part of her planned medication schedule. Iron helps prevent and treat anemia—low iron levels—caused by pregnancies. After taking the pill with a glass of water, my mother would place the bottle of iron pills back on the top shelf of the kitchen cabinet. One morning after she had done this and left the kitchen, I stayed in the kitchen. Being curious as I was, I opened the bottom cabinet door and slowly climbed my way up the cabinet and onto the counter top, then I opened the top cabinet and grabbed the bottle of iron pills from the shelf. The iron pills were small, bright red disks that I had mistaken for candy.

Shortly afterward, I climbed back down from the counter the same way I had climbed up. Then I opened the bottle of iron pills and began chewing and swallowing all of the pills in the bottle. When my mother returned to the kitchen, she saw that I was sick and throwing up on the kitchen floor. After my mother saw the empty bottle of iron pills on the kitchen table, she stood there for a moment, dumbfounded that I had climbed up on top of the kitchen counter. My mother remained calm but clearly upset and feared the worst because she knew that an accidental overdose of iron was a leading cause of fatal poisoning in children under six years of age.

After my mother dressed me, my grandmother, "Needie," picked us both up and rushed me to the hospital emergency. Upon our arrival at the hospital, I saw my father who was waiting for us. The hospital staff rushed me into the emergency room where a doctor actually stuck a tube down my throat and pumped my stomach. At first, I felt like the tube was going to choke me to death; but instead, it traumatized me, and I suffered in agony. Moments later, I began to relax. After a few hours, everything was good and they let me go home. Definitely, getting my stomach pumped was the first of many harrowing experiences that I would never forget.

"Sputdoll"

On December 27, 1957, my mother gave birth to her fourth son, my brother, and she named him Vernon Marcell Woodman. My mother named Vernon after her late brother. Also, my grandmother and my mother nicknamed him "Sputdoll," because of his doll-like look. The prefix "Sput" came from his birth year in 1957 with the Soviet launching of the world's first artificial satellite, Sputnik, then adding the suffix "doll." From then onward, Vernon was affectionately called Sputdoll by our family, relatives and friends.

After his birth, and within a few months as it was with the twins and myself, Sputdoll was baptized according to the "Rite of the Roman Catholic Church" at Holy Name Church near the beginning of the year, 1958. Our small family continued to grow, and now I was a big brother of three! My mom, my dad, the twins, Sputdoll, and me. We loved each other. We all were a family!

Brothers Forever

We're brothers forever—the twins, Sputdoll and me. What more can I say? Our friendship was special in so many ways! We liked eating cereal from our favorite bowls and napping together on our separate bedrolls. We liked watching our favorite TV shows, and which one did we watch? I would know. And playing with our toys, this we enjoyed!

We liked riding our bikes, it was nice. And flying our kites when the wind was just right. We're brothers forever, so we shared in our chores. We would put all our toys into closets and drawers. We would help one another with this thing and that, from doing our homework to swinging a bat. But what we liked best was just being together because we loved one another, and we're brothers forever.

Lost and Found at Inglewood's Hollywood Park

When I was a young boy, I went with my mother, grandmother, "Needie," and our family friend, Ernie Cruz, to Hollywood Park in Inglewood, California, for a fun afternoon at the horse races. Soon after arriving there, we found our assigned seats and then visited to the snack bar to buy some refreshments. Upon leaving the snack bar to return to our seats, it happened. As I was walking along with my mom, I recall either stopping to look at something or something distracted me; and when I looked up a minute later, alas, she was gone! Then realizing we got separated, I frantically began looking for her, and she was nowhere in sight. After not finding her, panic quickly swelled within me; and for the first time in my life, I was lost! While terrible thoughts began racing through my mind of never seeing my mother again, I started wandering around aimlessly like a lost puppy looking for her.

After minutes of being separated from my mother at Hollywood Park, a uniformed security officer suddenly appeared from nowhere. And he rescued me. The man understood I was lost and in distress, so he identified himself as an employee for the park, which was somewhat comforting and reassuring to me; but nonetheless, I cried out to him: "I can't find my mama!" Then gently, he held my hand and took me a short distance to the park's Lost and Found center. When we arrived, the Lost and Found center looked like a small jail with bars on a window which divided the reception area from the holding room, and standing behind the barred window was another security officer who seemed to be writing on something with a pen or pencil.

Afterward, the security officer who found and rescued me asked me, "What is your name, son?"

And I answered him, saying, "My name is Davion."

Then softly lifting me up, he handed me through the opened barred window to the security officer who was standing behind it, and in a kind manner, he sat me down on a bench in the holding room where I patiently waited for my folks to come and get me.

Next, I remember hearing the security officer's voice coming over the PA system. This paraphrases the security officer's words: "To the mother of a little boy named, Davion, who was lost. He is safe and waiting for you to pick him up at the park's Lost and Found center."

When I heard his voice over the PA system, I had hoped they would come get me soon because the holding room I was kept in and where I was alone seemed almost as traumatizing as the earlier separation from my mother.

Minutes after the announcement was made over the PA system, both my mother and my grandmother appeared at the barred window of the Lost and Found center to pick me up. Looking collected, they were relieved and very happy to see me as I was to see them! After I saw them, my mother signed a release form to take me back into her custody. Then the officer in the holding room opened a door and led me out to them where they were waiting for me in the reception area. Without hesitation, I walked toward them, and we all embraced each other with warm and affectionate hugs. Then they both expressed gratitude to Hollywood Park's security for their help in finding me safe and sound. Finally, the ordeal of being lost was over, and I spent the rest of the day with my family at the horse races where we enjoyed the sport of kings.

Baby Boomer: Tech, Media and Culture

I will always be part of a huge—and hugely influential—generation of Americans born during the post-World War II period between 1946 and 1964 known as the "Baby Boom Generation" or "Baby Boomers." As a baby boomer, I grew up in simpler times and reared on a narrative of goodness and rightness with television! The birth of television into American society was a huge influence on me as a baby boomer. Everything that was seen on TV was believable, and boomer parents like my mother considered it educational. TV just seemed realistic in the eyes of the youth of the 50s and 60s.

My mother remained a housewife as the independence movement began to move housewives into jobs. Nevertheless, TV became somewhat of a "babysitter" for many baby boomers, including me. Whether it was weekly musicals or drama, television grasped the nation. Its influences on my generation and myself could be seen in all aspects of life. Back then, violence on TV was never real. The bad guys and only the bad guys were killed and simply fell to the ground, looking like they had gone to sleep. No blood, gore, screams; no moans or tears. Most shows were either live or were movies converted for TV.

As a youngster, I watched many popular television series and movies. Whenever I did, I almost always watched them with my mother. Since living on 7th Avenue in the West Adams District or as far back as I can remember, the earliest TV shows that we watched together were *The Jack La Lane Show* (mom exercised in front of the TV with Jack La Lane), *The Cheyenne Show*, *Gun Smoke*, *I Love Lucy*, *Lassie*, *The Little Rascals*, and *Bonanza*, just to name a few. It was one of those things that we did together. I would lie on the living room floor in front of the TV set while my mother sat on the living room sofa with a TV guide on her lap.

Whenever I was curious about something shown on television, I'd ask my mother questions, and she'd lovingly and patiently answer me. My mother and I viewed many shows and movies from the late 1950s through the 60s, 70s, and even into the early 80s. As we grew watching TV together, the experience brought her and I closer to one another. Those moments helped shape our relationship. I enjoyed asking my mother questions about television because I always wanted to know her feelings and thoughts about everything. We had a blast watching TV together!

After World War II, the idea of the drive-in movie theatre didn't really take off until the baby boomers made it a hit. There was a kind of magic about the drive-in movie theatre. I can still hear the gravel crunching underneath the tires of our 1952 Chevy convertible as we entered to find the perfect spot to watch the scary movie, *Psycho*, in

June 1960. I can still smell the delicious aroma of the popcorn and hotdogs coming from the snack bar. Distant memories still exist in my mind when Mom and Dad loaded up the car that night with us wearing our pajamas.

While they were watching the movie, my siblings and I were all fast asleep with our favorite blanket and pillow. Strangely enough, I could not have awakened from my sleep at a more scarier moment than to have awakened during the shower scene at Bates Motel when horrified Marion Crane (played by the lovely Janet Leigh) who was standing behind the shower curtain in the bathtub screamed bloody murder after the maniacal transvestite, Norman Bates (played by the young Anthony Perkins), had quickly pulled the shower curtain open and then began stabbing her to death with a butcher knife! Startled as they were watching the shower scene, Mom and Dad seemed to have been filled with as much horror as the victim, Marion Crane. Sir Alfred Hitchcock, an English film director, who directed *Psycho* was indeed "the Master of Suspense and Macabre."

As a baby boomer growing up in Los Angeles, California, I also witnessed massive changes in technology, media, and culture over my lifetime. I grew up before smartphones and the Internet ruled almost every aspect of our lives. Here is a long list of the many things that I remember experiencing as a baby boomer:

Great film soundtracks were commercially recorded onto 33 1/3 record albums for easy listening, music that accompanied great movies and commercially recorded for easy listening added relaxing leisure time and entertainment for my mom and myself as we listened to beautiful music from film soundtracks on 33-RPM record albums such as *The Sound of Music*, a 1965 American musical drama film; *A Summer Place*, a 1959 romantic drama film; *Friendly Persuasion*, a 1956 American Civil War drama film; *Gone With the Wind*, a 1939 American epic historical romance film adapted from the 1936 novel by Margaret Mitchell, and many more...

Popular Dance Crazes of the 1960s

Taking a trip down memory lane with some of the classic dances, many of the popular dances of the decade were inspired and named after a song. As a kid growing up in the early 1960s, the following dance songs are the ones I remember and enjoyed the most with my family and friends:

- The Twist was an enormous hit back in the day. This dance involved twisting your lower body and kicking your legs while your arms moved from side to side in front of you. It was inspired by the 1959 song of the same name by musician Chubby Checker;
- The Watusi was a dance craze actually inspired by the 1950 hit film *King Solomon's Mines*, its sequel, *Watusi,* and the elaborate dances of the African Tutsi people. In 1962, "Wah-Watusi" by The Orlons was released, and the dance instantly became a hit with everyone;
- The Hitch Hike was Marvin Gaye's 1963 smash Motown hit. "Hitch Hike" inspired this dance craze that was one of the most-simple of its time. You'd simply hold your thumb out, wave it three times over your left shoulder, then point to the left and repeat on the right side;
- The Mashed Potato is a dance move which was a popular dance craze of 1962. The dance move and mashed potato song was first made famous by James Brown in 1959 and used in his concerts regularly;
- The Loco-Motion is one of the prime examples of a dance-song hit, solely written to accompany a new dance. "The Loco-Motion," recorded by pop singer, Little Eva, taught a whole new dance to a generation of teens. Carol King also co-wrote the 1962 smash dance hit.
- "The Jerk" was a 1964 single release hit song and popular dance for the Los Angeles band The Larks.

6

HEARING THE NEWS THAT PRESIDENT KENNEDY HAD BEEN SHOT

The assassination of President John F. Kennedy happened on my birthday, November 22, 1963. I had just turned eight years old. Everybody who was old enough knows where they were when this tragic event occurred. I was in my third-grade class at Saint Agatha Catholic School. I heard the sad news from my Lay teacher, Mrs. Feldon, and the nuns who were crying and clearly very upset. Though most baby boomers were young at the time, the assassination of President John F. Kennedy was an event that made a huge impact on me and people of my generation.

The Hippie Movement of the 1960s

When I think of the 1960s, I can imagine hippies as being a part of that era. Hippies were a subculture or a counterculture movement that began as a youth movement started on college campuses in the United States during the mid-1960s. I harken back when my stepfather took my family and me on a Sunday drive one summer day in 1965. We rode in the VW bus driving down Sunset Boulevard on the Sunset Strip at West Hollywood, California. This was the first time I had ever seen hippies up-close. They were walking aimlessly, wandering back and forth, to and fro, seemingly without a care in the world. Many were very strange-looking and unkempt with long matted hair, some below their shoulders. I remember one hippie in particular walking at the intersection of Sunset Boulevard and Doheny Drive. He looked sunburned and flea-bitten with long dirty blond hair hanging down to his shoulders. The youth wore tattered blue jeans with a fringed shirt, and he had on one foot a fin, and his other foot was bare; also, he carried on his back an old worn green backpack. For me, it was the most bizarre scene I had ever witnessed.

Dialing a Rotary Phone

It used to take a lot longer to dial someone's phone number. Most people born after my generation have no idea on how to dial a rotary phone. It worked like this: you'd pick up the receiver, listen for a dial tone, then dial the seven-digit phone number. If the called party's phone line was busy, then you would hear a busy tone.

Talking to an operator. If I needed information or any other telephone assistance, then I would dial zero and talk to a real live person to direct my call. I remember making collect calls from a phone booth in the barracks to my mother when I was in the United States Navy. Collect call or reverse charge call is a telephone call in which the calling party, myself, would place a call at the called party's expense, my mother's phone account.

Using a Payphone to Call Someone

Payphones in phone booths used to be on every corner, but today, finding one in a mile radius is impressive. While it might be sad, I can't deny how wonderful having a cell phone is...

Looking Up a number In the Phonebook

If you wanted to call a friend or a business, but you didn't have their phone number, you would have to flip through the phone book to find their number. And you would only find their number in the phone book if it was listed in the phonebook.

Listening to My Transistor Radio

These fell out of style once everyone started using portable cassette players, CD players, and other personal devices, but I remember how during the 1960s and 1970s, everyone had a transistor radio. When I got my first transistor radio in 1964, I remember hearing Petula Clark's hit song, "Downtown;" the Beatles number one hit song, "I want to Hold Your Hand," and the Supremes hit song, "Baby Love." How exciting that was! My best friend, Michael, and I even did a popular dance to those songs called "The Jerk" which was also a hit song by The Larks!

Buying My First Record

Whether it was the Supremes, Temptations, Beatles, Four Tops, Marvin Gaye, or Smokey Robinson and the Miracles, born in the 50s, I definitely remember buying my first vinyl record, the 45 record, and listening to it over and over again and memorizing the lyrics to impress the girls. Later generations have made records popular again, but baby boomers were doing this way before it was cool.

Looking Something Up in an Encyclopedia

Before the Internet and smartphones put the answer to almost every question right at my fingertips, I had to find the information I wanted in an encyclopedia. Our set, entitled *The World Book Encyclopedia*, which came with a bookshelf, was sold to our family by a door-to-door salesman—another thing that's basically a relic of the past!

Riding My 1964 Schwinn Deluxe Stingray Bicycle

On Christmas morning 1964, I received the coolest gift ever from my mom and my grandmother—a blue Schwinn Deluxe "Stingray" bicycle. My bike was designed to look like a chopper with the high handlebars, chrome fenders, chain guard, white-walled wide treaded wheel in the rear, and a smaller white-walled treaded wheel in the front with a white classic tuck-in-roll saddle seat. That bike served me well for several years with pure outdoor fun, adventure, and excitement! What a blast I had!

Putting Baseball Cards in My Bike Spokes

Using clothespins to attach the baseball cards to my bike spokes, it made the most satisfying noise when I rode down the street really fast; like the sound of a motorcycle!

Waiting for the Adohr Milkman to Deliver to our House

About 30 percent of milk was still delivered to homes, including our home, in the 1960s. The cold milk was delivered in glass bottles from the milkman off the milk truck; it looked so refreshing, I could hardly wait to drank from it! Got Milk!

The Helms Bakery Man

Many of us who grew up in Southern California in the 1950s and 1960s have fond memories of the Helms Bakery. The bakery itself was located only a few miles from where I lived in the bordering city of Culver City, California. Their unique mustard-yellow colored coaches and distinct "toot-toot" whistles would signal that the Helmsman had arrived in our neighborhood. Me and other kids would race to the Helms coach with excitement. Our moms would follow to buy fresh Olympic Bread and perhaps a delicious treat for dessert. The appeal to us kids was the long wooden drawers containing endless rows of the most delicious cookies, donuts, brownies, and cupcakes ever created. The goodies were individually arranged in each drawer, lined up like soldiers.

It was so hard to choose! Fortunately, the Helmsman was friendly and helpful, and he even knew most of the neighborhood kids by name. The Helmsman wore an official Helms hat, a tie, and a shiny chrome coin changer on his belt. It was such fun to get change! If you were especially lucky, like I was one time, he gave me a cardboard Helms coach! Afterwards, I played with the coach for hours, pretending I was the Helms bakery man, tooting its whistle! That was a fun time!

Here Comes the Ice-Cream Man

I can still hear it—the tinny amplified music that was so familiar. It alerted us kids that the "ice-cream man" (women were not hired as vendors until 1967) was in the neighborhood. The music motivated in me a response to run from wherever I was and whatever I was doing to find my mom so that I could get some change to satisfy my need for a frozen treat. My favorites were the ice-cream sandwich, ice-cream cone, Eskimo pie and the different flavored popsicles. They were very good, satisfying, and refreshing, especially on those hot summer days!

Having to Change the Channels Using the Knob on TV

I remember having to change TV channels by walking up and using the knobs before remotes were common in every household.

Seeing the TV Channels Sign Off at the End of the Night

It's almost unimaginable in the era of 24/7 cable TV, but TV channels used to sign off at the end of each night with no picture. You would only hear static and see snowflake like images. Many stations also played the National Anthem to close out the evening.

Looking Through the Sears Catalogue

I remember looking through the Sears catalogue, feeling totally amazed at all the things you could buy without leaving the comfort of home.

Shopping at the Five-and-Dime Store

Before we had Target, Amazon, and Walmart, we had five-and-dime stores where you could buy almost everything you needed. Our family's favorite store was F. W. Woolworth Co. 5 and 10 Cent Store. The first one was created in 1878. Today, the prices have changed, but there are still a few you can shop at.

Watching *Lilies of the Field* with Sidney Poitier at the Movie Theatre, October 1963

While I was attending Saint Agatha Catholic School, I watched *Lilies of the Field* with Sidney Poitier as Homer Smith, an African American iterant worker. It was awesome! In an act of charity, Homer Smith builds a chapel for immigrants from Germany, a group of Roman Catholic nuns who are impressed by his kindness and strong work ethic. The nuns come to believe that he has been sent by God to help build them a chapel. For an impressionable seven-year old kid, *Lilies of the Field* was probably the most surreal movie that I had ever seen. After I had watched *Lilies of the Field*, it made me feel proud to have been both an African American boy and a Catholic school student!

On April 30, 1964, Sidney Poitier also became the first African American to win the Academy Award for Best Actor for his role as a construction worker who helps build a chapel in *Lilies of the Field* (1963).

Actually Eating Spam

This canned cook meat product made with ham was in every baby boomer's pantry at some point. At the time it was introduced, it was the only canned meat product on the market that needed no refrigeration. My mom kept spam in our pantry, and I remember eating spam for lunch at school. It was a pretty good snack too! I still eat spam for a snack to this day.

Cassius Clay Defeats Sonny Liston

On Monday afternoon, February 25, 1964, while I was sitting down in the barber's chair at the barbershop getting my covatis haircut and listening to the radio with great excitement, the radio announcer suddenly announced that underdog, Cassius Clay, age twenty-two, defeats champion Sonny Liston in a technical knockout to win the world heavyweight boxing crown. And all the customers and barbers in the barbershop and people everywhere went wildly happy with the greatest upset in heavyweight boxing history. The highly anticipated match took place in Miami Beach, Florida. Clay, who later became known as Muhammad Ali, went on to become the first fighter to capture the heavyweight title three times.

Peyton Place TV Series

Near the end of the summer of 1964 when I was eight years old, everybody who lived on my block at South Spaulding Avenue in Los

Angeles eagerly waited for and watched every full TV episode of the new evening soap opera, *Peyton Place*. I watched every episode with my mom as I had always done when we watched television. *Peyton Place* was an American prime time soap opera which aired on ABC in half-hour episodes from September 15, 1964, to June 2, 1969. It was based upon the 1956 novel of the same name by Grace Metalious. The series was preceded by a 1957 film adaptation.

Seeing Long(er) Hair on Men and Women

Coming of age in the 1960s and 1970s, there were plenty of men, women, boys, and girls who had long hair—straight, curly, or afro. I began wearing my hair long in a natural way when I was twelve years old. My mom didn't like the natural haircut at first, but she eventually gave in to the idea. She was used to me getting the popular short haircut known as the covatis. Today, you'll still see men with long hair and women with really, really long hair, of course. My son has long braided hair, but it's definitely less common.

Riding in Our Family's 1964 Volkswagen Bus

The VW bus became especially popular in the 1960s and 1970s as a reliable but stylish family car. I remember having fun riding in our red and badge VW bus and going everywhere, including beaches, parks, and drive-in movies. We also rode in the VW bus to my favorite amusement parks throughout the years: Disneyland and Knott's Berry Farm. Occasionally, our passengers were friends and neighbors; there was plenty of seats for them too.

1965 San Francisco Giants Season

The 1965 San Francisco Giants' 83rd year in Major League Baseball, their eighth year in San Francisco since their move from New York following the 1957 season and their sixth at Candlestick Park. My favorite Major League Baseball team finished in a disappointing second place in the National League with a 95–67 record, two games behind their archrivals, and my brother Rene's favorite team, the Los Angeles Dodgers.

The Vietnam War Televised. Summer of 1965.

"We have no business being over there."

"Fighting for what?"

"Look at those American soldiers, they're just boys losing their lives for nothing!"

These were some of the comments I heard from my mother. As I lay on the living room floor in front of our RCA Victor color TV, totally engrossed with the news of the Vietnam War and witnessing some of the actual battles our American soldiers were engaged in with the Vietcong. Vietnam was the first truly televised war. The war and medium through which millions of Americans experienced it were inextricable.

Leo's Bar-B-Que

On the Fourth of July 1965, just before the occurrence of the Watts Riot, my stepfather for the first time loaded my brothers and I in the VW van and he drove us to Leo's Bar-B-Que joint on Crenshaw Boulevard and Adams Boulevard in the West Adams District of Los Angeles. Leo's was a very small restaurant with no dining area; it was take-out only. I remember sitting in the VW while my stepfather waited in a long line of Negroes that stretched from the cashier's order counter all the way outside and along the sidewalk to the end of the front of the building. But the line moved pretty fast.

After ordering from the large menu above the counter, he waited at least fifteen minutes or more for the food. I believe Leo's Bar-B-Que was the only black-owned restaurant in Los Angeles at that time. Leo's Bar-B-Que cuisine was excellent. The service was a bit slow, but we got our succulent food. I enjoyed their tender juicy, red hot, hot link (Pete's Sausage) sandwiches, pork ribs, bar-b-que beans, coleslaw, and yummy sweet potato pie for dessert. The choice of sauces: mild, medium, hot or a combination of all. Other BBQ restaurants in Los Angeles and Inglewood, California, where I enjoyed eating as I grew up were Woody's, Philip's, McClintock's, and Hungry Al's.

The Watts Riot

A relentless hot summer night…a minor arrest…a shrill cry: "Here comes Whitey, let's get him!" *Burn, baby, burn!* And suddenly…thirty-four dead, 1,032 wounded, 3,952 arrested. Property damage: $40 million. During the middle of August 1965, when I was a nine-year old boy, I witnessed what had begun as a routine arrest in a Los Angeles slum rage for six days and nights as the most violent, most destructive race riot in American history which infamously became known as The Watts Riot.

The Black Panther Party

The Black Panther Party was a radical African American revolutionary leftist organization cofounded by Bobby Seale and Huey P. Newton, headquartered in Oakland, California, which was active in the US from 1966 to 1982. When I was ten years old, it was stunning news to hear about the Black Panthers for the first time on television news and read about them in the headlines of major newspapers. My mother didn't agree with their philosophy and she thought they were black militants. I believed Mom, and I thought that they were armed thugs styling afros, donning black tams, black pants, leather jackets and arming themselves with rifles and handguns seeking to harm people.

But later after they established themselves, I came to understand the Black Panthers were ahead of their time, and for the most part, they stood for community social programs we now consider normal.

A Boomer's First Job—Paperboy

When I became a paperboy at eleven years old during 1966, I was living in Inglewood, California, and attending Daniel Freeman Elementary School in the fifth grade. This was my first and most exciting job with the *Morningside News Advertiser.* For me, it was a big job because I had to wake up every Tuesday and Thursday morning before sunrise. After I awakened and got out of my bed, I'd put on my clothes and shoes and walk outside to the driveway where two large stacks of freshly printed newspapers were lying. Then I'd pick up the stack of newspapers and carry them to my front porch where I had a big bag of rubber bands handy, tools of the trade.

Using the rubber bands, I'd wrap and secure each folded newspaper. After folding and wrapping more than one hundred newspapers, I'd place them neatly in a large double canvas paper route bag. Next, I'd lift the heavy bag of newspapers up off the ground and hang them onto the handlebars of my Schwinn Stingray bicycle. Then away to work I'd go, proudly riding my bicycle with the paper route bag on the handlebars.

My paper route was across Van Ness Avenue on the Los Angeles side east of Inglewood. I'd throw papers to every house from 76th Street to 73rd Street between Van Ness Avenue and Gramercy Place. Some newspaper subscribers requested to have their paper placed on the front porch; otherwise, I'd toss them in the driveway. The best part of this job was collections and getting paid once a month. At the end of the month, I'd go to every house and collect twenty-five cents from each newspaper subscriber. Back then, twenty-five cents could buy lots of things, especially if you were fortunate enough to collect from every customer! In addition to our pay, the newspaper publisher offered generous bonuses to paperboys who had the highest cash collections per month. The bonuses came in the form of generous material things like motorized minibikes to walkie-talkies, etcetera.

I left the *Morningside News Advertiser* during the summer of 1967 to throw newspapers for the *Inglewood Herald Examiner*. The paper route was much closer to my home, and I wrapped and threw newspapers in the late afternoon except on Sundays. The Sunday paper was delivered to the customers early in the morning. The paper route started on my block from West 79th Street to West 85th Street between 5th Avenue and 8th Avenue in Inglewood. *The Herald Examiner* was a seven days per week paper route which included a Sunday paper, and I threw newspapers to only thirty home subscribers. *The Herald Examiner* was a big step up from the *Morningside News Advertiser*. I kept it until I began junior high school. The last day I collected the monthly payment from my customers was a difficult one. This was the time for me to say and hear difficult goodbyes.

I collected a number of wonderful gifts and a lot of advice that last day of my paper route.

I think it's sad that the paperboy is almost another "thing of the past!" When I was a kid growing up in my neighborhood during the 1960s, becoming a paperboy was a milestone of growing up. For a boy eleven or twelve years old to wake up before the crack of dawn, fold, and bag all of his subscriber's papers, then have them delivered to fifty to a hundred subscribers all before 6:00 a.m. daily, rain or shine, was great character building and good work ethic the American way.

A Few of My Favorite TV Shows of 1967

When I was a kid, there were a few of many TV series shows I enjoyed watching with my mom in 1967, and they remain a nostalgic pleasure of mine today. Here are three main title sequences from Quinn Martin's Productions: *The FBI*, *The Invaders*, and *The Fugitive*: *The FBI* was a cop show starring Efrem Zimbalist Jr. as Inspector Lewis Erskine probing cases based on real FBI files. *The Invaders* was an alien invasion drama starring Roy Thinnes as David Vincent who pulls his car over to take a nap late one night only to be awoken by a spaceship landing nearby. However, he struggles to convince anyone of his story. The number of episodes were forty-three, and I didn't miss one. *The Fugitive* was a cop show starring David Janssen as Dr. Richard Kimble who is wrongly convicted for the murder of his beloved wife. Kimble, determined to track down the real killer, escapes from custody following a train crash while being transported to death row. What follows is a game of cat-and-mouse for both the true murderer and the good doctor. But while Kimble searches for the real killer, the authorities—notably Lt. Philip Gerard—are on the hunt for him. I watched all thirty episodes!

Another favorite 1967 TV show series I enjoyed watching with my mom was *The Virginian*. It was an American Western starring James Drury, the third longest running western, 249 episodes behind Bonanza at 430 episodes, and Gunsmoke at 635 episodes. I admired the Virginian's strong character and his black Stetson cowboy hat that he wore with a beautifully embroidered black leather vest. The series revolved around the tough foreman of the Shiloh Ranch, played by James Drury. His top hand, Trampas (Doug McClure), and he were the only characters to remain with the show for the entire run.

As in the novel, the foreman went only by the name "The Virginian." The Virginian's real name was never revealed in the nine years the show was on the air. The series was set in Medicine Bow, Wyoming. Various references in the first season indicate that the setting is 1898.

7

THE ASSASSINATIONS OF MARTIN LUTHER KING JR. AND ROBERT F. KENNEDY

I didn't know anything about Martin Luther King Jr. as I did with President John F. Kennedy until his tragic death on April 4, 1968. Dr. Martin Luther King Jr., at thirty-nine years old, was in Memphis, Tennessee, to lead a peaceful march in support of striking sanitation workers. When he was standing on the balcony outside his Lorraine Motel room, he was shot and killed by James Earl Ray. Martin's violent death saddened my mother and my grandmother deeply because it was ironic that he had always preached dealing with issues and differences in a peaceful way.

Afterward, I soon learned that Dr. Martin Luther King Jr. was an amazing man of God, spiritual leader, and America's most significant orator (made famous by his "I Have A Dream" speech) and leader of the black Civil Rights Movement during the late 1950s to the late 1960s.

After Martin Luther King Jr.'s assassination, I believe America thought that was it. No more. But on June 5, 1968, just two months later, another tragedy occurred. Robert F. Kennedy, younger brother of the late president, John F. Kennedy, had just won the California primary election, and he was at the Ambassador Hotel in Los Angeles giving his victory address. Shortly after midnight, he left the stage, going through a door of the hallway that led to the hotel service hallway. He was to meet the press, waiting for him in a nearby room.

As a security guard led him through the doors of the hallway into the service area, shots suddenly rang out. Along with the hopes and dreams of the youth of our country, Robert F. Kennedy died on June 6, mortally wounded by Sirhan Sirhan, a Palestinian immigrant. Robert Kennedy's assassination impacted my family as well as many Americans. His death was to be the final blow to a growing number of young people and Americans who thought another youthful Kennedy and new president could bring about a renewed vision of hope and peace for the country.

Not So Good for America

On the national stage, times weren't so good for America. The country was still staggering from the April 4 assassination of Martin Luther King Jr. and the June 5 assassination of Robert F. Kennedy. Chaos was exhibited by civil unrest, violence, and riots. The Democratic National Convention was scheduled for August 26–29 in Chicago. President Lyndon B. Johnson had declared that he was not going to run for a second term, and so the Democrats were seeking a nominee for their ticket ("Johnson was Constitutionally able to run for a second term because he had served less than half of John Kennedy's term, 1963–1964. Johnson ran and was elected in 1964, and could have run again in 1968 if he had chosen to do so.").

When the DNC convention convened, the streets of Chicago were flooded with demonstrators. As so often happens, it got out of hand and turned into a riot.

Hubert Humphrey ran on the 1968 Democratic ticket but was defeated by Republican Richard Nixon. In April 1969, Nixon escalated the military personnel in Vietnam to 543,400. In June, however, he withdrew 25,000.

The situation in Vietnam was extremely unstable. President Johnson realized that the war in Vietnam should be ended, so in October of 1968, he ordered that bombing cease in North Vietnam and peace talks commence. At the end of December, there were still 536,000 US military personnel in Vietnam.

The First Man to Walk on the Moon

On July 20, 1969, it was a very exciting and historical moment for the world and myself to witness because American astronauts Neil Armstrong and Edwin "Buzz" Aldrin became the first humans ever to land on the moon. About six-and-a-half hours later, Armstrong became the first man to walk on the moon. As he set took his first step, Armstrong famously said, "That's one small step for man, one giant leap for mankind." That night as I walked outside and looked up at the brightly lit moon, I thought it was incredible for the first time in scientific history that a man was actually walking on it!

The Tate-LaBianca Murders, 1969

When it was reported that on August 9 and 10, 1969, two grisly murders took place in Los Angeles, our nation was horrified. On the ninth, a gang of four people brutally killed the actress Sharon Tate who was married to director Roman Polanski and eight months pregnant, four of Tate's friends, and the son of her gardener. The next day, supermarket executive Leno LaBianca and his wife were killed in a similar fashion. Charles Manson and some of the Manson family, as his followers came to be known, committed the murders. Manson and three others were found guilty on January 26, 1971.

Using a Typewriter

When it came time to writing a letter in pre-computer days, you used a typewriter, and you'd hope for no typing mistakes because there was no backspace option, just the saving grace of liquid paper to cover your mistake. I remember when I was a freshman in high school, I took a typewriting course. During the 1970s, typewriting was a popular elective to take because it was a skill that was in big demand for job and employment opportunities. To prepare for job opportunities, I took the course, and when I had finished it, I could type up to a least 35 words per minute (WPM)! This skill came in handy later when I enlisted in the United States Navy and qualified for the yeoman rating.

As a Yeoman (YN), I had to perform clerical and administrative duties, including typing! My typing skill also helped me get promoted to Yeoman Third Class Petty Officer, YN3, within two years of my enlistment. My shipmates were impressed and at the same time green with envy.

Dancing the Night Away at the Sportsman's Park Record Hop

After I had graduated from the sixth grade at Daniel Freeman, my first encounter with a record hop was in the summer of 1968 when I was twelve years old. My classmate, Herold Nails, and his older sisters, Priscilla and Tamara, invited me to go with them to the County of Los Angeles, Sportsman's Park Record Hop at Western Avenue and Century Boulevard. The evening began at 7:30 p.m. in the park's gymnasium. Approximately 300 or more black adolescent/ teens attended the hop as we danced the night away until 11:00 p.m. For the hop, I was over the moon about my newly cut natural hair style, and I donned a pair of white trousers, a yellow and green leafed short-sleeved zipper shirt, and a pair of faddish white loafer dress shoes. I had a great time with Herold and his sisters at the dance.

I remember being amazed at the crowd of black teens dancing to the hit music as white American disc jockey, Hunter Hancock, from the local radio station, KGFJ, announced the various rhythm and blues titles of the records. Back then, the black-owned *Los Angeles Sentinel* newspaper rated Hancock the most popular DJ in Los Angeles among blacks. Record hops were also originally known as sock hops because dancers had to remove their shoes so they wouldn't scratch the polished hardwood floor of the school gyms where the dances were often held.

In Los Angeles, the Sportsman's Park record hops started in the mid-1960s post-Watts riot and pre-youth gang era as a way to keep teens off the streets at night. The dances were held on Friday and Saturday nights throughout the year at the Sportsman's Park gym for entertainment, fun, and to bring harmony amongst the teens.

Occasionally, when I hear an "oldy but goody" song, I'll reminisce about the excitement of being in the moment with hundreds of other like-minded teens who, for a few hours, enjoyed the company of one another while dancing the night away at the Sportsman's Park record hop.

Angela Davis (1944–)

Angela Davis, activist educator, and scholar, was
born on January 26, 1944, in the "Dynamite
Hill" area of Birmingham, Alabama. The area
received that name because so many African
American homes in this middle-class neighborhood had been bombed over the years by the
Ku Klux Klan. In 1969, Angela Davis was hired
by the University of California at Los Angeles
(UCLA) as an assistant professor of philosophy,
but her involvement in the Communist Party led
to her dismissal.

On August 7, 1970, Angela Davis became notorious and a news
sensation when she was implicated in a failed attempt to free prisoners who were on trial in California at the Marin County Courthouse.
During this failed attempt, Superior Court Judge Harold Haley and
three others were killed.

Although Davis did not participate in the actual breakout
attempt, she became a suspect when it was discovered that the guns
used by the perpetrator, Soledad Brother, Jonathan Jackson, younger
brother of Soledad Brother and Black Panther Party member, George
Jackson, were registered in her name. Davis fled to avoid the FBI's
most wanted list. Law enforcement captured her several months
later in New York. During her high-profile trial in 1972, Davis was
acquitted on all charges. I harken back to what my mother said of
Angela during her ordeal: "Angela Davis is a young and brilliant
black woman, but she lacks common sense."

Turbulent Times
I watched television with intense interest as the war in Vietnam
raged on. On April 30, 1970, the United States and South Vietnam
forces crossed into Cambodia to get at enemy bases. On the home
front, protests continued against the Vietnam War. One protest

ended in tragedy when, on May 4 1970, four students were killed at Kent State University during an anti-war rally.

The Sylmar Earthquake

On February 9, 1971, at 6:01 a.m., I was shaken awake in my bed by a 6.6 earthquake. My mom scurried into our bedroom and alerted my brothers and me to take cover underneath the doorways and tables for protection. So we jumped out of our bunk beds and did exactly as she said. At that time, it was probably the most shocking and scariest moment of my life and the worst recorded earthquake in Los Angeles history. The epicenter was in the San Fernando Valley, and some of the worst damage was sustained by Sylmar Juvenile Hall in Sylmar where in the summer of 1967, after a few hours of being in custody at that facility, I was scared straight to repentance.

This disastrous event became known as the Sylmar earthquake. The ground wasn't the only thing that was shaking, but so was my bed and I. When the shaking stopped on that February 9 morning, my mother made sure we were okay. Then afterward, we helped her assess any damage to our house. Miraculously, it sustained no damage, and life went on.

Back in the Day: Driver's Ed., Driver's Training, DMV Written and Driving test

It was a milestone on my sixteenth birthday, Monday, November 22, 1971, which marked the start of a new chapter in my life. This significant event was the excitement and adventure of driving an automobile instead of walking or riding on the bus. I remember how happy I was holding my California Driver's License after passing both the DMV written test and DMV driving test with 100 percent! And I used my mother's 1971 Volkswagen bus which had a clutch and a four-speed floor stick shift. When I was a sophomore at Inglewood High School in 1971–72, I was enrolled in a Driver's Education class.

I remember learning the rules of the road and passing the class with flying colors. Another thing I remember watching was those horrendous scared-into-driving-straight films like *Death on the*

Highway or *Red Asphalt* that featured graphic automobile accidents. After I took and passed Driver's Education, the next step was driver's training. This was where I actually drove an automobile with an instructor to put my driver's education classroom training into practice.

The first time I ever drove a car was with my stepfather on The Great Western Forum parking lot in Inglewood, California. He taught me how to drive the VW bus while using the clutch and stick shift. I learned quickly how fun and easy it was to drive a car with a gear shift.

On the day of my driver's test, I was at the Inglewood DMV on La Brea Avenue, and I was driving my parents' VW bus which had no power steering. Nonetheless, I parallel parked perfectly, and my tester gave me 100 percent on parallel parking, driving around the block safely while obeying all the signs and signals, and skillfully going through the maneuvers. Back in 1971, California, no auto insurance was required by law nor wearing of seat belts. Before I took the DMV written test, the only thing the tester asked me for was the green slip or certificate that proved I had passed both my high school's driver's education class and driver's training class; and the tester for the DMV driver's test only asked me for the car's registration before I took the driving test. Back in the day, indeed times were simpler.

The Godfather (1972). A Great Movie.

When I was sixteen years old, I watched this riveting crime movie with my mother in Inglewood, California, at the Century Drive-In Movie Theatre during the summer of 1972. According to Roger Ebert:

> *The Godfather* is told entirely within a closed world. That's why we sympathize with characters who are essentially evil. The story by Mario Puzo and Francis Ford Coppola is a brilliant conjuring act, inviting us to consider the Mafia entirely on its own terms. Don Vito Corleone (Marlon Brando) emerges as a sympathetic and even admirable character; during the entire film, this lifelong professional criminal does nothing of which we can

really disapprove. During the movie we see not a single actual civilian victim of organized crime. No women trapped into prostitution. No lives wrecked by gambling. No victims of theft, fraud or protection rackets. The only police officer with a significant speaking role is corrupt. The story views the Mafia from the inside. That is its secret, its charm, its spell; in a way, it has shaped the public perception of the Mafia ever since. The real world is replaced by an authoritarian patriarchy where power and justice flow from the Godfather, and the only villains are traitors.

8

THE HORROR OF WAR

Beyond the seas on June 8, 1972, an incident occurred in which photographer Phan Thi Kim Phuca captured a nine-year-old South Vietnamese girl running naked through the streets of a village near Saigon, the victim of a napalm bomb during a North Vietnam attack. The photographer took her to a hospital where it was understood she had been burned over 50 percent of her body. Fortunately, the little girl survived. The horrendous photograph became known as the picture that changed the world because it truly illustrated the horror, not only of war in general but specifically of the highly controversial conflict in Vietnam.

Watergate

On June 17, 1972, an incident at home occurred when burglars broke into the Democratic National Committee offices in the Watergate complex in Washington, DC. Five perpetrators of that crime were arrested. This event launched an impeachment investigation that ultimately led to the resignation of Richard M. Nixon on August 9, 1974, the only US president in American history to resign the presidency.

The End of the Vietnam War

The 1973 new year began on an encouraging note regarding the Vietnam War. January 27, 1973, marked the end of the US involvement in the Vietnam War when the peace pact was signed in Paris.

Saigon was now in the hands of the North Vietnamese. The war-weary United States was more than ready to get back to a normal life.

Dealing with Round-the-Block Lines Thanks to the Gas Shortage

In 1973 and again in 1979, Americans faced a persistent gas shortage. There were lines around the block and odd-even rationing was introduced, meaning that if the last digit on your license plate was odd, you could get gas only on odd-numbered days. Man, that was a nightmare for me because I was driving a gas-guzzler muscled car. It was a 1967 Chevy Malibu with a 396-horse powered engine and four-barrel carburetor. I remember those dreadful days when my car ran out of gas and I had to walk to the gas station with a gas can!

Heiress Patty Hearst's 1974 Shoot-out in Inglewood, California

About 6:00 p.m. on May 16, 1974, I was walking through the shopping center parking lot on Crenshaw Boulevard, north of Imperial Highway in Inglewood, California, heading toward the Brolly Hut Restaurant on my lunch break from Thrifty Drugstore when all of a sudden, I saw two gentlemen with authority who wore suits walking toward me. They both approached me with pictured ID in hand and identified themselves as FBI agents. The scene was a surreal experience, and I instantly knew why they were standing in front of me because everyone in the nation knew what had unfolded across the street at Mel's Sporting Goods two hours earlier.

On the other hand, one of the agents showed me a black and white photo of Heiress Patty Hearst, daughter of the American publishing magnate William Randolph Hearst on the FBI's ten most wanted list. And he proceeded to ask me, "Have you seen this person?" I answered him, "No, not around here but on every local news station." Then they politely thanked me and walked away as quickly as they had come before me. After they left, I safely assumed that these agents along with a large number of other law enforcement agents were canvassing the vicinity of the shooting for eye witnesses.

According to a Los Angeles Times article written by Sebastian Rotella on January 22, 1989:

The concrete light pole on Crenshaw Boulevard doesn't look like a historical artifact.

Two indentations in the pole are the only clues to its significance in urban archeology. They were made by bullets from a submachine gun fired by Patricia Hearst on May 16, 1974, after a bungled shoplifting attempt at what was then Mel's Sporting Goods.

The light pole, south of Imperial Highway, preserves in concrete Inglewood's part in the melodrama of Hearst and the Symbionese Liberation Army. Not much has been made of it, but Inglewood Police Capt. James Seymore and Detective James Boggs—then young patrolmen who responded to the call of a shoot-out at Mel's Sporting Goods—played small but vital supporting roles in the saga.

About 4 p.m., Inglewood police received frantic reports of heavy automatic-weapons fire at Mel's Sporting Goods. A van with armed suspects was reported fleeing east on Imperial Highway. Seymour and Boggs were first on the scene. A crowd had gathered at the store.

"I thought, 'Oh my God, we've had a slaughter here,'" Seymour said.

"It turned out no one was injured. Boggs spotted a man in the crowd with a gun in his waistband, grabbed him and put him against the wall. It was the manager of the store. The man had wrestled the gun away during a struggle with two shoplifters on the sidewalk, and he used it to return fire when a woman in the van across the street opened up with an automatic weapon, allowing the couple to escape."

Hearst and her kidnappers-turned-comrades got away, but Seymour and Boggs found a gun at the scene that they traced to SLA member Emily Harris. The next day, following that lead, police stormed a house in South Central Los Angeles. Hearst wasn't there, but most of the self-styled revolutionaries who had kidnapped her died in a blaze of flames and gunfire, an apocalypse televised in living color.

As numerous accounts—including Patricia Hearst Shaw's book, *Every Secret Thing*—later established, here is what unfolded:

> Hearst accompanied SLA members William and Emily Harris on a shopping excursion from their hide-out in South Central, Los Angeles. As Hearst waited in the van outside Mel's, a store employee spotted Bill Harris trying to steal a pair of socks. A struggle took place. Hearst blasted away from the window of the van, first with a submachine gun and then with a semiautomatic carbine. The three fled.

In her book, Hearst says she fired over people's heads, "aiming at nothing in particular," purely to help the Harris's escape.

At the end of her tragic ordeal, Patty Hearst Shaw, who had served almost two years in prison on a bank robbery conviction, was granted executive clemency by President Jimmy Carter before he left office, and she was released from prison in 1979. She was fully pardoned by Clinton in 2001.

Nixon Resigns

On August 8, 1974, President Richard M. Nixon appeared on television, announcing his resignation as president of the United States. He resigned in the wake of the Watergate burglary scandal. Nixon was the first president in American history to resign.

Seeing Billboards Advertising Tobacco

Back in the 60s and 70s, cigarette advertisements were everywhere. Everyone knew Joe Camel, the Marlboro Man, and the classic

Lucky Strike slogan: "It's toasted." Society, in general, accepted cigarette smoking. Cigarettes were also glamorized in Hollywood. Actors and actresses smoked cigarettes during the scenes in a movie. My preferred brand was Kool cigarettes in the 70s. But as we became more aware of the dangers of smoking, tobacco advertising on billboards were (thankfully) banned. I went to Schick Center for the control of smoking after I had listened to the actor Chuck Conner's (*The Rifleman*) television testimony, and by the power of the *Holy Spirit*, I quit smoking cigarettes in March 1986.

Smoking on Airplanes

Air travel has changed in so many ways, but I remember when it was common to see people smoking, including myself, on airplanes. It wasn't until the 1990s that smoking on airplanes was banned completely.

Watching *The Mary Tyler Moore Show*

Mary Tyler Moore made television history by being one of the first women on TV to wear pants. It was so outrageous that the producers limited her to one pants-wearing scene per episode. It's safe to say things have definitely changed since then! The Hollywood actress, Katherine Hepburn, also stirred up controversy wanting to wear her pants on the set.

Wanting to be as Cool as Paul Newman

Kids today (sadly) only know Newman as the guy on the salad dressing label or popcorn box from the store. But I knew that Paul Newman was the coolest guy ever. I mean, he was a movie star who drove race cars!

World Problems Winding Down

In 1974–1975, the world problems seemed to draw gradually toward an end when in April, all the US citizens were evacuated from Saigon. One of the major problems of the Vietnam War, despite everything, still dawdled and would for many years because the returning American soldiers were often treated very bad, hurling a dark blemish on our history.

Fall of Saigon

> The Fall of Saigon, also known as the Liberation of Saigon, was the capture of Saigon, the capital of South Vietnam, by the People's Army of Vietnam and the Viet Cong on 30 April 1975. The event marked the end of the Vietnam War and the start of a transition period to the formal reunification of Vietnam into the Socialist Republic of Vietnam.

9

WATCHING THE FIRST SEASON OF *SNL*

The first episode of *Saturday Night Live* aired on October 11, 1975. George Carlin was the host, and some of the first cast members were Chevy Chase, John Belushi, and Gilda Radner. More than forty years later, the show is still going strong. Now I enjoy watching President Donald J. Trump sketches from *SNL* played by Alec Baldwin on NBC. On December 21, 2019, one of *SNL's* most iconic cast members, Eddie Murphy, returned to host the show after a thirty-five-year hiatus.

The Home at South Genesee Avenue

After packing and moving from our 7th Avenue home in 1957, our family travelled southwest and settled into a small single-family residential home on the 2900 block of South Genesee Avenue at Los Angeles, California. Our new residence bordered east of the City of Culver City and north of the Baldwin Hills section of Los Angeles. Family members who lived in our new home were my dad, mom, the twins, and our newest addition, Sputdoll. By that time, I had grown older, and Mom would often say to me that I was a loving and affectionate child who also was responsive to the emotional needs of others. She observed in me that I was sensitive and bashful, and sometimes I would feel sorry or sad when others my age, especially my younger siblings, got upset. I liked pleasing my mom and I began to show her my independence early on.

According to my mother, when I was three years old, it was, "Watch out!" She described me as being charged with lots of physical energy. I did things on my own terms. My mind was like a sponge. Reading and socializing were essential in getting me ready for school. I liked pretending a lot and enjoyed scribbling on everything. I was full of questions, many of which were "Why?" I became fairly reliable about using the potty. Sometimes I'd stay dry at night and sometimes I didn't. Playing and trying new things out was how I learned. Sometimes I liked to share. I began to listen more and began to understand how to solve problems for myself. My mom made certain my needs were being met all of the time.

Mom allowed me to continue to explore this new world of mine, down the block and up the block, playing with other children, picnics at the park, and fun shopping at the grocery store, sitting and riding in the shopping cart, etc. Although I liked my routines, Mom gradually and slowly changed them as I grew older. She always made me feel happy when she noticed what I did well and *praised* me. I never felt unsafe nor insecure because she was always in control and made decisions when I wasn't able to do so. It seemed that I did everything better when Mom planned ahead for me, and she was *firm* about the rules, but *calm* when I forgot or disagreed. I loved Mom's patience with me when I did my best to please her, even though I may not have acted that way.

When I was four years old, and for the first time, playing outdoors on South Genesee Avenue was exciting and a new experience for me. I learned how to play with other kids who lived on my block. They were interesting and exciting to me because they were multiethnic, girls and boys consisting of African American, Caucasian, and Japanese who soon became my friends. My best friend's name was Raymond who was one year older than me, and he lived with both of his parents in a small house at the end of our block. Raymond's father owned his own carpet cleaning business. He once cleaned our carpet, and his mother was a housewife. Their house was located next to a large undeveloped land belonging to Department of Water and Power (DWP), that which we called "the vacant lot." Many years later, the vacant lot was developed into a community park named "Westside Neighborhood Park" by the City of Los Angeles, Department of Recreation.

Raymond and I enjoyed playing in the vacant lot because some parts of it looked like a real jungle with small swamp-like land, trees and tangled vegetation, but most of it looked like a large desert—dry, barren, having rocky soil with lots of tumbleweed and little vegetation. The vacant lot became our ultimate playground! Often, when we played there, Raymond and I would make-believe that we were cowboy and Indian fighting in the desert with toy six-shooter, bow and arrow, as well as soldiers, fighting in the jungle with toy hand grenades and machine gun. When we were not playing in the vacant lot, Raymond and I rode on our tricycles in our driveways and on the sidewalk; we also played with lots of toys at his house and my house, and we both played with the other kids who lived on our block as well.

My mom liked helping me make the most of outdoor play with these ideas:

- Hop-scotch, hide-and-seek or jump rope;
- Crawling through tunnels or climbing over fallen trees;
- Going on walks together and naming all of the different sounds I would hear;
- Building a castle out of boxes, clothes baskets, or outdoor play equipment or furniture.

I enjoyed sharing and exchanging outdoor playing ideas with my friends because this taught me how to give and take and play well with others.

I also remember becoming more active during this time, climbing, running, and jumping. I loved to question with "Why?" and "How?" I suddenly became interested in numbers and the world around me. I really enjoyed playing with the other kids on my block, especially with my best friend, Raymond.

Daddy and I

When I was a little boy growing up, Dad was my pal. He was a very handsome man, neat and trim in his appearance, always looked very dapper and up-to-date in his dress and manners. I enjoyed interacting with him every moment of the day. When I grew up, I had hoped of being a man just like my dad. I called him "Daddy" back then, and I believed he could do anything! Dad laughed and smiled more than anybody I knew. He was my strength and security, source of fun and laughter. He'd spend hours playing with me. Dad also liked tickling me and carrying me on his shoulders. Sometimes my dad would thrill me and excite me when he playfully tossed me up in the air and carefully caught me again and again.

As a musician, Dad delighted himself with playing his clarinet. Whenever he'd play music at home, I grew excited because he looked awesome just like with everything else he did. Dad's passion and favorite genre of music was jazz. He inherited his music talent from our family patriarch, my great-grandfather, William Woodman, who left the Woodman family a musical legacy. My family of jazz musicians were all successful as professionals, while Dad's Uncle Britt, an accomplished saxophonist, became famous and a member of the Duke Ellington Band. I loved being with my daddy; he was the greatest.

Mamma and I

As I developed and grew in weeks, months and years, I called my young and beautiful mother, Mamma, who without a doubt was the most important person in my life and the most complete individual I knew. She was truly beautiful with toned ivory-colored skin, hourglass shape, above average height for a woman, high cheekbones, naturally thick eyebrows, and she had the kindest emerald green eyes that I had ever seen. Not only did she work hard to ensure that I had a good upbringing but was also strict and often punished me whenever I went wrong. Even though I did not like the punishment then, I now look back and realize that it was meant to lovingly correct me and help me to follow the right path when growing up.

I had always taken pride in the appearance of my mom, especially her lovely curly sandy brown hair. I remember whenever she came to visit me at school or was my classroom mother, other kids liked seeing her and how pretty she was. Even though I had seen some beautiful people, few young women matched the beauty of my youthful looking mother.

One of the reasons why I was so fond of my mom was because of the way she used to take great care of me and my siblings, especially when we were ill. She was a very knowledgeable woman who made a variety of home remedies to help take care of the minor illnesses that we had as children.

I did not like to see Mom sad, and I would do anything to bring a smile to her face. Interestingly, even when she was worried or sad about something, she would always smile to make us stop worrying about her. My mom not only loved those around her but was also compassionate. Her compassion always moved her to help a neighbor or friend in need. She used to say, "I'll give you the shirt off of my back."

Mom was a good cook who always left me looking forward to the next meal, whether it was breakfast, lunch, or supper. She knew how to mix the right ingredients to end up with a meal that often left me licking my fingers. Just the memory of the foods that Mom prepared for me makes me salivate to this present day.

She continued to set reasonable limits for my own protection and for others. She'd let me know clearly what was or wasn't to be expected. My mom read to, talked to, and listened to me. I was given choices and I learned things in my own way. To help me learn new words and things, Mom labeled objects and she would describe my experiences and what was happening to me.

Always feeling abundantly blessed; I am forever humble and grateful to the Lord for my mom whom I will forever honor.

Mom and Dad's Greatest Gift to Me

When I was a child, Mom and Dad gave me the greatest gift of all—their love for one another. From their love came the foundation of our family, and I learned how to relate by watching how the two of them related. Dad made it a priority to greet Mom as soon as he came home, before engaging me and my siblings. He wanted us to know Mamma was the queen of the house.

They did weekly date nights with one another and created date night ideas around certain themes like play, laugh, dream, and adventure. The goal was to help spark conversation and creativity in their date nights. Mom and Dad always embraced joyful moments: These were daily ordinary moments that simply made them smile and appreciate the affection they had for one another. Since she was a child, and all of her life, my mom wanted to become a movie actress, and in 1954, she was chosen to be an extra in the movie, *The Egyptian*. It starred Gene Tierney, Jean Simmons, and Victor Mature. Being dramatic as she was, my mom enjoyed imitating her favorite actresses like Elizabeth Taylor, Bette Davis, and Joan Crawford in movie roles they portrayed. Her imitations were just adorable to my dad.

On days when Mom broke into her acting routine and memorized dialogues from her favorite movie scenes, Dad simply smiled, walked over to her when she finished, and embraced the moment. These ordinary moments were the same when Dad took out his clarinet and played his favorite jazz tune. The best moments I had were when I watched them and giggled along.

The safest relationship I experienced was seeing my mom and dad madly in love...

"Aunt Shirley"

It began with a visit one sunny morning during 1956 at the home of my mom's childhood friend who lived in East Los Angeles, California. Her name was Shirley Lumas whom I affectionately came to know as "Aunt Shirley." At the time of our visit, I was less than two years old, but I was walking and talking. When we arrived at her home, Shirley was in the backyard hanging out laundry on a clothesline. She was a Creole woman and the youngest of five children. When Shirley was a little girl, she came to Los Angeles, California, from New Orleans, Louisiana, during The Great Migration of the 1930s with both her parents and older siblings. During our visit, Shirley made a comment about my speech to my mom because I talked a lot and I talked fast. So she jokingly says to Mom: "Damn, Marlene, Davion speaks like he's Puerto Rican, I can't understand a word he says."

As I was growing up, my mom occasionally mentioned it in a fun way, how Shirley described my speech that morning in her backyard.

Shirley was a Louisiana Creole with a mix of French, Spanish, and African heritage. And often she was profane and boisterous, both at her home and at our home, but was generally on her best behavior in public. Shirley spoke using the local slang and phrases from New Orleans, which was of a French and West African hybrid language called Louisiana Creole or Louisiana Creole French. My mother described her childhood friend as being repetitious in her thinking, meaning well and telling it like it is. We all were very fond of Shirley. Actually, Shirley was my mom's best friend; they both were like loving sisters and two peas in a pod.

When we visited Shirley, her homecooked meals and New Orleans southern hospitality were my favorites. Her style of cooking, Louisiana Creole, originated in the bayous of Creole settlements. Shirley's food included French, Spanish, African, Native American, and Caribbean influences, making for a uniquely delicious culinary experience. My favorite Creole dishes were Shirley's jambalaya and gumbo made with succulent meats, vegetables, spices, stock, and rice; her jambalaya had many varieties including Creole or "red" jambalaya, straight out of New Orleans, and rural or "brown" jambalaya. Shirley's gumbo, another popular Creole dish I enjoyed eating, and a meal my mother and my grandmother also used to cook for me was a delicious hot stew containing onions, bell peppers, celery, a variety of tender meats and/or shellfish, and a thickener, which depended on the variety of gumbo she cooked. However, I recall Shirley's favorite food she enjoyed eating, and it was not Creole food but simply that of a "chili dog" with yellow chili peppers.

Like mom and myself, Shirley was a Roman Catholic as were her husband and her children, although some Creoles have been known to practice voodoo. Connected to her culture and heritage, Shirley practiced Catholicism all of her life, and she was my brother Vernon and my sister Leslie's godmother. Shirley married a Creole man named Irving Epps who we called "Uncle Irving" or "Big Irving," and Shirley often said of him: "He's an evil nigga."

Shirley and Irving were both the parents of two offspring named Kim Marie, the oldest child, and Irving Joseph Jr., who we called "Little Irving." Fondly, we considered ourselves as cousins, and we all began growing up together in Los Angeles. Afterward, both of our families moved to Inglewood, California, in the mid-late 1960s where we matured and became adults. I loved Shirley, and I know she loved me. She will always have a special place in my heart.

Moving to the New Home

During the year 1959, my family moved not far from our old house on South Genesee Avenue to our new house on South Spaulding Avenue (just two blocks northeast of our old house) located in the vicinity of West Adams Boulevard to the north, South La Brea Avenue to the east, Smiley Drive to the south, and South Fairfax Boulevard to the west. The seller of our new house was a Japanese family who had lived in it. They sold their house to my grandmother, "Needie," who bought it as a gift to our family. When we went to go see our new house, it had been freshly painted, and new carpet was put down in some of the rooms. While we were there, my dad introduced himself to the people next door. Their names were Newmar, who was an LAPD rookie cop, his wife, Maxine, a homemaker, and their two young sons, Tony and Raymond.

After escrow closed, we packed up our old house, which took many days for my mom and dad to sort out all of their things. Packing was hard work, and I made sure that all of my things were packed too. The twins and Sputdoll followed me. Then we began moving.

Early one morning, a big moving truck arrived to take our furniture to our new house. Ernie, who was a family friend and my dad, loaded everything into the big truck and drove it to our new house. Some of the smaller things we loaded into the trunk of our 1952 Chevy. Everyone helped unload the truck and the car. Ernie showed my brothers and me the inside of the big moving truck. Then we all started to take the things into our new house. Ernie and my dad carried the heavy furniture into the house. My mom showed them where to put everything.

My brothers and I shared our new bedroom which faced the backyard. Mom and Dad's new bedroom faced the front yard. Mom helped us get our room ready. They both went shopping and bought two new sets of western style bunk beds. One set for the twins and one set for Sputdoll and me—the beds had a matching dresser and four drawers. Rene and Sputdoll slept on the top bunks. Andree and I slept on the bottom bunks. Mom put up the curtains to cover our bedroom windows, and she helped us unpack. We were very excited about our new house because it came with a big backyard, beautiful plants, flowers, trees, green grass, and a built-in brick charcoal grill with a woodburning fireplace, chimney, and an attached garage.

Our entire family met the people next door. That afternoon, we'd go for a walk down the street where there were lots of people to meet. My brothers and I had new friends to play with. That evening, we all went to bed late because we were excited after the move and fell fast asleep in our new home.

The Home at South Spaulding Avenue

After we moved into our new home at 2635 South Spaulding Avenue, Los Angeles, California, my mom helped me make the moving transition easier. In the first few weeks after we had moved, she took me on a tour. She walked through the space, discussing what each room would be, describing how it would look, what activities would happen there, and asked me what I thought about organizing the space. Mom covered every room and space, including the yard and garage, then she let me take my own time to explore it.

Mom made sure I packed a box for myself. This included my favorite things, such as toys, games, and clothing. She encouraged me to pack everything together so that all the things that were meaningful to me could be unpacked first. These boxes were taken with me instead of the movers, just to make me feel a little sense of home my first night.

The first room Mom unpacked was a beautiful yellow kitchen. She just unpacked the basics, the things that would be needed for the next few days. After the kitchen items were unpacked, she helped me with my room. I unpacked my own stuff (with Mom's help, of course), and Mom talked to me about how I'd like my room arranged. This helped me to feel like the new space was mine, and I soon settled into my new room.

I got back into routine as soon as it was possible. I like routine. In the first night, Mom let me stay up a little longer just to make the night special, but after that, she established a daily routine. Keeping bedtime hours, mealtimes, and playtimes consistent, this helped me to feel more settled. After settling our family in the new home, Mom and Dad took time out too to enjoy the new home and neighborhood.

Mom and Dad gave many cocktail parties when we lived on South Spaulding Avenue, especially during the years 1959 through 62. I enjoyed watching her, Dad, and often my grandmother, Needie, having fun with their guests. Even though it was late at night; past midnight, I couldn't fall asleep because the excitement of the party kept me awake. Therefore, I'd get out of my bed and walk to the bedroom door, then I'd open the door slightly and peek into the living room where everybody was finger-popping. Mom would catch me every time and say to me that I was like a night owl and I needed to go back to bed and go to sleep. However, it was fun watching them and their guests dance, laugh, and enjoy one another to the music of Ray Charles, Johnny Mathis, Frank Sinatra, and jazz legends Duke Ellington, my Uncle Britt, John Coltrane, and Dave Brubeck, to name a few. They had a blast! And I did too!

After I had felt comfortable in my new surroundings, I wanted to settle into my new neighborhood. So I'd peek into yards to see if there were any signs that kids lived in that house, looking for swing sets, bikes, and toys. I also spent time outside in the front yard, rode my tricycle, went for a walk, and hung out on the front porch. I spent a lot of time outside where I would be discovered by neighbors and local kids.

Michael Williams, a local kid on my new block, became my best friend. He lived just two houses from me on the left. Michael was five years old and only eleven months older than me, and his older brother's name was Gregory who was three years older than me. Michael was full of energy and was fun to play with! It seemed like he had everything, including every kind of toy, game, and other things that kids like myself wanted! He was a nice-looking Creole-cultured kid; tall, chubby, and pigeon-toed. Michael and I shared many childhood experiences as we grew up together, including our friendship, religion, education, culture, recreation, and sports.

I also became friends with a girl whose name was Paige. She was my age, and her older brother's name was Craig. Later I discovered that their dad, Woodley Lewis, played professional football for the Los Angeles Rams in the NFL! Paige and her brother, Craig, were both mixed-race kids; their father, Woodley Lewis, was an African American, and their mother, Mitzi, was Japanese American. Surprisingly and coincidentally, many of my childhood friends who lived on my block were Roman Catholic, and they attended the same Catholic School that I did; but some of my other neighbors and friends who were non-Catholic attended the local public schools.

I really enjoyed living in my new multicultural neighborhood because I met a variety of people and I made many new friends.

"Gretchen"

On January 22, 1960, my mom gave birth to her fifth child, a baby girl whom she christened, "Leslie Denise Woodman." After Leslie's birth, my mom and grandmother nicknamed her "Gretchen." Gretchen is a German female baby name meaning pearl. When I heard the news, I jumped up and down with great delight because my baby sister was coming home that night. It was very exciting. My family would grow! But after I stopped cheering, there were a few things I didn't know.

Baby sister was darling. Baby sister was cute. But I let her looks fool me because here was the truth: My sister would drool. She would smell. She would scream. She sometimes would pull my hair. And she would do things that seemed to be mean.

She had expected me to share, even things that were new. And it was not just my toys, but the ones I loved too. Sometimes I would look for a hug when I wasn't feeling great. But when Mom was feeding the baby, I just had to wait. And since I was the first, that made me feel mad. But my family still loved me. So there was no need to feel sad.

It's just that my sister didn't know what to be. She needed help all the time. She wasn't smart yet, like me. I became her first teacher, showing her things that I knew. Giving her patience and love, then she just grew. And when she grew up, watching all of my deeds. She became amazing, for she was just like me!

Baby Sister's Whooping Cough

I remember my mom's unyielding faith, love, and persistence when she nursed (which seemed like an eternity) my then two-year-old baby sister back to sound health. This situation took place after Leslie had contracted the whooping cough (pertussis) or 100-day cough, a symptom of walking pneumonia which is a highly contagious respiratory tract infection. Being a young six-year-old boy myself, I had never seen or heard anything like it before. This disease was shocking in nature, and Leslie became very sick from it. The onset of it was like the symptoms similar to those of the common cold with a runny nose, fever, and mild cough.

But then, this was followed by weeks of my sister having severe coughing fits. Following a fit of coughing, she had a high-pitched whoop sound or gasp that occurred as she breathed in. The coughing lasted for ten or more weeks (hence the phrase "100-day cough"). Sometimes Leslie coughed so hard that she vomited and became very tired from the effort. Also, due to a loss of fluids and body fat, my baby sister experienced a significant weight reduction turning her virtually into skin and bones. I felt sympathy for her and my mom. Leslie's illness had both frightened and saddened my mom. But thanks to her faith and prayers to God, Mom's loving care for Leslie helped her make a full and healthy recovery from the whooping cough. Selah.

Kindergarten

In the prior weeks before I started kindergarten, my mom discussed it with me. She understood that being separated from her for the first time in my life would be stressful, so she expressed enthusiasm and excitement at all I was going to learn. Her compassion and comforting words about my first day at school made me feel good. Even though I feared going to kindergarten, it was something exciting that I looked forward to. When I was four years old, I started kindergarten at Marvin Avenue Elementary School in the Los Angeles Unified School District. It was just before the start of fall and near the very end of summer, September 6, 1960.

On the first day of kindergarten, Mom spent some time with me in my classroom. She introduced me to the teacher, but I don't remember her name. I was a bashful kid. So it was difficult for me to settle in to my first day of school. I wasn't used to all of the attention I was getting from my teacher and the other kids.

Mom remained cheerful and reiterated that she would be back to pick me up at noon, the end of the school day. She reminded me that I would be learning exciting new things, and she made time for me to talk to my teacher. Her strategies at comforting me seemed to have worked for the moment. But after she waved goodbye and left me there, I became anxious because I thought I wouldn't see her again! But I relaxed after the teacher had comforted me.

However, I had still missed my mom. Then suddenly, I had an idea of leaving school and walking back home. After recess, when my teacher wasn't paying attention to me, I left school through the opened gate and walked home. This was my second most daring act yet. Just a few years earlier, at the age of one, I had climbed up on the kitchen counter and grabbed my mom's iron pills out of the kitchen cabinet. Surely, I had become a little boy risk-taker.

This was an amazing feat for me because I was only four years old and had never done anything like that before. The walking distance from Marvin Avenue School to my home at 2635 South Spaulding Avenue was almost one mile (0.8 mi) and it took me about twenty minutes to walk it. With confidence, I knew my way back home after studying the route my mom drove to get me to and from school. Therefore, I was able to walk home.

After I had made it safely back home, I walked up to the front porch and rang the doorbell. When my mom answered the front door, she did not expect to see me standing there. Although I was okay, my mom was surprised and upset that I had left school and walked home by myself. She chastised me for leaving school without permission and expressed her concern that I could have been kidnapped or run over by a car. Scared and confused, I didn't know what to do! Immediately, Mom put me in the car and she drove me back to school. When we returned to the classroom, the teacher looked both concerned and happy that I was okay. Afterward, she seemed relieved that nothing bad had happened to me. Some of my classmates were also happy that I came back, and they wanted to be my friend.

Subsequently, I felt much better about being in kindergarten and I wanted to stay in school and have fun! After my mom made her goodbye cheerful and brief, she reminded me when she would return to pick me up. From then on, kindergarten would become the most joyous and successful educational experience in my life! I made lots of friends and learned how to interact with my classmates. I also learned how to count numbers from zero to fifty, say my ABCs, read stories like *Jack and Jill* and *The Three Little Pigs*, sing songs, draw, paint, and perform many other life tasks. Kindergarten became fun, interesting, and exciting for me.

10

DAD THE MILKMAN

My dad was a milkman for the Adohr Milk Farms Company. He was employed as a delivery driver at the Culver City, California, plant located on Washington Boulevard at La Cienega Boulevard near the historic Helms Bakery. On his route, he delivered milk and other dairy products to people's homes. Back in 1959 to 1961, Dad would leave our house early in the morning before anyone else was awake. When his milk truck was ready, he delivered the milk to the customers on his route. The milk was delivered in glass bottles with a round piece of cardboard capping the top. Deliveries were usually left at the customer's front door, and it was up to him or her to bring the milk inside before it got too warm or too hot, especially in the summer.

Milk came whole or homogenized. Whole milk was about a one-quarter cream which separated and floated to the top, forming a layer. People poured that off and used it for coffee or for whipped cream or shook the bottle to mix it and before pouring it into a glass or on cereal. Yummy-yummy! No one worried about milk fat back then. Skimmed milk was available, though. At the dairy, the fat raised to the top of the vat and was skimmed off before bottling. Now I rarely hear it called skimmed milk. Instead people say nonfat or fat-free. As far as 1 percent and 2 percent milk, I'd never heard of it in my childhood. Occasionally, Dad would bring home in small cartons pints of cold "chocolate milk"—mmm-mmm! Now that was a treat!

Sometimes, if Dad had finished his milk route by the time I was leaving for school, he would give me a ride in the truck. This was pretty exciting for a little kindergartener like myself. When I stepped off the truck and onto the playground, my friends gathered round. "How did you get a ride in that milk truck?" With a sense of pleasure, I proudly responded, "My daddy is a milkman!" My friends were green with envy…

At some point, and I'm not sure when, Dad didn't work for Adohr Milk Farms, and he didn't drive a milk truck anymore.

Mama Dear's Kitchen: 1958–1962

My siblings and I spent much of our early childhood visiting and sleeping over at my great-grandmother Mama Dear's house. After my dad was separated from us, Mama Dear stepped in and helped my mom tremendously with all of our needs and necessities. She was the matriarch and heart of our family. I played at her house, watched TV, went grocery shopping with her at the grocery store, and before she owned her own car, I would occasionally travel with her on the city buses! Mama Dear was a wonderful great-grandmother, and she would fill us up with lots of her love and joy! She and her husband, John, who was employed with the City of Los Angeles in the Sanitation Department, lived in a house on South Thurman Avenue just south of Smiley Drive at Los Angeles.

My favorite room in Mama Dear's house was her kitchen. Mama Dear's kitchen was where her food was prepared with love and seasoned with soul. Her soul food kitchen was a southern taste sensation, Texas-style! For as long as I can remember, Mama Dear proudly and carefully prepared every dish by hand and with love from her homemade recipes. Mama Dear's focus was on serving made from scratch true southern fare.

One of my favorite meals that Mama Dear cooked was her fried chicken dinner. The preparation for this, I remember, was an interesting process. Mama Dear would go to the local butcher's shop. The smell would greet us well before we stepped in the door to the tiny storefront selling chickens, turkeys, ducks, and supposedly rabbits. It's bearable, you might have told yourself, as you would peer a bit anxiously into the dark feather-strewn interior from which a cacophony of squawks occasionally erupted. Trying not to breathe too deeply, you'd step inside and join the queue, which had moved with briskness of a well-tuned assembly line. You're going to purchase live poultry? Well, I thought it might not be live when we leave with it, but it won't be the frozen variety from your grocery store.

Then Mama Dear would select a live chicken of her choice. The butcher would kill it and defeather it in front of her! Then he would clean it, wrap it, package, and sell it to her. Later that afternoon, she'd cut up the chicken parts which included the neck, back, and two wishbones from the breasts, and she'd season the fresh chicken with seasoning, salt and black pepper, dip it into flour, lay it into a black skillet of very hot Crisco oil, then she'd fry the chicken until it was golden brown. Delicious! The best very fresh and tender fried chicken ever!

The southern fare of other foods Mama Dear cooked and I enjoyed eating were fried pork chop, fried catfish and shrimp, oxtails, meatloaf, burger with fries, chitterlings, pork roast, and baked turkey wings! Mama Dear's was the best in Texas soul food cuisine.

Mama Dear's side dishes were just as good as her fried chicken! My favorites were her hot macaroni and melted cheese, mustard greens mixed with turnip greens, hot diced turnips and ham hock, hot rice and gravy with dabs of green onion, buttered corn on the cob, and hot sweet potatoes with vanilla extract, cinnamon, brown sugar, and melted butter on top! Very good!

Saving the sweets to eat for last. Some of Mama Dear's baked desserts and my favorite dishes were her hot sweet potato pie, peach cobbler, white coconut cake, devil's food cake, and banana pudding. Hmm-mmm, delicious!

The Pivotal Years: 1960 to 1965

All was well with me,
growing up in LA during the early 1960s;
I enjoyed my life!
Given the birthright as a firstborn child, was very nice!
When my baby sister came home that night,

she indeed became my delight!
I thought it was cool riding my bike,
but it was a "barrel of fun,"
when I played with my pal, big Mike!
All in all, I have expressed,
great things have been done for me,
and I'm feeling truly blessed!

Starting Kindergarten

Starting kindergarten on September 6, 1960, was a crucial step for me. Kindergarten was a place where I began to grow in a natural way. I learned how to play, sing, draw, and interact socially with other kids and people. Kindergarten really helped me to succeed in my transition from home to school. Kindergarten also helped promote my growth and development. It provided a safe and happy environment to learn skills that I would build on throughout my life.

With Mama Dear on Election Day, JFK

The day before election day, Monday, November 7, 1960, I spent the night at my great-grandmother's house on South Thurman Avenue. That next morning, on November 8, 1960, she served me a hot breakfast of oatmeal, bacon, and toast with a glass of whole milk, and then she drove me to my kindergarten class at Marvin Avenue Elementary School. That afternoon, Mama Dear picked me up from kindergarten and drove me back to her house. Later that afternoon, she explained to me that it was election day, and we were going to go vote for the democratic candidate, John F. Kennedy for the presidency of the United States. She described JFK to me as that handsome young man who people had been talking about lately, hearing about, and whom we had watched on television.

This was interesting and very exciting to me! So she held my hand and we walked down the street to a private residence that was being used as a public polling place. When we arrived, there were only a few people who were standing in line, waiting to vote. Then Mama Dear took her place in line with me standing next to her. The house had the American Flag hoisted on a staff in front. There were colorful banners, signs, hats, and badges decorated like the American flag in red, white, and blue with pictures of John F. Kennedy on them!

When Mama Dear was next in the line, she walked up to the voting booth with me still standing next to her. It was a small, enclosed area where she stood and cast her ballot. After she had cast her ballot and finished voting, I saw in her joy and a sense of pride. We both smiled and quietly rejoiced together. Then Mama Dear took me by my hand again, and we walked back to her house. Indeed, for a kid just like me, this was truly a wonderful experience in civility and patriotism. Since then, I have cherished and held on to that fond memory. John F. Kennedy ultimately won the general election. He was the youngest man and the first Roman Catholic ever elected to the presidency of the United States.

"Daddy" Takes Too Long

Sometimes Dad had to pick me up from kindergarten, but instead of driving me directly home, he would occasionally stop at a house nearby my school and visit with whomever. While I anxiously waited for him inside the car, which seemed like an eternity, my thoughts were, *Dad is taking too long inside that house! Why can't Dad take me inside that house with him?* or *Dad has forgotten about me!* And so forth. Consequently, I began to dread those days when Dad had to pick me up from kindergarten because I didn't want to go back to that house and wait for him again.

Emotionally, I had felt neglected and abandoned. Sometimes I would weep and cry out to dad! Yet, joy would come over me when I saw him leaving that house. But in fear that Dad would find me upset and teary eyed, I'd quickly use my hands and wipe away the tears from my face before he reentered the car. After he was inside the car, dad would look at me and smile.

I would also look back at him and smile because after waiting alone in the car while he was inside that house, I was happy that we were finally going home! I also had missed my mom and I wanted to see her warm smile and feel her comforting hug. Then Dad would start the car, and he'd drive us home. However, I never told Mom about Dad's indiscretions because I wanted to protect her good heart.

Up to now, I still don't know what business Dad had inside that house, except that he probably was gambling because he had once told me that he won money from somebody inside that house.

My First Birthday Party

I was going to be five years old and was looking forward to my first birthday party. I had been dreaming of that day for months, and I had imagined a huge party outside in our backyard with my best friend, Michael, all of my family, and a clown. My fifth birthday was on November 22, 1960; it was the best birthday party that I can remember as a kid. On that same day, after kindergarten, I went directly home to celebrate my birthday.

When I opened the door to the backyard, I saw a big sign hanging there, saying, "Happy birthday, Davion!" Everybody wished me a happy birthday, then my mom played a song on my record player called "For He's a Jolly Good Fellow," a popular song that was sung to congratulate me on my fifth birthday. And everybody at my party sung along with that song.

My fifth birthday party was just as I had imagined because my best friend, Michael, was there; a clown who was sitting down blowing up the balloons was there; and all of my family and relatives were there too! I also saw a big patio table full of food, a bowl of punch, and a birthday cake with five candles and my favorite devil's food cake with vanilla ice-cream.

However, that wasn't all, they had also prepared different games to play altogether. To sum up, I enjoyed my birthday party on that wonderful day in November, and I learned that it doesn't matter how you hold a party as long as your loved ones are there.

My First Bicycle: Christmas 1960

After I was five years old, I remember how excited I was on Christmas day when my mom and Needie gave me my first bicycle. It was a new red bicycle, trimmed in white, with a battery-operated headlight. My bike also had pretty red and white streamers hanging down from the handle bars. It was the largest gift of all the gifts, standing upright on training wheels alongside our beautifully decorated white flocked Christmas tree with red ornaments hanging all around it. My gift was placed in our living room next to the front window.

I did not know how to ride a bike, but I was grinning from ear to ear just thinking about learning. My dad began teaching me how to ride my new red bike. The training wheels on it helped me to get my balance. I would ride up and down the sidewalk, hoping that all my friends could see this wonderful new Christmas gift that was given to me.

Once I got the hang of riding, my dad raised one wheel up so that I could get comfortable with one training wheel not touching the ground. Soon my dad took both training wheels off, and I remember feeling nervous and excited all at the same time.

For a few days, my dad held on to the back of my bike while I would ride. I felt very safe knowing my dad was right behind me. Then one day…he let go. I didn't know he had done that until a few minutes later. I was so excited when I realized that I was riding my bike all by myself!

After that day, I went everywhere on my bike. I loved riding and I loved my bike.

I have a photo in one of my photo albums. It's one among my many favorite ones. I'm smiling, and there beside me is my red bicycle, and standing on both sides of me are the loves of my life, my mom and my grandmother, Needie. It has been a great reminder of their love for me. As I have grown and matured, I've looked at that photo from time to time, and it has helped me to always be thankful to God for all the love and benefits which I have received from him each day.

The Williams Family

They were there for me, even when they didn't have to be. There hadn't been a time that I didn't look forward to going to the Williams' house who lived just two houses to the left of our house on South Spaulding Avenue at Los Angeles. They were Catholics and a typical nuclear family consisting of both parents: father and patriarch, Mr. James Williams who was from Chicago, Illinois; he was a hard worker and good provider for his family; and mother, Mrs. Mayola Williams who was Creole from Baton Rouge, Louisiana; she was a highly educated woman with a master's degree in education; big brother, Gregory Williams, who was a smart and disciplined child; and my best friend, Michael Williams, "Big Mike," who in my mom's opinion was the sweetest of the two brothers. They could all be gathered up in the living room or spread around the house. But the first thing I was greeted with was so much love. Even though they had their own family to nurture and care for and busy work schedules, the Williams' time and time again took me into their home and made me one of their own.

Each and every one of them played such an important role in my friendship with Michael whether it was his parents who had given me the very gift of his presence or his big brother, Greg, who was there for him when I couldn't be. I never took for granted how much they meant to him. Not only did they welcome me into their own home to be a part of their family, but they made me want to be a better part of my own family.

It didn't matter if they argued or struggled with each other. Each one of them refused to give up on each other. They were a family that never stopped fighting for each other and that inspired me every time I stepped foot in their home. I'm thankful that I got the chance to be in their lives.

There can never be enough ways to put into words how grateful I was that my best friend had the family that he had. Once in a lifetime is really all I can say to describe the Williams family. Through thick and thin, ups and downs, they molded my best friend into a compassionate and fun-loving person. Everyone who had encountered the Williams family experienced a friendship unlike anything else.

I was always able to count on all of them for a laugh, even when it was at the expense of being made fun of. No one will ever be able to replace the spot they took in my heart.

I never knew the day when I met my best friend in 1959 that I would gain something so much more than a friendship. I will forever be thankful for the Williams family investing in our friendship and truly caring for me as their own. They are once in a lifetime, and I am so joyful and grateful God blessed my lifetime with them.

Last Day in Kindergarten

I came to understand the significance of the year I had just completed. Nine months earlier, I had walked into this place called "Kindergarten." I was scared. I cried and didn't want to stay. Instead, I didn't stay. I left and walked home; but when my mom brought me back to kindergarten, I stayed. I stayed that second time because my teacher held my hand while I said goodbye to my mom, and she let me sit next to her on the carpet while I was sad. We read a story together and played a game to learn everyone's name.

In our time together, I learned what it meant to sit in a circle, walk in a line, hold a pencil, use scissors, zip up my coat, and be part of a group. I learned how to read, become a mathematician, scientist, inquirer, and more. I learned what it meant to be a friend. I played with others, took turns, worked through problems, and practiced patience.

I smiled, laughed, and sometimes cried. Not all of my days were easy, but most of my days were filled with learning, excitement, and happiness. I gave her lots of hugs and high fives and still called her "Teacher" no matter how many times she told me her name.

Fast-forward nine months, and I was losing some of my teeth! I was also five years old now and nearly a first-grader. Time had seemed to fly by, and I was excited for the summer. I was ready to go! Surely, I had graduated from kindergarten and promoted to the first grade. Hooray!

Mamma Recalled Taking Me to Kindergarten on the First Day

Mamma recalled taking me to kindergarten on the first day. She said we walked into the classroom, and I just stood there, shy at first, but then the teacher came over and introduced me to the other kids, and I went off to play. Mamma watched me for a few minutes to see how I would do, and then I came up to her and said, "Mamma, you can leave now."

And she just laughed and said, "Okay." Then she hugged me and said, "I love you and that I'll be back soon to get you."

And I said, "Okay, I love you too" and then went back to playing. She hated to leave me there, but knew she had to go.

Mamma really thought I would be crying like she had seen some of the other kids doing, but I didn't. She was the one crying. Mamma thought about me the whole time I was gone, just wondering what I was doing until I shocked her when I walked back home and stood at the front door. But after she returned me to school that morning, and when she came to get me, I was so excited, and before getting in the car, I was telling her about my day. She said my eyes were so bright and I was just filled with so much information. She swore I didn't stop talking until we got back into the house.

Hody's

Hody's Coffee Shop was once located on the northeast corner of La Brea Avenue and Rodeo Road near the Baldwin Hills section of Los Angeles and just across the street from the historic Thrifty Drug Store, now Rite Aid. It was a carhop drive-in type of restaurant in 1961. Whenever my grandmother, Needie, took my younger siblings and me for a treat, she'd load us up in her Buick La Sabre and drive us to Hody's. When we arrived at the coffee shop, she'd order delicious cold flavored malts for us to drink. Depending on what flavored malt we wanted, my siblings and myself would sit in the car and sip on either a vanilla, chocolate, or strawberry malt. Needie always ordered for herself a hot pastrami sandwich to eat. Pastrami was her favorite sandwich.

We also went to Hody's and ate their excellent hamburgers and French fries smothered with ketchup. The food was brought right to our car on a tray and then hung on the driver's window. I enjoyed Hody's carhop type restaurant. It was fun just to watch the young ladies as they went from car to car, bringing food and beverage. When we ate there, it always was a pleasant experience. The atmosphere and food were out of sight, but the cold vanilla malt with whipped cream and red cherry on top was my delight. Whenever we wanted a treat, Hody's indeed was the place to go eat!

A New and Friendly Backyard

In the spring of 1961, Dad paid a construction contractor cash to rebuild a beautiful new backyard at our house on South Spaulding

Avenue. It was a dynamic place to hang out. "Kid-friendly," the basic design had an area closest to the house as a shared-use area. It was a patio with black and white colored metal awnings, paved concrete deck, built-in brick barbeque grill and fireplace, with spots for the adults to sit and relax. At the same time, they could easily keep an eye on us while we played outside in the backyard.

Further out in the yard was a newly constructed fenced-in basketball half-court on paved concrete ground; it included a handball court and an area with a tetherball and pole. The other part of the backyard, which ran parallel to the patio, was a green manicured lawn. For walking on the lawn in the backyard, there were two paths of stepping stones. One path lead from the patio to the backyard/side yard wooden gate, and the other one lead from the patio to the chain-linked gate at the entrance of the basketball court. Planted in the center of our new yard was a large maple tree. Also, an assortment of beautiful plants, roses, and flowers were planted between the lawn and patio with nicely trimmed hedges. The hedges were planted alongside the fenced property line on the north side of our new yard. The hedges extended from the backyard/side yard gate to the fenced-in basketball court.

After our new backyard was completed, I jumped up for joy in high spirits! It was a kid's paradise, and the kids on my block of all ages, girls and boys, came to play at my house in our new backyard. For a five-year-old boy, this was very exciting to me; I was as proud as a peacock. After construction, some of the kids who came over to play looked covetously at my new backyard. They were amazed to find so many exciting and fun things to do in it. Certainly, our new friendly backyard made me feel like I was over the moon!

From then on, and in the following years, my mom and later stepfather, Dick, enjoyed lots of barbeques, marshmallow roasts, and countless parties. In our new backyard, either day or night and on weekends, we enjoyed ourselves! Especially during the summer months, we had hours of fun playing games of croquet on our backyard lawn. Also, I enjoyed outdoor activities with my brothers and neighborhood kids; we played games of tetherball, handball, and we shot hoop-games of horse with the basketball. In addition, the neighborhood kids and myself enjoyed swinging and sliding on my outdoor swing set, cooling off in my aboveground rubber wading pool or climbing up on our large maple tree. When warm sunny California days arrived and I wasn't in school, I enjoyed playing in my new backyard. Now looking back is indeed a real blast from the past.

11

THE LOS ANGELES POLICEMAN WHO SHONE HIS FLASHLIGHT IN MY BEDROOM

During the spring of 1961, when I was only five-and-a-half years old, I believed that I had experienced the most horrific rude awakening in my life, and it happened one late evening while my brothers and I were fast asleep in our beds. We were suddenly and unexpectedly awakened by a loud commotion coming from the living room. Then I was surprised to see that our bedroom door was slowly opening. When I looked up, I saw this tall and strange-looking white man with a medium build walk through my bedroom door; he was a Los Angeles policeman wearing a dark navy-blue uniform carrying a holstered gun fastened around his waist and a shiny badge pinned on the front of his shirt. He quickly began shining his flashlight all around our bedroom, and he shone it on my brothers and me. As I laid in my bed, I immediately began tingling with anxiety as well as excitement while I watched him shine his flashlight under our beds and inside of our closet.

Meanwhile, I remember seeing several other uniformed police officers; one in particular had distinguished himself from the other policemen. He was wearing a dark stingy brim fedora hat with the brim snapped down in the front, a white dress shirt, a dark navy-blue suit and tie (he reminded me of the fictional police detective, Dick Tracy). The policemen kept coming and going. They walked in and out of our house, through the front door from the front yard and through the back door to the backyard, and vice versa. The policemen went in and out of our adjacent garage, and around the outside of our house from the front yard through the side yard gate to the backyard. With eyes like a hawk, they shone their flashlights circumspectly, diligently looking everywhere and leaving no stone unturned in their search.

Commotion in the Living Room

Initially, I was awakened from my sleep and distracted by a commotion in the living room which had happened moments earlier. The commotion in the living room occurred between my mom and the policemen. Mom was furious over why LAPD had come to our house so late in the evening, which caused an unexpected and unpleasant disturbance to our family's peace and tranquility. Even though Mom had been furious with the policemen, she was merely acting on her love and motherly instinct by protecting us, her small children, from danger and keeping us safe from harm.

> A mother's love for her child is like nothing else
> in the world. It knows no law, no pity, it dares
> all things and crushes down remorselessly all that
> stands in its path.
>
> —Agatha Christie

After everything had calmed down, the policeman wearing the hat, suit, and tie was a robbery and homicide police detective and lead investigator on the case. He interviewed my mother in the living room. When the police detective showed her the search and seizure warrant from a Los Angeles County judge, giving them the authority to search our house and property for stolen money and firearm(s), she began trembling with fear because my father had been charged earlier that day with the crime(s) of armed robbery. Also, the police detective was investigating my mother to find out whether or not she had knowledge of the crime(s), and/or if she was involved with my father in the commission of the alleged crime(s). But of course not! My mother was an innocent child of God. She had never been involved with my father in any alleged criminal act(s), and she knew nothing concerning any crime(s) he was accused of and/or charged with. So my mom was ruled out by the detective as a possible suspect because she had a strong alibi as a God-fearing, loving, and caring mother.

Later that night, police recovered some of the alleged stolen money my father had stashed away in the garage. The money was tucked in a small toolbox and hidden under a pair of work gloves. However, I'm uncertain whether or not the police recovered the firearm(s) used by my father to commit the alleged crime(s). In fact, while that horrendous occurrence was happening to us in our home, my father had been apprehended and placed into police custody.

A Heartrending Visit

Since that dreadful night in our home several months earlier with the Los Angeles Police Department, I saw my father for the first and last time while he was incarcerated. Dad had been transferred from the Los Angeles County Jail to the California Institution for Men, a major minimum-security prison in Chino. When we faced each other, it was during a heartrending visit in a booth behind a plexiglass window. My voice wobbled with emotion as we talked on the phones. I had missed my daddy terribly and I wanted to embrace him, but the prison's security perimeters prevented it. The California Institution for Men was the first state penitentiary where he began serving a five-year prison sentence. I would not see him again until three years later after he was released on parole in 1964.

Single Mom after Dad's Incarceration

After Dad's incarceration, my mom was presented with a challenging issue—how would she respond to my questions about him, a convicted felon who was serving a long prison sentence? Mom suddenly and unexpectedly became like a widowed single parent with five young children to care for. I was left without a dad and a role model, but I still had three great role models in my mom, my grandmother, and my great-grandmother. However, my mom was still concerned that I would somehow end up identifying with my dad's example, and she had to deal with the emotional trauma of telling me that my dad had been incarcerated. This is illustrated in the following prison poem by Alison Henderson:

How do you sit down and talk to your son
and tell him that his Daddy has gone?
It's easier explaining the meaning of death
and why people die and draw their last breath.
But Daddy, he's gone to no peaceful heaven.
Instead he's in prison and serving a seven,
so how do you sit down and tell your own son
the whys and the reasons his Daddy has gone?
"Listen, my son, you'll need to be strong.
Daddy has done something terribly wrong.
He's gone into prison for quite a long time,
and this is what happens when you commit crime."
"Daddy still loves us, he'll phone and he'll write,
ring you to wish you goodnight and sleep tight.
We can sit down together and write him a letter.
It'll make Daddy smile and make him feel better"
"We can go and see Daddy, perhaps once a week,
to give him a hug and a kiss on the cheek.
You can draw Daddy pictures and paintings at school
to put on his wall, which will look really cool."
I tried telling my son with emotional tact
the truth of the matter, but you can't hide the fact.
His Daddy has gone and has gone for a while.
You can't say it with flowers or manage a smile.
So how do you sit down and talk to your son
and answer his questions why Daddy has gone?

All you can do is just tell him your way
and pray to the Lord he'll be home soon one day.
—Alison Henderson

Even though I had become fatherless, I lived my life in high spirits, knowing that I was blessed to have my mom who loved me and my siblings so much. Her concern for our well-being was consistent, and she would keep moving in this same positive direction throughout my childhood. As I grew, Mom cultivated an awareness of my inclinations and interests. She would always compliment me on my positive attributes and affirm in me for who I was: a unique and special creation of my heavenly Father.

At first, when I asked Mom questions about Dad, she looked sad and ashamed regarding what had happened to him; so she wouldn't tell me the truth about his absence, but she told me that my dad was in the army instead. Then I told everybody that my dad was in the army too. When I persistently asked my mom questions about my dad, she finally told me the truth about what happened to him. Mom explained to me that my dad had done some bad things in the past and that he had to be punished for them.

After hearing the truth from my mom, it was another rude awakening for me and just another episode in the ongoing saga of our family's enormous personal tragedy. I broke down into tears, assuming that I was the blame for the brokenness in our family. While feeling sad and assuming the blame for what had happened to my dad, without hesitation, my mom made sure I understood that my dad was absent because of his own mistakes, not because of anything I had did. Mom told me that it was okay to be sad about not having a dad, and sometimes even feeling angry about it. This was only natural. My mom also helped me grasp the point that God didn't want me to hold grudges against anybody because it saddens God when we become bitter against other people, and resentment only hurts the person who nurtures it.

Although I didn't have any other positive male role models, it was encouraging to know that I had been blessed with other positive female role models in my mom, my grandmother, and my great-grandmother.

Their affirmation and attention gave me a deeper sense of how special and valuable I was. They also shared God's love with me, which helped me to understand that while my earthly dad was not around, my heavenly Father would never leave me nor forsake me.

Andree's Accident

When I was five-and-a-half years old, a car accident occurred that involved my four-and-a-half-year-old brother, Andree, who was the youngest twin; it happened one late afternoon on a weekday during the summer of 1961. We had just returned to Mama Dear's house from shopping at the grocery store. She lived in a beautiful house on South Thurman Avenue at Mid-City, Los Angeles. After we had carried the groceries inside of her house, I asked Mama Dear and Mamma for permission to play outside in the front yard; they both said yes. But my mamma affectionately warned me not to play in the street; and since I was the oldest child, she urged me to be safe, to take care of my younger brothers and play only in the front yard. I assented, and jumping with joy, we hurried outside.

After we had went outside to play in the front yard, Andree and I walked over to Mama Dear's car, which was a 1958 Oldsmobile, and it was parked in her driveway. Then I curiously walked around to the driver side door, and as I was peeking through the driver's side car window, my brother, Andree, was standing next to the passenger side door. When I looked inside of the car, I observed that both car doors were unlocked; and at that moment, it came to my mind the idea of having fun would be to get inside of Mama Dear's car and pretend like I was driving her car, just like she had driven it. After that thought, and tingling with excitement, I opened the driver side door and sat down in the driver's seat. And at the same time, Andree opened the passenger side door and sat down across from me in the passenger front seat.

Next, I closed the driver side door, shifted the gear into neutral, and released the emergency brake as I had watched Mama Dear do many times before, and suddenly, her car began rolling in reverse down the slightly sloped driveway. This happened before Andree could close the passenger side door. While the car was still moving,

Andree reached out and attempted to close the passenger side door, but he lost his grip instead and fell out of the car onto the driveway below. While Andree was lying in the driveway on the ground below, the front passenger car wheel rolled over him, and the weight of the car nearly crushed his skull.

Afterward, I began to panic, and the car rolled to a complete stop in the street. Then pumping with adrenaline, I jumped out of the car and ran around it to see about Andree. It astounded me at what had just happened to my little brother, and it was horrendous seeing his unconscious and lifeless body lying there on the concrete driveway. Andree wasn't screaming or anything, but he lay there unconscious and out of it. Feeling weak, helpless, and scared, I began crying. Next, I ran into the house, telling Mama Dear and my mother what had just happened to Andree. They both immediately went into shock and couldn't quite believe it.

Moments after, they both scurried out of the house and came to Andree's aid. Mama Dear gently picked him up and held him. Then they both provided Andree with as much comfort as they could. Without any hesitation, Mama Dear quickly carried his lifeless body inside of her house, and she softly laid him on the living room sofa. By that time, I had felt wretched with grief and was deeply saddened.

Then I heard a loud prolonged sound of a siren; it was an ambulance responding to the medical emergency for Andree. The siren from the ambulance sounded louder and louder as it came closer and closer to Mama Dear's house. After the white Cadillac ambulance with flashing red lights and Red Cross symbols with the word Mercy written on the doors arrived in front of Mama Dear's house, the loud sound of the siren all of sudden fell silent. Red lights still flashing, two paramedics who were wearing white uniforms quickly emerged from the front of the ambulance, and they walked to the rear of it, opened its rear door, and lifted up a gurney, and then they lowered it down onto the street. Next, both men, one who was carrying a red paramedic box, pushed the gurney on wheels and rolled it up to the front porch, lifting it up the steps, and through the front door where they had entered Mama Dear's living room.

While both men were in Mama Dear's house, the paramedic who was carrying the red paramedic box immediately rendered first aid to Andree. He checked his vital signs. After he had finished checking Andree's vital signs, the paramedic gently lifted him up from the sofa and laid Andree softly on top of the gurney. After that, they strapped Andree securely onto the gurney and rolled him out of the house to the waiting ambulance. Then they lifted him up and rolled him into the rear of the ambulance.

As it was becoming dark outside, and the ambulance was leaving for the hospital, the paramedic who had carried the red paramedic box sat next to Andree in back of the ambulance while the other paramedic drove the ambulance. I still remember hearing the loud prolonged sound of the siren and seeing its red lights flashing as the ambulance drove away from Mama Dear's house. After the ambulance was out of sight, and moments later, the sound of the loud siren became faint and finally quiet in the far distance. Andree was rushed to the Children's Hospital of Los Angeles in critical condition.

While Mama Dear took care of me and my other siblings, Needie and Mamma drove to Children's Hospital Emergency. It's where they saw Andree before he went into surgery. For Needie and Mamma, that's when reality had kicked in. Andree was in an induced coma, and they told me that they were horrified at the sight of him because the size of his head had swollen to twice the size of his normal head. They had felt completely helpless.

After more than one month of intensive care and therapy at the Children's Hospital, my brother, Andree, miraculously recovered from his traumatic head injury, and he was discharged from the hospital. When he returned home, Andree was ecstatic over reuniting with us. My family was in high spirits, and I was elated! We had truly missed Andree, and I loved him very much. Since Andree's accident, and from that day forward, he became my special brother because inside of my heart, I would always hold a soft spot for him. One of empathy and compassion.

God's grace had truly touched our family on that wonderful homecoming day when He reunited us with Andree, who had fully recovered from his head concussion and who also was in good health!

Swimming Lessons

After I had graduated from kindergarten at Marvin Avenue Elementary School in June 1961, the most exciting thing happened to me that summer. Just when the season was heating up, my mom's childhood friend and classmate, Joan, invited me to join her son, Michael, for swimming lessons at Los Angeles High School. My mom and I thought that swimming lessons were a wonderful idea, and we both were happy and excited about it. So she accepted Joan's invitation on my behalf.

Then it followed; Joan would pick me up in her 1960 Ford Thunderbird, and she'd take her son, Michael, and me to and from LA High School for our swimming lessons. Joan would never leave us alone at the pool, but she'd stay and sit in the bleachers to watch us while we learned how to swim with the other kids. My swimming class was multicultural; it had only a few African American kids, twice as many Japanese kids, and three times as many white kids; it was comprised of both genders in the same age group: four, five, and six years old...

LA High School's swimming pool water was dark blue in color and it had a strong chlorine smell. As a common disinfectant, chlorine is used more directly in swimming pools to keep them clean and sanitary. The pool was an old-fashioned Olympic-sized rectangular-shaped indoor swimming pool made of ceramic tile with the high school's colors: royal blue and white. The depth of the swimming pool ranged from three feet on the shallow end, gradually sloping down deeper and deeper into twelve feet on the deep end. It had stairs on every side to climb in and out of it. The deep end of the swimming pool was equipped with three diving boards, one low diving board on each side, and a high diving board in between them.

On that first day of swimming lessons, having my swimming trunks on, wearing my beach thongs, and carrying my towel, I walked from the locker room with my swim class to the swimming pool area. Upon seeing the swimming pool for the first time, it gave me a surreal feeling. But after I had climbed down into the swimming pool, it felt awesome! Pumping with adrenaline and tingling with anxiety and excitement at the same time, I was ready to learn how to swim!

Joan's son, Michael, was a tall and handsome boy with a slim build whom was one year older than me. He was already in an advanced swimming class because he had taken swimming lessons one year before me. We became best friends that summer, riding together to and from swimming lessons with his mother. He was the one with whom I liked being with, and I believed he liked being with me. We shared all of our feelings with each other, and we liked talking about everything. It was always fun and laughter when we were together.

I will admit that I did have a crush on his mother, Joan. She wasn't beautiful in the classical way, no flowing golden curls or ivory skin, no piercing eyes of green. She was shorter than average and certainly larger than a catwalk model, but in her ordinariness, she was stunning. Something radiated from within that rendered her irresistible and attractive to me. Sometimes I could hardly wait for her to pick me up and take me on the next trip to the swimming pool. Joan cared for me like my mom did, and she was exciting and fun to be with.

After I had learned all of the basic swimming techniques, safety rules, and passing my swim test for the summer session, it was time, and I was definitely ready for the final swim test; that is, to jump off the high diving board into twelve feet of deep water, resurface to the top of the water, and swim to the edge of the pool. I told my mom I was going to jump off the high diving board into deep water that day. "Really?" she said with a smile. The diving board was very high, and the water was very deep, both maybe a little scary, but I was excited and ready to jump. So on my last day at the swimming pool, I watched the other kids climb up the long ladder to the top.

They'd walk all the way out to the end of the board, like tiny creatures. Then they stood on the edge. They'd spread their arms and bend their knees and spring up, up, up! And then they dove down, down, down. Splash! It looked easy, I thought.

Feeling a little nervous, I was next in line. I stood at the bottom of the ladder. Then I looked up. I began to climb, thinking that ladder was very tall, up and up until I got to the top. I reached the top and I stood straight up. Then I walked all the way to the end of the board. My toes curled around the rough edge. I looked out as far as I could see. I felt like I was ready. I took a deep breath and spread my arms and bent my knees. Then I sprang up! Up off the board! Flying! I hit the water with a *splash!* Down, down, down I went, underwater in the deep. And then back up with my head above the water! *Whoosh!* After I had resurfaced, I swam to the edge of the pool.

"Davion! You did it!" said my swimming instructor.

I did it! I thought to myself with a big smile. *I'm a great jumper and swimmer!* And my chest stuck out proudly... Then jokingly, I said to my swimming instructor, "Do you know what?"

"What?" said my swimming instructor.

"Surprise double backflip is next!"

After my swimming class had finished the qualifying jump from the high diving board into the deep twelve feet of water, which was the final test to advance to the next level, those who passed received a red ribbon certification. When the swimming instructor announced my name to come and get my ribbon, I was in high spirits as I walked up to receive it! I had done this wonderful thing; I learned how to swim successfully by my own effort, courage, and skill. This amazing new gift from God significantly impacted my character and my life in the most positive way from then on until this day.

All in all, I was elated about my recent swimming achievement. At the same time, I broke down into tears that my swimming lessons had come to an end for the summer. And I was equally saddened not knowing when I would see my friends, Joan and Michael, again.

After that day, the Lord gently touched my soul with his compassion. And I was filled with great joy and comfort from the Holy Spirit. Feeling blessed! It was time for me to move on to my next adventure.

12

THY NEIGHBOR

While I was playing in my front yard one sunny afternoon, our neighbor, a teenage boy who lived in the house across the street from my house, approached me with an illicit proposition. He asked me to walk with him to the rear of a neighboring vacant house. So I hesitantly walked with him toward the backyard of the vacant house. As we approached the backyard through the side yard, it became apparent to me that he wanted to commit an act that was sexually immoral in exchange for a red plastic Duncan yoyo. Feeling nervous and afraid, I declined his offer and quickly departed from there.

Leaving him where he stood, I ran as fast as I could back home. After my encounter with him, whenever we were outside at the same time, he avoided looking at me because I think he despised himself for tempting me to do wrong. Then I soon realized it was foolish of me to have been too trusting of my neighbor. Eventually, I felt sorry for him and hoped he'd get over his shame; but I don't believe he ever did. From then on, and seemingly remorseful, my neighbor kept his distance and he never attempted to approach me again.

My Dad's So-Called Friend Who Became Our Stepfather

Richard, whose nickname is Dick, proved himself to be my dad's "so-called friend." His friendly pretense became apparent after my dad was sentenced to a state penitentiary for the conviction of his crime(s). Within a short time afterward, Dick started dating my mother. He subsequently married her. I believe a true friend doesn't date and marry his friend's ex-wife with five children. When my mother and Dick began dating, it wasn't clear to me that she was a divorcee yet.

Nevertheless, because of my mother's vulnerability, Dick, the foolish knight in shining armor, came to her rescue after my father had put her in a difficult situation. During this very trying time, Dick drove a neat-looking late 1950s black on black Austin Healy sports car. And sometimes, with my mother in the passenger seat, he'd picked me up after school. Although I did not like him, it was only on those rare occasions when I rode with him in his sports car that I liked him. That is, I only liked Dick when I rode in his sports car, especially when the convertible top was down.

I had met Dick approximately one year earlier when my dad had taken me to visit him at his apartment. After graduating from high school, he left his birthplace in Ohio and came to live with Aunt Dorothy (his mother's sister) and Uncle Connie (Dorothy's husband) in Los Angeles. Soon after Dick's arrival in Los Angeles, he befriended my dad and mom when they were in their late teens, and both were later betrayed by Dick who also destroyed our family.

When I first met Dick, I thought he was a peculiar and strange-looking man with a large wart on the left side of his nose. After he married my mother, I often wondered why he didn't have the wart removed from his nose with cosmetic surgery.

Most of the time, I thought Dick was creepy. He always looked mean and he rarely cracked a smile. In spite of the fact that he was welcoming toward my dad and me during our visit with him, I felt as though he disliked me from the very beginning. And he acted like or it seemed like he despised the father-son relationship my dad and I had with one another. Dick also reminded me of the Hollywood actor Boris Karloff in the 1931 DRAMA/science fiction movie *Frankenstein*.

After graduating from Los Angeles Trade Technical College, (LA Trade Tech) Dick as a young man landed a career as a machinist with Rockwell International in the aerospace industry. My dad once described him as being like the machines he worked on. His heart was hard and he always had a stoned face. Even though Dick had become my stepfather after my mother divorced my father, we never were close nor affectionate. Unfortunately, our stepfather-stepson relationship has always been virtually nonexistent and adversarial, even to this day. Actually, Dick is a stranger to me because I have never known him, and he has never loved me or anybody else for that matter.

Holy Spirit Catholic School: First Grade

On September 5, 1961, the day after Labor Day holiday, I began attending a new school, Holy Spirit Catholic School, where I was in the first grade. It was located on Burnside Avenue at Pico Boulevard in Los Angeles, California. My father had recently been incarcerated and separated from our family. My beloved mother was like a widowed single parent and homemaker. My siblings and myself were left fatherless. My younger twin brothers, Rene and Andree, were both in public school kindergarten attending Marvin Avenue Elementary School where I had attended during the previous semester. My youngest brother, Vernon "Sputdoll," and my baby sister, Leslie "Gretchen," not of school age yet, were still at home in the loving care of my mom.

My mother attended Catholic school for twelve years, and she benefited greatly from it. After I had graduated from kindergarten and promoted to the first grade, my mother had decided to send me to Catholic school where she believed it would offer me a much a better education than the local public school. Aside from this, she liked the fact that Catholic school combined academic lessons with those on morals and good behavior. Also, the Catholic religion required that my mother uphold the obligation to preserve and ensure the baptism and education of her children in the Catholic church.

It was the beginning of my first day in the first grade as I entered the two-story brick building at Holy Spirit Catholic School. My mother was with me on that bright sunny Tuesday morning, September 5, 1961. I was feeling a little excited and scared at the same time. I was afraid that I would not make any new friends, but my mom said it was going to be okay because I was going to meet new friends just like I did in kindergarten. I was wearing the parochial school's prescribed uniform: a pair of salt and pepper corduroy pants, black dress shoes, a white dress shirt, and a light grey cardigan sweater with the Holy Spirit School emblem displayed on the right-side pocket of the sweater. I was five years old and one of the youngest students in my first-grade class. Most of the boys and girls in my first-grade class were already six years old except for a few of my classmates who were born after me. Almost all of my first-grade classmates were born in 1955, the same year of my birth.

My Christian journey and Catholic education started with discovering and learning while I was growing in God's love. When my mother and I went into the classroom, we met my new first-grade teacher. She greeted us with a smile and introduced herself. She said her name was Sister Angela. I replied in kind and said, "Hi, my name is Davion." Even though the nun seemed very nice, I was still a little scared because I did not want Mom to leave me. My teacher was a Catholic nun who looked strange to me because I had never seen a school teacher who looked that way. She was wearing a black robe with a rosary bead around her neck and a black habit and veil on her head. Later, I would learn that the nun's all black clothing was symbolic of repentance and simplicity.

After Mom and I met my teacher, we started looking around the classroom. My mom pointed out all of the cool things that I was going to learn in the first grade, especially religion. I would soon learn how to recite prayers, retell Bible stories, identify the members of the Holy Family, recognize Peter as the first pope, identify the parts of the Bible, and understand the importance of the Sacraments, especially Baptism. My first-grade curriculum included the general education lessons in reading, English/language arts, listening/speaking, mathematics, social studies, and science.

Even though I was still a little scared, I started to relax and got excited by the things I was seeing. When I looked about the classroom, I saw a tall boy who looked really happy. I said, "Mom, look at that tall boy, he looks so happy."

Then my mom said to me, "Why don't you go over and introduce yourself?"

Delighted to do so, I immediately walked over to the tall boy and introduced myself as Davion. He looked down at me and replied with a big smile, "My name is Michael Shannon." To this day, I've never forgotten Michael Shannon because he became my first and best friend at Holy Spirit Catholic School.

After we became friends, Michael Shannon and I always had fun laughing, playing tetherball, doing other fun activities, and we ate lunch together. He also had protected me from a bully on the playground. The kid was light brown-skinned with thick curly brown hair. He was in the second grade and was older and bigger than me. So one afternoon while I was eating my lunch, he tried to take my metal lunch box and thermos from me. My lunchbox was unique-looking. It looked like a barn with farm décor on it, and the metal thermos looked like a grain silo with farm décor on it. So that second-grade boy wanted it. But Michael stopped him in his tracks and told him to leave me alone.

Suddenly, he froze! Then after looking at Michael and me momentarily, he got scared and ran away to the other side of the playground. I think Michael's height and my good courage intimidated the bully, and he never messed with me again. Wow, the idiom was true! "A friend in need is a friend indeed." From then on, Michael watched my back, and I watched his back. Since our first meeting in the classroom, Michael Shannon was whom I would have a bond with for the rest of my first-grade school year. After I had left Holy Spirit Catholic School and transferred to Saint Agatha School, September 4, 1962, I would not see my friend, Michael Shannon, again until almost two years later in 1964 at a Cub Scout Pack meeting. What a reunion we had as fellow Cub Scouts!

Although this story may sound eerie, nevertheless, it is a true story that I have found to be endlessly amusing. The gothic fiction movie, *The Hunchback of Notre Dame* was a 1939 American film starring Charles Laughton as the Hunchback. Before I started Catholic school in the fall of 1961, I had recently watched that movie during early 1961 on television with my mom, and I misinterpreted the hunchback's physically disfigured and severely deformed character as being the evil and hideous bell ringer of Notre Dame Cathedral in Paris, France, during the late Middle Ages. Later, I understood contrarily that the hunchback's character was one of goodness, meekness, gentleness, and compassion. He was the one and only Quasimodo, the humbled and deformed bell ringer of Notre Dame Cathedral.

When our first-grade class took its very first tour inside of our school's Catholic church during prayer time, I was afraid that at any moment, Quasimodo the hunchback, whom I thought was lurking in the darkness high above the dome in the church's bell tower, would suddenly come swinging on a rope from there, down to the pew where I was sitting with my class, and get me because I thought he would become mad at me for invading his dwelling, the church! But instantly, I had understood and realized that the church was the Body of Jesus Christ where His members, we the believers, dwelt and fellowshipped with one another. It was not the dwelling of the fictional character, Quasimodo.

Much to my relief, and at that moment of fear, I felt the indwelling comfort and power of the Holy Spirit. Then I thought to myself, *Away with you, hunchback!* And his spirit fled from me never to scare me again.

The Popes

After I had begun Catholic school at Holy Spirit, and during my time as a student at Saint Agatha School, I came under the papacies of two Catholic popes: The papacy of Pope John XXIII and Pope Paul VI. When I was in first grade, I remember my mom referring to somebody as the pope. From then on, I would hear her talk about the pope regularly as an important man, who was the bishop of Rome as head of the Roman Catholic Church worldwide. I soon learned more about the pope while I attended Catholic school from nuns who taught catechesis to priests at Sunday mass services.

When I started Catholic school in 1961, Pope John XXIII had been the Pope since 1958. Pope John's papacy was short-lived. He died on June 3, 1963, and then on June 21, 1963, Pope Paul VI was elected by the College of Cardinals as the bishop of Rome to head the Roman Catholic Church. I attended my last two years of Catholic school during the papacy of Pope Paul VI. On August 6, 1978, Pope Paul VI's fifteen years as pope ended when he died of a sudden heart attack.

13

No Meat on Fridays

Traditionally, as a member of the Roman Catholic faith, I had to abstain from eating red meat on Fridays year-round as part of a penance to mark the day of Christ's death. That is, no meat on Fridays! Romans crucified Christ, and he died on Friday, the day before the Hebrew Sabbath which is celebrated on Saturday. Since Mom's Catholic school childhood days, she had abstained from eating red meat on Fridays, and she consistently enforced this penance on my younger siblings and me as we were growing up. I actually looked forward to Fridays because it was the beginning of the weekend and time off from school. And I also liked eating a variety of delicious seafoods and healthy vegetables my mom had prepared for our family on Fridays. Thus, as a devout Catholic, I enjoyed practicing abstinence from red meat Fridays and indulgence in seafood instead.

Mom's Divorce, Remarriage, and Remorse

When my mother told me that she was getting divorced from my father, I was only six years old, and it saddened me immensely. As she broke the news, it was heartrending to see the hurt in her eyes. Since my father's incarceration, I had hoped that after his parole and ultimate release from prison, he would return home to be reunited with us. However, my feelings of expectation and desire for his eventual homecoming quickly dissipated into despair because I knew that divorce meant my parents' marriage had ended. Although I was disappointed about their impending divorce, I had already suffered anxiety to some extent after my mother and father were forced to live apart due to his conviction and imprisonment throughout the course of the prior year.

My mother's divorce from my father was difficult for me to understand and accept, but her assurance to me and my siblings that we would be cared for and loved, no matter what, comforted me significantly. While adjusting to the divorce, I needed a lot of my mother's affection and attention. Moved with compassion, my mother knew what I needed, and she gave me more snuggle time and read an extra story to me at night. I also received extra hugs and kisses from her.

Although weeks and even months had passed after the news had sunk in, I continued to ask her questions again and again, so in preparation for my questions, my mother patiently went over the same explanations and repeatedly answered all of my questions with wise understanding and gentle kindness. Even when my mother really wanted to stop talking about it, she made sure that I knew she was open to questions about the divorce at any time.

While the disruption of divorce was an unpleasant experience to my family, all the same, it didn't interfere with our household routine. My mother maintained our routines and even kept our house tidy while she continued with our regular schedules, which made me feel safe and secure. As much as was possible, basic mealtimes, with traditional Christian mealtime blessing and other rituals, including The Lord's Prayer, remained consistent in my mother's household. My mother also made sure we kept going to school and that things would remain the same for us.

In the aftermath of the divorce and my father's imprisonment, I responded well to my single mother's new household. Finally, making a point of remaining positive, my mother reaffirmed me that we would still do lots of fun things together.

My mother's divorce and remarriage filled her heart with remorse. The Catholic Church had excommunicated her, not because she had divorced my dad but as a result of her subsequent remarriage to Dick. Since her remarriage to Dick was not recognized by the Catholic Church for the reason that she didn't get her first marriage annulled, my mother incurred auto-excommunication and could not receive communion. As a devout Catholic, losing the Sacrament of Holy Communion caused my mother great grief. Divorce is always very sad, but sometimes it is necessary, especially when your partner commits adultery.

In my mother's case of divorce and remarriage, it was caused by my father's long-term imprisonment which consequently led to his reckless abandonment of our family. Whenever my mother was sad or unhappy about anything, it was heartrending seeing her that way. When circumstances occurred that caused my mother to become sad, I would not hesitate to encourage her that everything would be okay. Her response often brought me joy, especially when she would say to me: "Davion, my son, you always comfort me." My mother and I lovingly and consistently tried to keep each other's spirits high throughout our lives. We had a unique and wonderful mother-son relationship.

Stepfather

Since the age of seven, I have spent most of my life forgiving my stepfather for his shortcomings, including his sin of covetousness. Most disturbing of all was his defiance and disobedience to God. After marrying my mother, he became the stepfather from hell, and my life as I had known it before him would never be the same again.

The Tenth Commandment says, "You shall not covet your neighbor's house; you shall not covet your neighbor's wife, nor anything that is your neighbor's."

Well, stepfather Dick, who was my biological father's so-called friend and an opportunist from Ohio, couldn't wait because soon after my father's incarceration, stepfather coveted everything that had belonged to him. Stepfather moved into my father's house and made it his house, and he coveted what had belonged to my father and took my father's wife (my mother) who was in a vulnerable position, and for himself, he made her his wife; and he coveted everything that had belonged to my father and he made it his, including my father's five children (my siblings and me); and then he who had become my mother's husband and our stepfather desired that all of us submit to him.

I knew right from the start we were going to have problems with my stepfather. He was much like a wolf in sheep's clothing, which "is an idiom of biblical origin used to describe those playing a role contrary to their real character with whom contact is dangerous." I harken back to his frequent angry outbursts of profanities and using God's name in vain. Dick's irreverent behavior and his obscene language was always aimed at my siblings and me. From the start, when he began living with us, I constantly felt a sense of dread and impending unknown danger. I just didn't know what he was capable of doing to my family and me.

Although only a child, months earlier, I had just completed my first year of parochial school and I had applied good common sense to my life. I had already been blessed and introduced at my grade level with some knowledge and understanding of Christianity and Catholicism. Most significantly, I was beginning to believe in the birth, life, teachings, death, and resurrection of Jesus Christ. After just coming to understand the Ten Commandments from catechesis, there was no doubt in my mind, Dick was a sinner indeed. His vulgar behavior was evident enough for me to know that he didn't understand God's Ten Commandments. Dick's evil ways disrupted the holiness of my mother's loving, peaceful and joyful home.

Strangely enough, I seldom, if ever, witnessed stepfather getting mad at my little sister, Leslie. Still to this day, Dick has always been jealous, possessive, and unjustifiably overprotective of Leslie who was the only girl in our family. It didn't matter whether Leslie's actions were right or wrong. Dick insanely and cruelly defended her to spite my mother, my brothers, and me. He also did it for other strange and unknown reasons only God knows. From the very beginning, he often attempted to and sometimes he succeeded at undermining every good deed that came from my mom's heart to us, her children, and every good deed that came from our hearts to my mom and to each other because of his extreme jealousy and envy toward our family, and the love that we had for each other. He also enjoyed inflicting emotional pain, mocking everything good that we did and causing division amongst family members.

One of his major character flaws was his frequent acts of mental cruelty and utter abuse toward my mother and us. It was horrendous coexisting with him; his ways reminded me of the character in the 1987 thriller/slasher movie, *The Stepfather*, but without the brutal physical murders. To this day, I truly believe that my mother would have been better off without a husband in so many ways, especially spiritually, and my siblings and I would have been better off in so many ways without a stepfather as well. My family as a whole would have been better off without this narcissistic impostor who respected nobody and thought that he was the center of the universe at all times. My mother once accused Dick of not having any humility because of his lack of humbleness and unforgiveness. She often called Dick "cabbage head" because he was a thick-witted man who lacked common sense. The most serious character flaw that my mother believed hardened Dick's heart was that of an atheist, his lack of belief in the existence of God.

Although difficult at times because of his nonpenitent heart, as I pray to Jesus every day for mercy, I still ask Him to forgive my stepfather for his lifelong trespasses against me as well. According to the teaching of Jesus Christ concerning forgiveness in Matthew 18:21–22, "The Parable of the Unforgiving Servant," thus it is written:

> Then Peter came to Him and said, "Lord, how often shall my brother sin against me, and I forgive him? Up to seven times?" Jesus said to him, "I do not say to you, up to seven times, but up to seventy times seven."

Accordingly, I have learned and practiced my faith to continuously forgive others, no matter how many times they offend me always giving the glory to Jesus Christ. So after fifty-six years of "my stepfather's shenanigans," who has tested my patience no end, I focus on his forgiveness and not his person which has allowed me to move forward in my life toward the prize of redemption and eternal salvation with my Lord and Savior, Jesus Christ.

My mother dated Dick for at least one year before they were married. After her divorce from my father on the grounds of his imprisonment, my mother was legally freed to get remarried to Dick. So they tied the knot, and Dick became my stepfather. My mom thought Dick was a good person because she had befriended him when they were in their late teens. I recall her telling me a story about how Dick was a gentleman who always drove a nice car and had a good paying job which was impressive to most young women in her generation.

In fact, my mother was so fond of her new husband, she asked my siblings and me at the beginning of their marriage if we could find it in our hearts to call him *Dad* instead of Dick. God knows I wanted to call him *Dad* because I loved and honored my mother. But as I've mentioned before, I always wanted to please her and make her proud of me. But it never happened. I couldn't come to calling him *Dad* because we didn't connect with one another. I never felt the genuine love and affection of a father-son relationship with Dick.

Furthermore, Dick had never shown any interest in adopting and giving us his surname, Carey, like some stepfathers who truly love their wives and stepchildren often do. In time, I know my mother understood why I wouldn't call my stepfather *Dad*. As I also understood, Dick didn't want to adopt us because he didn't love himself; therefore, he was incapable of loving my mother, my siblings, and me. However, my sister, Leslie, called him *Dad* because she was only a toddler when he became her stepfather, and he was the only father that she had ever known after our biological father's imprisonment. Much of the same reason that I had understood, Dick's love for Leslie was highly unlikely, and I am certain that there is nobody on God's green earth who could ever be the love of his life.

Unfortunately for my mom, she really didn't know Dick's ways until she came to understand him during their very odd marriage. In the beginning, she made exceptions for his erratic behavior. Mom forgave Dick for his shortcomings, uncontrollable outbursts of profanities, apparent vulgarities, including his lack of common sense, humility, compassion toward people in general, and most importantly, his lack of faith in God until she had enough of it. At the end, during the early 1980s, without a divorce decree, my mom permanently separated herself from Dick. She explained to me that he had lost control of everything for a long time and he wasn't fulfilling his spousal nor his parental responsibilities. While his hatred toward my mother, my grandmother, my siblings, and me became increasingly apparent in his acts of cruelty, all kinds of neglect and abuse, except physical abuse. I wasn't surprised, but I was terribly disappointed in Dick's obvious and gradual meltdown.

According to the teaching of Jesus Christ, I likened my stepfather to the thief in John 10:10 of the Bible. Thus, it is written: "The thief does not come except to steal, and to kill, and to destroy."

Beloved Matriarch: Mama Dear

It often was on bright and late sunny afternoons, almost daily, during the first few weeks in the summer of 1962. When my mother took all five of us in my grandmother, Needie's yellow 1960 Buick La Sabre, to visit my beloved great-grandmother, Mama Dear, who was in the hospital at UCLA Medical Center. My mother had told me weeks earlier before Mama Dear was hospitalized that she was sick and not feeling well, which explained why we hadn't seen her lately. Then I received news that her condition had worsened, which is why she was admitted to the hospital. According to the doctor's medical diagnosis, Mama Dear was suffering from a malignant tumor which had invaded surrounding tissue behind her stomach. In fact, she was dying from pancreatic cancer.

However, hospital rules restricted small children from visiting patients because of childhood diseases; therefore, my siblings and I could not see Mama Dear in her hospital room. Leslie was only two years old, Vernon was four years old, the twins were five years old, and I was six years old. So we had to wait for my mother in the car while she visited with Mama Dear. Each visit lasted approximately thirty minutes. Since I was the oldest child, my mother put me in charge to watch over my younger siblings while we waited in the car for her.

When I rode in the car on the way to the hospital and waited in the car during my mother's visits with Mama Dear, I had often walked down memory lane, reminiscing about the wonderful and joyful times I shared with my great-grandmother. The most memorable times I had with her were the many fun-loving days and nights during the years that I had spent over her house. Most of the fun-filled times were spent in her kitchen, watching her cook and bake while I sat and ate. Also, I delighted in the chilled and sweet watermelon pink fruit slices that she carved out from the rind for us to eat on those hot summer days in her backyard patio. To top off, of course, with a piece of her chocolate candy, she always kept a box of See's Candy laying on top of the living room coffee table.

I remembered the times when I had sat down for a short while after I had played outside to watch Mama Dear sew on her 1950s black Singer sewing machine. "Sew, Mama Dear, sew"—I thought it was interesting watching her place the machine on a sewing cabinet, turning it on, threading the needle, and finally I would watch her make beautiful clothing, especially the nice-looking colorful shirts she made for my brothers and me and the pretty dresses that she made for my little sister, Leslie.

I remembered the fun city bus rides (RTD) I traveled with her in the city before she bought her late 1950s Oldsmobile. We'd travel to various places in Los Angeles, especially nice places like "The Original Farmers Market" on West 3rd Street where she'd shop and buy fresh fruits and produce. I also recalled the many fun times I had with her when she'd push me in the shopping cart while we were at the grocery store and when she took me with her to the butcher's shop for a fresh chicken to fry. I also thought about her swift discipline when I disobeyed. I missed Mama Dear and wanted to see her and I wanted to hug her and I wanted tell her I loved her. I was sad and I cried! I remember our last visit to the hospital when my mom said to us that Mama Dear looked out of her hospital room window into the parking lot and saw all of us sitting in the car. The sight of us for the final time had made Mama Dear smile, and we, her great-grandbabies, had filled her heart with joy.

Within a couple of weeks, my great-grandmother passed away and was able to go home to heaven and be in the presence of the Lord and her grandson, my Uncle Vernon Landry. My prayer for the death of Mama Dear, had I known it then, would have been the following prayer I've learned now during my Christian walk of faith:

Remember, Lord, those who have died and have gone before us marked with the sign of faith, especially for whom we now pray, "Mama Dear."

May she, and all who sleep in Christ, find in Your presence light, happiness and peace.

Through Christ our Lord. Amen.

14

Needie's Nervous Breakdown

After Mama Dear's hospitalization, which was followed by her death, it caused and triggered my grandmother's nervous breakdown, also known as mental breakdown. Needie had experienced a complete emotional and psychological collapse during the summer of 1962 while we were living in our South Spaulding Avenue home. It happened suddenly and unexpectedly. As I had noticed, my grandmother went into a deep state of depression, and she couldn't perform her social roles anymore. Compassion and empathy helped me to understand the onset of my grandmother's depression and her feelings of not being in touch with reality.

I had believed that my grandmother's depression occurred, not only at the loss of my great-grandmother, Mama Dear, but many years earlier when she had experienced the tragic loss of her son, my Uncle Vernon. The stress and grief of her son's death was never dealt with right away. Worst of all, the loneliness from the separation of her prior two husbands consequently led to my grandmother's alcoholism.

The first thing I will harken back to and I remember clearly because of her memory loss is that Needie did not recognize me nor my siblings, and she would ask us questions like, "Where is Mama?" referring to my great-grandmother after her funeral and burial' and, "What time is it?" Or "What day is it?" and so on. My grandmother often repeated the same questions moments later. For me, it was heartrending to see her in that way. Since the triggering of her depression, and for a period of time after, Needie would sleep too much, which caused her to miss Mama Dear's funeral. On the day of my great-grandmother's funeral while lying down on the sofa in our living room, Needie slept right through it.

Needie's inability to function happened both in her work and personal areas, which resulted in her inability to fulfill her obligations. It truly felt like I had suffered two losses, one after the other. First, the death of my great-grandmother, Mama Dear, and then immediately following her funeral, the loss of my grandmother, Needie, because of her mental breakdown. It would take years for Needie to recover from her nervous breakdown. However, she would never fully recover from it.

Afterward, my grandmother never returned to work again as the secretary and office manager for Patterson's State Farm Insurance Agency nor did she fulfill her other personal obligations. For example, maintaining her separate residence and driving her car, etcetera. My grandmother stayed and lived with us permanently under the love and care of my mother. Meanwhile, she'd help my mother with her household chores and cook our family meals. My grandmother also received a monthly social security disability check, which helped Mom with our family finances.

Later, my grandmother's long-term memory was restored, and she once again shared words of wisdom and true stories about our family history. However, her short-term memory did not improve completely, but my grandmother's love for me remained and it became stronger than ever. Indeed, I felt truly blessed. I loved her, but she loved me more!

Too Young

My mother didn't take me to Mama Dear's wake nor her funeral service. She thought that I was too young at age six and I would not understand why she was lying inside of an open coffin. I knew that she had died and I missed her, but my mother comforted me by saying that the angels were always with us; we just couldn't see them. Mom's comforting words made me feel good about Mama Dear's death. Since that time, I would close my eyes daily and pray and think about her. It gave me great comfort to feel that I could continue some connection with Mama Dear, even though she was not with me in this world, and whatever the truth may have been, this comfort had been a wonderful gift to me. Thus, I've always honored my mother and believed in her love for me.

Mama Dear's Estate

After her funeral, my great-grandmother Mama Dear's estate was handled by her husband, John, which involved selling their house. Since she had recently suffered a mental breakdown, my grandmother was not involved in any aspect of handling her mother's estate. John took full responsibility of distributing the assets. The assets that my grandmother and my mother received from John included furniture, personal property, and money. The only thing that disappointed my mother in the way John handled the will was that he either intentionally or unintentionally took some very important sentimental things that belonged to both my grandmother and mother.

These things were her late brother Vernon's priceless vintage toy soldiers, large-sized Union and Confederate Army with horses and cannons. John also walked away with priceless family photographs and other invaluable mementos. Emotionally, my mother was disappointed with my grandmother for the reason that she was sick and literally let everything go. My mother felt that if my grandmother had not fallen ill, then she would have soberly and vigilantly been involved with the handling of Mama Dear's estate, and John wouldn't have walked away with their precious and treasured memories.

I knew what had happened regarding Mama Dear's estate grieved my mother, and I felt nothing but empathy and compassion for her. Soon afterward, John left Los Angeles and moved back to his birthplace in Louisiana. I had missed John, and I don't remember ever seeing or hearing from him again.

Mom's Love and Spiritual Strength: Inspirational

I couldn't have written it better about my mom's love for her children. The mother's love for her children in this story parallels to what I believed in my mom's love for me. This is one of the most beautiful stories about a mother's love and spiritual strength. It was written for *Good Housekeeping* in 1933 by Temple Bailey.

"Is this the long way?" asked the young mother as she set her foot on the path of life.

And the guide said, "Yes, and the way is hard, and you will be old before you reach the end of it. But the end will be better than the beginning."

The young mother was happy, and she would not believe that anything could be better than these years. So she played with her children, she fed them and bathed them, taught them how to tie their shoes and ride a bike, and reminded them to feed the dog and do their homework and brush their teeth. The sun shone on them and the young mother cried,

"Nothing will ever be lovelier than this."

Then the nights came, and the storms, and the path was sometimes dark, and the children shook with fear and cold, and the mother drew them close and covered them with her arms. The children said,

"Mother, we are not afraid, for you are near and no harm can come."

And the morning came, and there was a hill ahead, and the children climbed and grew weary, and the mother was weary. But at all times she said to the children,

"A little patience and we are there."

So, the children climbed and as they climbed they learned to weather the storms. And with this, she gave them strength to face the world. Year after year she showed them compassion, understanding, hope, but most of all unconditional love. And when they reached the top they said,

"Mother, we could not have done it without you."

The days went on, and the weeks and the months and the years. The mother grew old and she became little and bent. But her children were tall and strong, and walked with courage. And the mother, when she lay down at night, looked up at the stars and said:

"This is a better day than the last, for my children have learned so much and are now passing these traits on to their children."

And when the way became rough for her, they lifted her, and gave her strength, just as she had given them hers. One day they came to a hill, and beyond the hill they could see a shining road and golden gates flung wide. And Mother said,

"I have reached the end of my journey. And now I know the end is better than the beginning, for my children can walk with dignity and pride, with their heads held high, and so can their children after them." And the children said,

"You will always walk with us, Mother, even when you have gone through the gates."

And they stood and watched her as she went on alone, and the gates closed after her. And they said,

"We cannot see her, but she is with us still." A mother is more than a memory. She is a living presence. Your mother is always with you. She's the whisper of the leaves as you walk down the street, she's the smell of certain foods you remember, flowers you pick and perfume that she wore, she's the cool hand on your brow when you're not feeling well, she's your breath in the air on a cold winter's day.

She is the sound of the rain that lulls you to sleep, the colors of a rainbow, she is your birthday morning. Your Mother lives inside your laughter. And she's crystallized in every tear drop.

A mother shows through in every emotion—happiness, sadness, fear, jealousy, love hate, anger, helplessness, excitement, joy, sorrow—and all the while hoping and praying you will only know the good feelings in life.

She's the place you came from, your first home, and she's the map you follow with every step you take. She's your first love, your first friend, even your first enemy, but nothing on earth can separate you.

Not time, not space—not even death!

15

LAST DAY OF CATHOLIC FIRST GRADE

When my class finished the first grade at Holy Spirit Catholic School in June 1962, I remember that there wasn't any formal graduation ceremony held. However, Sister Angela congratulated me on a job well-done! After she had finished congratulating me, and if my memory serves me correctly, she said something like this:

> The completion of Catholic school first grade was truly a Spirit-filled historic moment in your academic career. When you look back, you'll realize that your public kindergarten, which seemed seriously important only last year, was just a warm-up for the grade you have just completed. In kindergarten, teachers had to reinforce basic ideas such as "Share" and "Take turns" and "Don't laugh when another kid burps loudly in class."

In the first grade, here at Holy Spirit Catholic School, marked the start of a *real* Christian journey and Catholic education because you had to face homework every weeknight.

In religion, you learned how to recite prayers, retell Bible stories, identify the members of the Holy Family, identify the parts of the Bible, understand the importance of the Sacraments, especially Baptism. You also learned how to read and write. You learned basic arithmetic. And you learned that if a kid actually had burped loudly in class, it was okay to think it was funny as long as you didn't actually laugh out loud. These lessons, she said, would serve you well in your future endeavors.

As I was listening to the nun speak, I received my final report card grade and promotion to the second grade. While my eyes were still on her, she said, "This transition from the first grade to the second grade is most crucial in your Catholic education. While most of you will be seven years old in the second grade during this current year, it means that those of you who plan to celebrate their sacraments of First Reconciliation, and First Holy Communion, have already participated in the first-grade religious education program, here at Holy Spirit Catholic School. Accordingly, you are ready to celebrate the sacraments of First Reconciliation and First Holy Communion at any Catholic school that you may to attend in the second grade."

After finishing her speech, the nun said to my class, "Thank you, boys and girls, now go in peace and may the grace of God and the joy of the Holy Spirit be with all of you."

Devout Catholic and Christian Discipleship

After finishing first grade at Holy Spirit Catholic School for the summer break, my mom loved having me home without the stress and routine of school. However, it was difficult to entertain myself for three whole months, and it was not the best summer ever, but the summer of 1962 was an incredible time for me and it would shape my life in a very special and unique way. After all, I was six years old, and there would be no other time in my life when I would have as much freedom and as much energy as I did then. Harnessing both the energy and freedom allowed for the boredom and structured activities to take place that summer, which enhanced my spiritual character, deepened my family bonds and helped me create special memories.

Even though I was very young and while being a baptized practicing devout Catholic, I believed during the summer of 1962, I had consciously become a disciple of Jesus Christ because suddenly, He was my center and purpose of everything I did. I was committed to following Jesus Christ. In my mind, I had conceived of God as a person with whom I could have a relationship with and I chose to commit to that relationship. According to Matthew 4:20 in the Bible (NKJV), "They immediately left their nets and followed Him." Like Peter and his brother Andrew who were fisherman, I made the decision to dedicate my life to following Christ.

We all know the story, but the lesson is essential to understanding my discipleship at the tender young age of six. People brought infants and children to Jesus, and his apostles rebuked them. Jesus fired back at his apostles, telling them that, in fact, the kingdom of God belongs to those who accept the kingdom like a child. As a child of God and disciple of Jesus Christ, my mom had me baptized when I was an infant, and during my preschool ages, she took me to mass regularly, and with her help, I learned how to pray daily. Once I was able to talk, my mom talked to me about God, and I did not question his existence. I had no doubt that God was a "he" with whom I could talk to.

Throughout my early childhood before I attended Catholic school, I remember often having exchanges with my mom about God's existence. I asked her many questions like, for example, "Mom, why do we have to pray to God all the time?"

She'd answer me, "Well, Davion, it's impossible to do anything without God's help. Why do you pray to God?"

My response, "I want him to watch over me."

She'd answer, "That's a very good reason."

To further illustrate my faith in God, when I was seven years old, I recall on Christmas day in 1962, my grandmother had given me a battery-operated toy car dashboard for a gift, and the windshield wiper stopped working. Feeling sad that my toy was broken, I prayed and said, "God made it, I sure hope God can fix it." From then, that story was told over and over again by my mother's friend, Irving Epps, who always shared it with everybody, even when I was an adult. I believe it amazed him that I had so much faith in God at the age of seven.

I can't say my mom was a perfect parent, but I do believe that she did a good job witnessing to her personal faith in God to me. Why? Because I learned from her to view God as a reality with whom I could know and have a lasting relationship. I understood that when we went to church, we were going to see Jesus. When she prayed, I knew she was talking to God. She constantly referred to God as a someone rather than a something. Prayer, mass, and my catechesis were all related to Jesus. As a young child, referring to God as a person, expecting to see Jesus like I saw other people, and asking God to watch over my friends and family, these acts of faith confirmed my willful discipleship in Jesus Christ.

"Pepper"

On July 22, 1962, my mom gave birth to my half-brother, Richard Landry Carey, whom was nicknamed "Pepper." His middle name, Landry, was my mom's maiden name. I believe my half-brother was nicknamed Pepper for his dark-colored hair which was the color of a peppercorn. He was the firstborn son of my stepfather, Richard Dick Carey, and my mom's sixth child whom she had given birth. Pepper was born nearly seven years after my birth. Following Pepper's birth, I became the oldest and proud big brother of five siblings: the twins, Sputdoll, Gretchen and now my brother, Pepper! Sadly, there was no baptism for Pepper after his birth because of my stepfather's unbelief in Christianity.

Saint Agatha School

As the summer of 1962 was coming to an end, I was in high spirits because many new and exciting things were about to happen for me! First, I was transferring from Holy Spirit Catholic School to newly built Saint Agatha Catholic School where I was going to begin the second grade. I also would be joined with my twin brothers, Rene and Andree, my best friend, Michael Williams, and his big brother, Gregory, my neighbor, Craig Lewis, and his sister, Paige Lewis (Paige was going to begin the second grade along with me). It was a great joy for me to attend the new school with my friends and family for the first time. As I continued on my path to Catholicism and Christian discipleship in the second grade, I had felt a sincere desire to make my First Confession and then receive my First Holy Communion, and I was still more curious about what God and Jesus were like.

Super Second Grade

Second grade was an exciting time for me at Saint Agatha Catholic School as I began a year of important changes and the learning of new skills. I would receive two Sacraments that year: I would make my First Reconciliation and First Holy Communion. Receiving these Sacraments were important occasions in my life as they would allow me to develop a closer relationship with God and the Catholic Church. This relationship was nurtured through daily prayer, weekly Mass/Prayer service, and classroom discussion. Second grade was also a time when I matured academically and socially. Besides this, as a young devout Catholic and religiously ambitious, I dreamed of entering the priesthood and becoming a Roman Catholic priest as soon as I became an adult.

This was a pivotal year for me when I had to make the transition from learning to read toward reading to learn. I would become an independent reader and learn to read with understanding, fluency, and expression. I also would become more of an independent writer with daily assignments that asked me to respond to writing prompts and literature. Consistent practice of those skills helped me to become a more creative writer too. In arithmetic, I would learn to work, place values, and build fluency with addition and subtraction. My second-grade experience at Saint Agatha School would help me to continue to grow into an inquisitive, creative, loving child of God; but my bashfulness and difficulty understanding the basic operations of arithmetic would prove to be great stumbling blocks for me as well.

My First Confession

In 1962, while I was attending Saint Agatha Catholic School in the second grade, my classmates and I learned about God's love and forgiveness. We learned that when we pray and ask God to forgive us for our sins, he is able and willing to forgive us. Through Sacrament of Reconciliation, we can ask for God's love and forgiveness. Reconciliation means to be friends again. My First Confession was an important day for me because I had received the Sacrament of Reconciliation for the first time, and this very holy occasion was a reason to celebrate!

In class, my teacher, Sister Ann Regina, helped us prepare for our First Confession. She instructed us to read animated but true Bible stories about God's forgiveness. I read about Jesus helping all kinds of people with their problems:

- Jesus helped a blind man to see;
- Jesus helped two people to be friends again;
- Jesus hugged children and taught them how to pray.

Everywhere Jesus went, he taught people to love God and each other. We learned what Jesus had done is what God wants us to do too. To help us, God gave us a special set of rules called the Ten Commandments. These rules help us make good and loving choices and live a happy life. Sometimes, even with the Ten Commandments to follow, we can forget what Jesus taught us. I'm witness for myself because during my lifetime, I've done many wrong things that has made me feel sorry for doing them. When this has happened, I've felt small, lonely, and not very happy.

When we choose not to love each other like Jesus wants us to, I understand it's a sin. I learned that a sin is not a mistake or an accident. Mistakes and accidents are not done on purpose. A sin is something we choose, even though we know it's wrong. Sin hurts our friendship with God and each other. It pulls us away from God's family.

When I say I'm sorry to someone I've hurt and do something nice for them, I've felt much better. Afterward, I've understood that I needed to make it better with God too. So I harken back to Sister Ann Regina who read us a story from the Bible about God's forgiveness:

> The Prodigal Son
> Once there was a father who had two sons. One day, the younger son asked for his share of the family's money so he could go out on his own. The father agreed. The son left home and spent all his money on wasteful things. Soon, he was hungry and lonely and sorry for what he had done. He realized he had sinned against God and

his father: He decided to go home. As he was on the road, his father saw him and was so happy that he gave the son a robe, a ring, sandals, and a big party to celebrate his return.

We are like the younger son. Sometimes we think about what we want and not what God wants. God is like the loving and forgiving father. He will always be there to welcome us back when we ask. After I had learned how much God wanted to forgive me when I turned away from Him, I was ready to receive the Sacrament of Reconciliation.

On the day of My First Confession, I recall standing in line, inside of the church sanctuary with my class and waiting my turn to go into a small room called the confessional. In preparation for the Sacrament of Reconciliation, our class visited the confessional together, so I knew what it was like. Inside, there was a kneeler with a screen in front of it. On the other side of the screen, there was a chair for our priest, Father Crowe. Across from him there was an empty chair. You could either kneel on the kneeler or sit in the chair facing the priest. It was up to you.

While I waited to make my first confession, I tried to remember things I had said or done that had hurt someone else. This was called an examination of conscience. My mom had helped me with this at home. She told me to ask the Holy Spirit to help me remember my sins. She also told me that we do things we wish we hadn't. The important thing was that God will forgive us every time!

When it was my turn, I started to feel a little nervous, but then I had remembered that Father Crowe was my friend. He wasn't there to scold me or punish me. He was there to listen and to help me. He was there to give me God's forgiveness! So I went inside the confessional and kneeled on the kneeler facing Father Crowe who was sitting in a chair behind the screen, facing me.

Father Crowe who was a friendly priest, he gave me a big smile and he put me at ease. "Hello, Davion," he said. He seemed glad that I had come to celebrate God's forgiveness! I knew God was happy too. Then Father Crowe said, "Let's begin now by praying together in the name of the Father and of the Son and of the Holy Spirit."

I made the sign of the cross.

Afterward, Father Crowe read a passage from the Bible about Jesus forgiving a woman, Mary Magdalene, for her sins of adultery. I had remembered that story from class. I felt happy for Mary Magdalene. I knew God would forgive me too.

I told Father Crowe that this was my first confession. A confession is when we talk to the priest about our sins. A priest is not allowed to tell anyone else what he hears in confession. So I could talk to Father Crowe about anything. Father Crowe listened. He understood. He remembered feeling the same way when he was my age.

We had talked about how I could make changes so I could be a better follower of Jesus. Then Father Crowe gave me a penance. A penance is something we do to help make up for what we did wrong and to help us not do it again. Sometimes it may be a prayer. Sometimes it may be an action. My penance was prayer to say the "Our Father" and "Hail Mary" a few times each.

I told God I was sorry for hurting my friendship with him. Then I prayed an "Act of Contrition" that told God I wanted to change. I could have used my own words, but that day, I said a prayer I had learned in class:

> Oh my God I am heartedly sorry for having offended thee, and I detest all of my sins because of thy just punishment, but most of all because it offends thee my God, who is all good and deserving of all my love, I firmly resolve with the help of thy grace to sin no more and to avoid the near occasion sin.

After I had prayed the Act of Contrition, it was time for the Absolution, the words of God's forgiveness. Father Crowe placed his hand on my head and gave me God's blessing. He told me to go in peace. I felt wonderful! Then I left the confessional and smiled at my family and friends waiting in line. I was happy to be close to God's family again. Being forgiven by God was a great feeling, also knowing that I could receive the Sacrament of Reconciliation anytime I wanted to! I invite you to come and experience God's love and forgiveness too.

16

My First Holy Communion

When I was seven years old, I experienced a very special occasion on a bright and warm sunny day during the spring of 1963. It happened inside of the Saint Agatha Catholic Church building. I had been preparing for it for a long time. This celebration was my First Holy Communion. It meant that I had invited Jesus into my heart in a new and wonderful way. I was amongst all of my second-grade classmates who were going to celebrate their First Holy Communion too.

That day was a good day because we were required to wear formal clothing. The girls wore beautiful white dresses with a carnation attached to the front of their dress, and they wore a white veil on top of their head. The boys wore navy-blue colored suits with a white carnation attached to the left lapel on their suit coat. However, it really wasn't important how we looked on the outside that mattered but how we felt on the inside—happy and ready to receive Jesus!

When the celebration was about to begin, I remember seeing my classmate, Gregory Lamont, who was standing just outside of the church building; we complimented one another for looking nice in our navy-blue suits. As we walked in, I smiled at everyone. I saw moms and dads, brothers and sisters, aunts and uncles, grandmas and grandpas, cousins and friends. We sang a song about all the people in church belong to one family in Jesus. That's a big family! I sang extra loud.

Sister Ann Regina had taken charge and made our First Holy Communion class form a double-file line which we had learned to do during our celebration rehearsals. Before entering the church building for the celebration, the girls formed a single-file line on the left, one behind the other, and the boys formed a single-file line on the right, one behind the other. Then on Sister Ann Regina's signal, we followed her in a double-file line, walking down the center aisle toward the front of the church sanctuary, and we occupied the first two pews. The boys entered the front two pews on the right, and we kneeled down, and the girls entered the front two pews on the left, and they kneeled down.

Mass began just like it always had. My mom had brought me to Mass every Sunday to learn about Jesus, so I felt right at home in church. After Mass began, Father Moran, Senior Pastor who was at the pulpit, led us in prayer.

"Together, we ask God to forgive our sins. Now it was time to sit and listen to the word of God. That day's readings were all about Holy Communion."

My friend and classmate, Gregory Lamont, read a letter from Saint Paul: "[t]he Lord Jesus, on the night he was handed over, took bread..."

I knew that story. It was about the very first Communion. Communion means to join together. Jesus, on the night before he died on the cross for us, had a last supper with his good friends, the apostles. Jesus wanted his friends to know how much he loved them. He wanted them to know that he would always be with them. So Jesus gave himself in a very special way through bread and wine—a way that would join him to his friends forever: "Take and eat. This is my body. Take and drink. This is my blood. Do this in memory of me."

The next story we heard in church that day was read by Father Moran. It was the Gospel, the good news of Jesus. We stood for that important reading. "[t]aking the five loaves and the two fish, and looking up to heaven, He said the blessing over them..."

I knew that story too. It was about how Jesus fed 5,000 people. He took two fish and five loaves of bread and said a special blessing. Then he told his apostles to feed the people. There was plenty for everyone! It was a miracle. At Mass, the same kind of miracle happens when Jesus tells his priests to feed the people. This time, Jesus fed us with his body and blood during Holy Communion.

After the Gospel was read, Father Moran talked to us. He said that our First Holy Communion was a good reason to dress up. It was fine to have a party on that day with cake and gifts, but the best gift we would ever receive was the gift of Jesus. Father Moran reminded us how Jesus is the Bread of Life. Jesus promised that no one who comes to him will ever be hungry. Now we, too, were ready to be fed.

Next, we sang a song of preparation. While we sang, two altar boys carried bread and wine up to Father Moran. Bread and wine are gifts from earth which God created. Father Moran placed them on the altar. We give thanks to God for all his gifts. We thanked him for the bread and wine. We thanked him for his love. Most of all, we thanked him for giving us his Son, Jesus.

Another word for Communion is Eucharist. Eucharist means to give thanks. There was so much to be thankful for. Blessed be God forever! Then Father Moran held up the host, a flat white bread in the shape of a circle. He held it high so we could all see it. He said the same words Jesus said to his friends at the last supper. "Take this, all of you, and eat. This is my body given up for you."

I bowed my head quietly. I knew Jesus was there with us then and now. Then Father Moran held up the chalice, the cup of wine. That too he held high so we could see it. "Take this, all of you, and drink. This is the blood of the new and everlasting covenant. Do this in memory of me."

I bowed my head again. Even though I saw bread and wine, I knew they had become the body and blood of Jesus. This is called the consecration. Now Jesus is really and truly present. In a way that we don't fully understand, the bread and wine are changed forever; so are the people who receive Communion.

When I received Jesus that day, I became joined to him in a special way, just like the apostles were at the last supper. But I wasn't the only one. All of the people who received Communion that day were also joined to Jesus and to each other. To show our communion with one another, we pray for the church and for people who have died. We pray the Lord's Prayer. And then we give each other the sign of peace.

Finally, it was time to receive my First Holy Communion. One by one, in a single-file, my class walked up to Father Moran. My classmate and friend, Gregory Lamont, was ahead of me, walking toward the altar. I had learned in class that the host could be a thin white circle or it could be brown and thick like a cracker or it could even be pointy if it was broken off from a bigger piece. We always received the white circled host.

We had practiced how to receive Holy Communion on the tongue:

1. With prayer hands, eyes closed, raising our bowed head up, we learned to open our mouths wide, making our mouths into a landing pad, not a quarter slot.
2. Not being embarrassed, we learned to stick our tongues out. Why keep our eyes closed? Because if we left our eyes open, we'd be tempted to move toward the priest. Moving targets are hard to hit. So we closed our eyes and kept our heads still.
3. Don't bite the hand that feeds you! Sticking out our tongue insured that the priest's hand wouldn't come into contact with our teeth (or lips—gross!).
4. Please do not chew the Holy Eucharist! We learned to let it soften in the mouth and then swallow. By doing this, we avoided having the smallest particle of our Lord stuck in our teeth where it might be desecrated later by coming into contact with the profane.

A very special thank you to Father Thomas Logan for sharing these tips on receiving the Blessed Sacrament on your tongue. Also, a special thanks to Dr. Taylor Marshall for sharing these tips on a blog...

Back then, only priests sipped wine from a cup.

I also learned never to be afraid to come to Jesus. No one is perfect, and we all make mistakes. God loves us anyway and forgives us if we ask. We were taught a special prayer to ask for forgiveness. I still say it to myself now:

"My God, I am sorry for my sins with all my heart. In choosing to do wrong and failing to do good. I have sinned against you whom

I should love above all things. I firmly intend, with your help, to do penance, to sin no more, and to avoid whatever leads me to sin."

When it was my turn to receive My First Holy Communion, my heart pounded hard. I walked up to Father Moran. Without a smile, he said, "The body of Christ, Davion."

"Amen," I answered. That meant, "I agree." I opened my mouth wide and stuck out my tongue, then Father Moran placed the small white host on my tongue. Afterward, I closed my mouth and swallowed the host. I knew then that Jesus was very near to me.

When I sat down at my seat in the pew, I closed my eyes and thought about Jesus sitting next to me with his arms around me. I had felt very close to him. I know Jesus loves me and wants to be with me. I know he wants me to bring his love to everyone I meet. My mom and grandmother smiled at me. They were very proud. I had felt proud too. To celebrate Jesus with us, we sang another song about being God's people. My family smiled and waved to me as I walked out. My grandmother, Needie, took a picture of me.

Outside, there was lots of laughing and hugging. And more pictures! My grandmother handed me a gift. It was a First Holy Communion pin. I remembered what Father Moran had said about Jesus being my greatest gift. My First Holy Communion had been a happy day. But the best part was going to Mass, and every time after that, I'd receive Jesus all over again! He would be with me this special way for the rest of my life.

17

UNDERSTANDING LENT AS A CATHOLIC SCHOOL BOY

While attending Catholic school, I became aware of the significance of Lent, which was explained to me by my mother, teachers, and priests. First, I understood that Lent was a time of preparation for Easter, the Christian Holiday that celebrates the resurrection of Jesus Christ. I also learned to think of the forty days of Lent as an opportunity to change my daily life and become closer to God. However, as I learned this concept, it became challenging to me. Sometimes it made me upset by Jesus's death, confused me by changes to my normal routines, and sometimes I was resistant to the Lenten ideal of sacrifice. But by my mother compassionately discussing the details and traditions of Lent in a kid-friendly manner that aided me in my understanding, especially when she made it a point for us to experience Lent together.

Stations of the Cross

Each year during Lent on Good Friday, I participated in an awe-inspiring "Stations of the Cross" with all of the other Catholic schoolboys and girls from the first grade to the eighth grade. Traditionally, as we sat in the pews of the church sanctuary. The devotional began with an opening prayer:

My Lord, Jesus Christ, You have made this journey to die for me with unspeakable love; and I have so many times ungratefully abandoned You. But now I love you with all my heart; and because I love You, I am sincerely sorry for ever having offended You. Pardon me, my God, and permit me to accompany you on this journey.

You go to die for love of me; I want, my beloved Redeemer, to die for love of You. My Jesus, I will live and die always united to You.

The Stations of the Cross or Way of the Cross, also known as the Way of Sorrows or the Via Crucis, refers to a series of images depicting Jesus Christ on the day of his crucifixion and accompanying prayers. The stations grew out of imitations of Via Dolorosa in Jerusalem which is believed to be the actual path Jesus walked to Mount Calvary. The object of the stations is to help the Christian faithful to make a spiritual pilgrimage through contemplation of the Passion of Christ. It has become one of the most popular devotions and the stations can be found in many Western Christian churches including Anglican, Lutheran, Methodist, and Roman Catholic ones.

Commonly, a series of 14 images will be arranged in numbered order along a path and the faithful travel from image to image, in order, stopping at each station to say the selected prayers and reflections. This will be done individually or in a procession most commonly during Lent, especially on Good Friday, in a spirit of reparation for the sufferings and insults that Jesus endured during His passion.

The style, form, and placement of the stations vary widely. The typical stations are small plaques with reliefs or paintings place around a church nave. Modern minimalist stations can be simple crosses with a numeral in the center. Occasionally the faithful might say the stations of the cross without there being any image, such as when the pope leads the stations of the cross around the Colosseum in Rome on Good Friday. (From Wikipedia, the Free Encyclopedia)

Jesus Death and Resurrection.

The story of Jesus life was told to me often when I was a boy. My mother understood that if she wanted me to accept the Christian faith and its major traditions, it was important for her to talk to me about Jesus regularly and not just during holidays. Additionally, I read about Jesus life at Catholic school during catechesis. In the context of Lent, Catholic catechism emphasized that Jesus was born and lived on earth for one purpose, to show everyone how to achieve salvation and everlasting life, and that he accepted and embraced this calling, despite his own suffering because of the eternal glory that it would make available to all of us.

When they explained Jesus's death, the Catholic nuns and teachers never dwelt on the gruesome details of his crucifixion, which could have upset and frightened me. But they did introduce Jesus's death to me. They emphasized the reasons for his sacrifice. They taught me that he gave up his earthly life so that we, the believers, could have eternal salvation. Jesus showed that death is not the end, but rather the beginning of eternal life.

The meaning of Easter was formally introduced to me in Catholic school. Catechesis taught me that Easter was the most important Christian holiday—yes, more important than Christmas—and far more than just bunnies, eggs, and chocolate. Easter Sunday celebrates Jesus's return from the dead. The concepts of resurrection and life after death are fundamental to the Christian faith. So I learned about them early in my childhood. I was told as a young kid and Catholic school student that all the celebrating that surrounds Easter should remind me of the joy of knowing how much Jesus loves me, and that he showed us the path to eternal life. Therefore Lent, then, is meant to be a time of reflection and focus so that the faithful can be truly prepared to comprehend the power and glory of Easter Sunday.

The Crucial Days of Lent

Lent begins with Ash Wednesday which, for me, included a symbolic drawing of a cross with ashes on my forehead. The ashes are meant to remind everyone of human mortality (i.e., "ashes to ashes, dust to dust"); however, this idea was not necessarily pushed too forcefully on me as a young kid. It was more of being matter-of-fact about the tradition. My mother thought it helped me to talk less about death. And she'd emphasize how the drawn cross was meant to be a reminder of the main focus of Lent—Jesus. My mom explained to me that Lent lasts forty days because that was how long Jesus wandered in the desert, fasting, while he resisted Satan's temptations. She told me that I had an opportunity during the forty days of Lent to be like Jesus. And I too could resist temptations and use this time to become closer to God. Lent wasn't simply a "countdown" or something to "get through." But it was a chance to set aside distractions and focus on my relationship with the Lord.

18

HONORING HOLY WEEK TOGETHER

As a child, I understood that the last week before Easter was especially important. My mother made sure that I knew this last part of Lent led up to the celebration of Easter. Note that Palm Sunday marks Jesus's entry into Jerusalem to cheering crowds but that within a few days, many of those same people would turn against him. Accordingly, my mother explained to me that this showed how quickly anyone can succumb to temptations of evil and turn away from God. She also used Holy (Maundy) Thursday to tell the story of the night before Jesus died, and how he chose to spend his last supper with his family of disciples. My mother always considered making our family meal to correspond with the last supper too.

She occasionally made special notes of Good Friday. The day that Jesus died was a sad one for Christians, but it still resonated with me. As I matured and grew older, every Lent, my mother would discuss the details of the crucifixion and she'd focus on the sacrifice Jesus made for everyone and the glory he knew was to come afterward. During the Easter holiday, we'd dye eggs together, but Mom pointed out to me that we were not just making something for the Easter Bunny. She explained to me that the eggs represented the promise of new life, and we could focus on Jesus's coming rebirth, even as we commemorated his death.

As Catholic Christians, our family ended Holy Week by looking to the joy of Easter. On the Saturday before Easter Sunday, there was typically no liturgy so that we faithfully could focus completely on Easter. My mother always talked about Easter with joy and enthusiasm, and she'd explain the symbolism of painted eggs and the wonder of resurrection, salvation, and life with God after death. Finally, we'd welcome Easter Sunday with unbridled joy, praying, singing, celebrating, and wearing our best clothing to church for the Easter Sunday Catholic worship service and spending the day together with our loved ones.

Altar Boy Tryouts

After making my First Holy Communion, I was eligible for training to become an altar boy. My desire as a devout Catholic to serve Jesus motivated me to seek out altar boy tryouts. Serving Jesus by assisting our Catholic priests—Father Moran, Senior Pastor, and Father Crowe, Junior Pastor of Saint Agatha Catholic Church—at the altar was a great privilege, and altar boy training would help me learn the responsibilities, expectations, and procedures to become an altar boy. The altar boys had a special relationship with and would work for Saint Agatha Church priests. Saint Agatha parish was honoring the tradition and practice of having boys serve their priests at the altar, and any boy who had received his First Holy Communion was eligible to be trained to become an altar server.

When altar boy tryouts took place, I was happy for the opportunity and I had hoped to fulfill my goal of becoming an altar boy. The altar boy tryouts were held inside the Church sanctuary in the morning while classes were in session. The head pastor, Father Moran, an Irishman, was the altar boy coordinator assigned to work with us on training, scheduling, and enforcing the rules. A small group of boys, including myself, showed up in the church sanctuary, and we sat down in the first two pews close to the altar. Then Father Moran called our names for the attendance.

Father Moran was regarded by some of our students as the mean priest in contrast to Father Crowe whom was regarded as the friendly priest. Rumor had it that Father Moran was also an alcoholic. No sooner than the altar boy meeting had begun, it had ended with no interaction from Father Moran. Sadly, and for no apparent reason, Father Moran sent me back to the classroom with my hopes of becoming an altar boy shattered. Thus far, this was the most dispiriting act of rejection that I had ever experienced in my young life at the age of seven. Furthermore, I wouldn't be able to serve as an altar boy with my best friend, Michael Williams, who had passed the altar boy tryouts. Since his attendance at Saint Agatha School, Michael's big brother, Gregory, had been an altar boy, and I had seen him serve at several Sunday Masses. I would soon see Michael serving Mass too. During the early 1960s, I recall Catholic Mass was spoken in Latin by both the Catholic priests and altar boys alike.

I was disappointed by my failure to become an altar boy and I thought it would also disappoint my mother. But what really disturbed me about my discharge from the tryouts was that Father Moran never gave me a reason why he denied me the opportunity to become an altar boy. After all, I had the qualifications to become an altar boy in every respect. I thought probably he had rejected me for some silly reason(s). Perhaps he had despised me because I was good-spirited, intelligent, or was a nice-looking boy—only God knew.

When my mom picked me up from school that afternoon, I immediately told her what had happened. The first thing she said was, "Davion, you'll bounce back." My mom was comforting to me. Because I knew at that moment, I had not disappointed her for failing to make it as an altar boy. I also agreed with her that this was an act of God's divine intervention; that is to say, for God's purpose, it wasn't time for me to become an altar boy yet. Then my mom looked at me and said, "Davion, next year you can apply for altar boy tryouts again." And sitting down in the front seat with contentment, I smiled all the way home with my twin brothers sitting in the backseat.

Setback

After attending Saint Agatha Catholic School for the second grade, I began to have difficulties academically with arithmetic. My second-grade teacher, whose name was Sister Corona, observed me struggling with class assignments and tests. She did everything she could to help me, encouraging me and practicing arithmetic problems with me one on one. However, I was somewhat of a bashful child, having trouble with the accelerated arithmetic lessons which had begun in the first grade at Holy Spirit Catholic School. In consultation with my mom, Sister Corona made a tough decision. She had me repeat the first grade; thus, I was put back from the second grade to the first grade.

I was feeling uncomfortable because I had to move my desk from the second-grade classroom to the first-grade classroom, which was next door. What made matters worse, I had to join my twin brothers back in the first grade. My new first-grade teacher's name was Sister Ann Regina. She seemed very strict at first, but soon she showed warmth and compassion for me, and I began to excel in her first-grade class. Friends and classmates alike were not empathetic with my setback, but some were.

My mom felt like a failure at the time, thinking that it was her fault, but looking back months later, she was pleased at my progress. At seven years of age, I was just blossoming, and I drew praise from my new teacher. The decision to set me back was good after all because it encouraged my mental, social, and physical development. Fortunately for me, I always had a healthy self-esteem and social skills with fewer achievement problems; therefore, I did better after being held back a grade.

At the end of 1963 school semester, I passed the first grade satisfactorily and got promoted back to the second grade. Hooray! Fortunately for my twin brothers, Rene and Andree were held back in the first grade for the same reasons that I had been set back, but my mom remained positive, spiritually strong and committed to our welfare.

The "Rookie Cop" Next Door

Newmar was our next-door neighbor and a young rookie cop with the Los Angeles Police Department. He was married to a cute and friendly young woman named Maxine, and they had two young sons whose names were Raymond and Tony. On one sunny morning during the summer of 1963, my best friend, Michael, who was excited and smiling from ear to ear, ran to my house. He boasted about his big brother, Gregory, and our mutual friend, Craig, himself—and assuming I was invited—were going to the LAPD shooting range with our next-door neighbor, Newmar, who was a policeman! "We're going to watch him shoot his gun (service revolver) at the targets!" said Michael.

Suddenly, my feelings were hurt because Newmar had unfairly excluded me from going with them to the LAPD range. Feeling unjustifiably ashamed, I told Michael that our neighbor did not invite me to go with them. Michael was shocked, and we both wondered why he didn't invite me. Since I was his best friend, Michael knew we'd have more fun at the range if we were together. However, I thought of several probable reasons why he didn't invite me:

1. He stigmatized me for the LAPD raid on our home by his fellow police officers that late spring night in 1961, which resulted in my dad's subsequent incarceration.
2. Once my mother called him a "bastard" because he constantly griped to her about us playing near his yard and on his fence next to the property line.
3. Newmar envied and lusted after my beautiful young mother whom he couldn't have.
4. A severely flawed character; Newmar was cruel and abusive toward his wife, his sons, and people in general.
5. As a police officer on-duty and off-duty, rookie cop Newmar had been severely reprimanded on several occasions by the LAPD for police brutality and unjustifiable shootings of suspects, which ultimately led to his termination from the police force. He was a real nutcase!

As traumatic as it was, with the passage of time and comforting grace of the Holy Spirit, I forgave my neighbor, the rookie cop, for his acts of cruelty toward my family and me.

Trauma: Eleven Stitches

One summer day back in 1963, while I was playing with my friend, Paige, in her front yard, she suddenly picked up an empty Coca Cola tin can, and without any coordination, Paige crookedly threw it at me. The tin can hit me on the right side of my head between my right eye and my temple. Then it bounced off of my head. And falling to the ground, it rolled to the edge of the grass. Everybody, including my best friend, Michael, and some other kids from the block started laughing because seeing the tin can bounce off of my head appeared to be funny to them. I had laughed too.

But after the tin can had bounced off of my head, blood started oozing from the wound on my head. So the laughter on my friend's faces quickly turned to horror when they saw the bleeding. Immediately after seeing my own blood, I began crying loudly with crocodile tears. Paige's next-door neighbor, whose name was Helen, heard me crying and she emerged from the front door of her house and walked briskly to my aide. Helen put an antibacterial ointment on the wound and applied pressure using a sterile gauze. And moved with compassion, she was comforting, which helped calm me down, and I stopped crying.

My friends and neighbors, especially Paige, showed empathy toward me, and Paige was sorry that she had hurt me, but I forgave her because it was an accident and she didn't mean any harm. Helen and Michael walked home with me and told my mom what had just happened. My mom and stepfather, Dick, took me to the doctor, and I got eleven stitches. Dick's employer sponsored family health care insurance covered the doctor's visit, diagnostic, and medical treatment. I have to admit, it was awkward for me to receive medical services covered by Dick's health insurance because I knew that he had despised me. However, I was still thankful to him for taking care of me when I needed it.

Although it was natural for me to feel a little anxious about getting stitches, especially after I had just experienced trauma, the procedure was almost painless. And the stiches helped my cut heal with only a little scar and no infection. I had only felt slight pinching as the doctor threaded the needle through my skin to piece together the edges so that the skin and other tissues could fuse back together. Then within one week, the stitches were painlessly removed.

Strangely enough for me, the small scar on the right side of my head was a battle scar that I would proudly display for years to come.

19

I WAS A CUB SCOUT

On November 22, 1963, I turned eight years of age. It was a special birthday for me because I was then old enough to become a Cub Scout! However, it had been a sad day in America because President John F. Kennedy was assassinated at Dallas, Texas. After hearing the news of his assassination, I immediately recalled election day back on November 8, 1960, when my great-grandmother and me went to the polls and she had voted for him. If my great-grandmother had still been alive during this awful tragedy, I know she would have been racked with grief because of her love for President Kennedy.

I was assigned to Den 7, Pack 12, and Mr. Woodley Lewis, my neighbor, who was a former wide receiver in the (NFL) and also Craig's dad, was the Cubmaster. To my delight, Mr. Lewis had selected my mom to be my Den Mother. When I heard the good news, I raced all the way home and gave her a bear hug. Mom suggested that I could help her turn the enclosed patio into a cub den. She thought it would be a pleasant place to hold our den meetings.

First exciting thing that I did was go and get my new Cub Scout uniform from J. C. Penney. The next Thursday after school, five good friends gathered together on my patio. They were Michael, Craig, Jeffrey, Victor, and myself. Our new den picked Craig as our leader because he was the oldest boy and he had already earned his bear badge. Also present was Michael's older brother, Gregory, a First-Class Boy Scout who had been selected as Den Chief.

As our Den Chief, Gregory told us that he would teach us many new and exciting things to do such as run like a fox, leap like a deer, and build like the beaver! I also asked Gregory to show us how to start a fire without a match. He said he would, all in good time. Then my mom gave the Cub Scout Sign for quiet and attention. Five hands shot into the air to give the signal right back.

Afterward, we faced the flag in a straight line. Then we gave the Cub Scout Salute and said the Pledge of Allegiance. Craig, being the leader, collected the weekly ten cent dues from each of us. Mom said the money would be used to pay for badges, handicraft material, and re-registration. And whatever was left over would be put into a good will fund.

The next thing we did was make a living circle. Then we sang "Be Game, Be Square." And our first weekly meeting was over. Finally, Den Chief Gregory reminded us not to forget our first pack meeting, which occurred on the following night. Our first big Cub Scout Pack Meeting was held at Burnside Elementary School in the auditorium, and it was exciting!

My Cub Scout friends and I knew that several dens joined together made Pack 12. And our whole pack was led by Craig's father, Cubmaster Lewis. At the pack meeting, the next evening, I wore my new blue Cub Scout uniform and cap for the first time. In the school auditorium, I walked bravely on stage with the rest of Den 7 while many people watched. The lights dimmed, and I saw a big Indian Chief standing before a red cellophane fire.

Then I heard the words, "Welcome to the Fire of Friendship" from the Chief who was really Cubmaster Lewis. "Now say the Cub Scout promise."

So I stood at attention with the other Cub Scouts, and I said, "I, Davion Woodman, promise to do my best. To do my duty to God and my country. To be square and obey the law of the pack."

When the ceremony was over, each of us received our Bobcat Pin from Cubmaster Lewis. He said that we had to wear our pins upside-down until we had done one good deed. I gave Cubmaster Lewis a real Cub Scout handclasp. Then I whispered and told him that I was going to do lots of good deeds.

At the next meeting, each of us bought a Wolf Cub Scout Book. The book instructed us about the twelve achievements we had to learn to become a wolf. Den Chief Gregory told us that feats of skill was one achievement to be mastered. He showed us the many simple stunts to do on a gym mat—front rolls, back rolls, and falling forward rolls. Gregory showed us how to tie our shoestrings with a square knot. This was part of our knot achievement. I could hardly wait to start work on my individual achievements.

For feats of skill, I learned how to swim with a kickboard. I also walked a two-by-four plank, pretending I was a tightrope walker in a circus. For Helps in the Home, I swept the patio where we held our den meetings and did errands. I held yarn for my grandmother, Needie, while she wound it up into a ball. And I threaded the eye of a needle for her sewing.

Den Chief Gregory had to help *all* of us with our Whittling Achievement. He showed us how to open and close our scout knives easily and safely. For Collections, I decided on stamps. And every time I finished an achievement, my mom signed for it in my Wolf Book. Those were proud moments for me as Cub Scout!

One Saturday, Cubmaster Lewis took our whole pack on a field trip to the Shelter for Homeless Animals. Another time, our pack visited the firehouse where we learned many things about fire engines and fire prevention. And once we went on a treasure hunt to look for leaves, acorns, and rocks to add to our collections. And the time had come for the big Father-and-Son Cookout in the forest preserve. Sadly, I didn't have my dad to share with me in this wonderful experience. And stepfather Dick wouldn't volunteer for it. When Cubmaster Lewis realized that I was fatherless, he adopted me that day for the sake of the Father-and-Son Cookout.

Den Chief Gregory started the campfire with his fire-by-friction set. Our pack cooked hotdogs on sticks and roasted potatoes wrapped in aluminum foil. We ended the cookout by toasting marshmallows, playing games, and singing scout songs. I was grateful to Mr. Lewis who had adopted me for the Father-and-Son Cookout. It was a lot of fun.

At our next meeting, the Den Mother, who was my mom, asked each Cub to answer the roll by telling of some good deeds they had done. When it was my turn, I proudly answered the roll by describing a good deed I had done in an act of compassion; I had helped an older woman with groceries by pushing the shopping cart to her parked car, and she expressed her gratitude to me. Since the Cubs, including myself, had performed at least one good deed, we earned the privilege to wear our Bobcat Pins right side up. This was a proud moment for all of us!

As the weeks went by, Den Chief Gregory taught us how to make many things out of wood, seashells, pine cones, and vegetables. Soon the handicraft table was full of things that we had made. There was a tom-tom made from a coffee can; a red racing car that I had made from wood (it really moved!); a fiddle made from a cigar box; six hand puppets; and a tin can telephone that really worked!

My fellow Cubs learned many skills and hobbies from their Den Dads. Fortunately, the Den Dads taught me together with their sons because I didn't have a dad who would. We learned how to shoot with bows and arrows, how to use hammers, screwdrivers, and other tools, and how to read animal tracks in the woods.

And Mr. Lewis showed me how to make a plastic lanyard to hold my cub scout knife and my whistle. Now every Cub in Den 7 had finished all twelve achievements. We were now ready to move up from Bobcats to Wolf Cubs. Hooray! After I had passed my Wolf Cub Achievement, I became an ambitious little Cub Scout! I told my mom I wanted to become a Bear Cub, and next, become a Lion!

Then after I'd earn my WEBELOS, I would be ready to become a Boy Scout. I liked scouting when I was a boy. And I had hoped to go all the way up to Eagle Scout.

The Dickerson Family

During the summer of 1963, my new neighbors moved into the house next door to our house on the south side of the property line at Spaulding Avenue. They were the Dickerson family. Taylor Dickerson and Midge Dickerson, who were both in their mid to late twenties, had a brood of three young children in my age range. Their oldest child's name was Ava and was ten years of age; second to the oldest child, her name was Arlene, and she was nine years of age; and Jeffrey, the youngest child, he was seven years of age. The Dickerson family made it easy for us to get to know them because they were warm and friendly. Their benevolence had opened the door for a close and long-lasting friendship.

I had always called Midge and Taylor by their first name because they considered themselves as either hip or cool folks relative to their African American culture for food, dress, music, religion, and family. They both had an attitude, a stance in opposition to the unfree world, and that's how they enjoyed their lives. Therefore, I didn't address them by Taylor's surname, Mr. or Mrs. Dickerson, as I had typically done out of respect for my elders. The Dickerson family were also Roman Catholics. Ava, Arlene, and Jeffrey had come from Transfiguration Catholic School and attended the newly built Saint Agatha School where they were in the same classes with Craig, Michael, and myself. That is, Craig and Ava were in the same fifth-grade class, Michael and Arlene were in the same fourth-grade class, and Jeffrey and myself were in the same second-grade class.

Taylor Dickerson was short in stature with a muscular but thin body and was a good-looking man. He had a reddish-brown complexion with a freckled face, and the color of his hair was red. Taylor wore a pompadour hairstyle. He worked for a GMC/Buick dealership as an automobile mechanic on Pico Boulevard. It was located within a block of my mom's alma mater, Bishop Conaty High School at Los Angeles, south of downtown. The nickname, Red, was sewn on his employee identification badge.

Midge complimented Taylor because she was also short in stature, petite, and an attractive woman. She was a brunette and regularly wore her hair short. Midge had a light-skinned complexion. I think she was of a mixed race. They both seemed to be happy in their marriage as Taylor was the typical dominant husband, and Midge was the loving and submissive wife. When cigarette smoking wasn't taboo, Midge and Taylor were both chain-smokers, and I rarely saw them without a cigarette.

The Dickerson children were attractive, smart, and fun to play with. As neighbors, we did everything together. Within a short time, we were not only friendly neighbors, but we also became a family. We enjoyed sleepovers, picnics at the beach and parks, house parties, and barbeques. Taylor grilled the best barbeque ribs and chicken that I had ever eaten, and sometimes for dessert, he would spoil us with his delicious vanilla ice-cream made at home from his wood bucket ice-cream maker. We also attended Saint Agatha School together where we learned and prayed to God. On Sunday mornings, our families went to Mass together at Saint Agatha Catholic Church.

After Sunday morning church service, we looked forward to eating and enjoying a delicious doughnut. My favorite doughnuts to eat were glazed and chocolate doughnuts. They were provided to our congregation by the church parish. I also recall the aroma of freshly brewed hot coffee. All of the refreshments were served every Sunday morning after each Mass by our church volunteers. A small portable food cart was used to facilitate the delicious treats. The doughnuts and coffee were usually located just outside of the sanctuary in front of the rectory hall.

I thought Arlene was the prettiest girl I had ever seen. She had a milk chocolate-colored complexion and long dark hair that she wore with two pigtails and bangs in the front. Arlene had a great personality; she was both funny and smart. I enjoyed playing with Arlene, especially when we went swimming together because I liked seeing her wear a bathing suit. She had the nicest pair of long pretty legs. I used to tease Arlene about her knees, calling them golf ball knees. She'd laugh, and with her open hand, gently and playfully tap me on my back.

Actually, I had believed that Arlene was my girlfriend and there was a mutual attraction between us because she treated me like I was her boyfriend. I remember when our families would take trips to fun places together. During those trips, I would sit next to Arlene in the backseat of our VW bus and put my arm around her shoulders. Our parents would get a kick out of us. "Look at Davion and Arlene snuggling!" they would say. What fun we had!

Jeffrey was an interesting boy to play with because he was intelligent, active, and energetic with everything he did. He was the same age as my twin brothers, Rene and Andree. We did lots of fun things together, which included scouting in the Cub Scouts, swimming, and bicycling. Jeffrey and I also were in the same class at Saint Agatha School. We spent much of our time sharing the same educational and religious experiences with one another.

Ava was the Dickersons' oldest child and she was sort of a loner. She spent some of her time fussing and creating confusion. Thinking or saying this wasn't nice, but occasionally I would refer to Ava as "the bad seed." After seeing the movie, *The Bad Seed,* starring Patty McCormack as Rhoda, Ava had reminded me of her character in some small ways. Like Rhoda, Ava was an attractive ten-year-old girl with light-colored eyes, perhaps hazel, blondish colored hair, and she wore two pigtails with bangs in the front. She also was bright and mischievous. However, unlike the character, Rhoda, Ava was not an evil and murderous demon child, but she was a good neighbor, and I loved her too.

I always will remember the Dickerson family for their love, kindness, and friendship.

Catastrophic Man-Made Disasters at Los Angeles, California
The Los Angeles Hollywood Hills Fire May 1961

As I was sitting down on the sofa in our living room, watching one of my favorite TV shows on the evening of May 12, 1961, *Breaking News* suddenly flashed across the TV screen. It was the esteemed local KTLA News Anchor, Harold "Hal" Fishman. He was reporting on the disastrous Hollywood Hills fire of May 12, 1961, which had started at the northern edge of Beachwood Canyon. The Hollywood Hills fire was near and below the Hollywood sign. The fire's enormous dark smoke emitted from the canyon's heavy dry brush due to the high winds and low humidity encircled the Hollywood sign like a dark cloud.

After minutes of watching the emergency news broadcast, I hurried outside and stood in front of my house at South Spaulding Avenue. After looking up far to the north at the Hollywood sign, I watched in astonishment as the flames from the fire roared down the hills below it. I could only see a few letters of the Hollywood sign. Within fifteen minutes of its reporting, the fire became a major one in great proportions. I smelled the smoke from the burning brush, and I witnessed from my front yard the fire burning out of control toward Mt. Lee and the Griffith Park Observatory to the east. The fire spread and developed into a large inferno, consuming large areas of the Hollywood Hill's canyons.

Due to the heavy dry brush, high winds, low humidity, and rugged terrain, the fire spread and continued to burn out of control. I watched it race up one canyon and down the other. Only on local TV news did I see the extent of the fire and news reports that seventy-five Los Angeles Fire Department firefighters were deployed to extinguish it. As I looked up in the sky above the dark clouds of smoke, I watched while several local news helicopters recorded and reported aerial views of the fire. In addition to seeing TV news coverage of the firefighters on the ground, I saw in the sky aerial firefighting which was also used to combat the wild dry brush fires in the deep canyon terrains of Hollywood Hills.

According to local news reports, two types of aircraft were used to fight the canyon fires: they were fixed-wing aircrafts and helicopters. Also, it was reported that the chemicals used to fight the fires were water, foams, and retardants. For a five-year old boy who had never seen an enormous fire before, the spectacular Hollywood Hills fire was an awesome catastrophic event to watch on TV and witness live from my own front yard! In the aftermath of the 1961 Hollywood Hills fire, seventeen houses in Beachwood Canyon were either damaged or destroyed by the fire; and figuratively speaking, the fire left a four to five-mile perimeter of scorched earth. There was no loss of human life. The wild dry brush fire was extinguished and 100 percent contained the next day by the Los Angeles Fire Department.

20

The Los Angeles Baldwin Hills Dam Disaster and Flood December 1963

I harken back to December 14, 1963, when I was eight years old and living at 2635 South Spaulding Avenue, which was only a few miles north of the Baldwin Hills section of Los Angeles where a major disaster had occurred. The Baldwin Hills Dam had just collapsed, sending a fifty-foot wall of water down Cloverdale Avenue, slamming into homes and cars. My mom and I were glued to the TV as we watched KTLA local newsman, Hal Fishman, report on the flood disaster most of that afternoon and evening. We watched moment by moment news of the flood. In addition to watching the Baldwin Hills flood on local TV news, I also stood in my front yard, which was at a safe distance, of course, and witnessed the Baldwin Hills reservoir flood water gushing out from the ruptured dam wall. The flood water came rumbling down the hillside like a raging river.

When I looked up at the sky, I saw and watched a squadron of local news helicopters, Los Angeles City and Los Angeles County rescue helicopters lifting people up and off of their rooftops. At the same time, I heard the sounds of numerous sirens from the Los Angeles

Police Department, Los Angeles Fire Department, and ambulances. It was a shocking sequence of events which unfolded before my very eyes.

In the wake of the Baldwin Hills Flood, five people were killed, few injuries were sustained, and hundreds of homes and cars were either damaged or totally destroyed. Early warnings from the local news stations, the Los Angeles Police Department, and the Los Angeles Fire Department with vigorous rescue efforts prevented a greater loss of life and injuries, perhaps in the hundreds.

Burn Baby Burn! The Los Angeles Watts Race Riot August 1965

When I was 9 years old, my family and I watched in shock at the local TV news. News reporter Hal Fishman was again reporting on another major disaster. He was reporting on the melee of rioters thronging the business district and public streets of Watts. While thousands and thousands of Negroes—men, women, and children—had gone on a frenzied rampage, they were burning up and destroying everything in sight. Looters ran through the streets of Watts, carrying furniture, appliances, and merchandise they had stolen from plundered stores, and they prowled both sides of street after street, searching for unburned stores to ransack. Rioters were assaulting people, especially white motorists, and snipers with guns were shooting live bullets at police and firemen on the ground and at news and police helicopters in the air!

It was a horrendous event to witness because I had never seen anything like it before! The Watts riot became so dangerous that in fear for their lives, my mom asked stepfather Dick to go and pick up our Aunt Nora whom we affectionately called "Earntie"—she was my great-grandmother's older sister—and her husband, Uncle George, from their home on East 123rd Street and Central Avenue. After picking them up, stepfather Dick brought them back to our home on South Spaulding Avenue in Mid-City, Los Angeles, where they would be safe from the perils of the uproar. They had lived just a few blocks north of Centennial High School in Compton and several blocks south of perilous Watts in a small section of Los Angeles County, which was in the midst of South Central Los Angeles. Officially declared a disaster area, it was in Watts where most of the rioting was developing and uncontrollably out of the hands of the Los Angeles Police Department, Los Angeles County Sheriff's Department, and Los Angeles County Fire Department.

Definitely, I had to look to my mom for understanding of the Watts riot as it was unfolding before us on TV. My mom expressed her disgust for the way the rioters were grandstanding before the cameras of the local news stations. Sadly, they were making a mockery of everything happening during that awful insurrection. Some of the rioters, whom were of all ages, had the audacity to bow before the local news cameras as if they had just finished a great acting performance on Broadway. My mom thought that their actions were despicable, and the entire incident dumbfounded me.

After the National Guard had restored order, stepfather took Aunt Nora and Uncle George back home. He drove them in our red 1964 VW bus, eastbound on Adams Boulevard, and then he turned right onto southbound Central Avenue. He then proceeded to drive, heading toward 123rd Street in South Central, Los Angeles. As we rode through the Watts section on south Central Avenue and 103rd Street, it was surreal having the appearance of a bombed-out block in a war-ravaged land like the destroyed cities of Hiroshima and Nagasaki by atomic bombs dropped from American bombers during War World II. This location was the heart of Watts following the August holocaust, which now was like a charred and eerily quiet burned down ghost city. The Central Avenue district was totally destroyed, and I saw, in person with my own eyes as Dick drove through the disaster area, ruins of burned-out store buildings and cars, mounds of debris and rubble from the explosive fires, and widespread devastation all around me. Residential homes in Watts were not burned except for those that incidentally caught fire which were in proximity to the burning retail stores and commercial buildings.

A Relentless Hot Summer Night and a Minor Arrest

What had begun as a routine arrest in a Los Angeles slum raged for six days and nights (August 11 to 16, 1965) as the most violent, most destructive race riot in American history. A minor arrest...a shrill cry: "Here comes whitey, let's get him!"

"Burn, baby, burn!"

And as sudden as the Watts riot had started, suddenly, order was restored by the California National Guard. In the wake of the riot, thirty-four dead, 1,032 wounded, and 3,952 arrested. Property damage: $40 million.

Val Verde Park

Val Verde, California, was once considered the "Black Palm Springs." During the 1930s through the 1960s, black people had their own recreation haven—Val Verde Park. This resort was where they could gather for family outings or just have a weekday outing with family. In 1939, the resort called Val Verde (Spanish for Green Valley) featured a community house, tennis courts, baseball fields, hiking trails, and a nine-hole golf course. In 1940, a $125,000 Olympic-sized pool was opened, complete with a bathhouse.

Through the years, jazz bands played at the community center. Visitors rode horses through the surrounding hills. And thousands of picnickers and vacationers summered and wintered there. Bill "Bojangles" Robinson helped establish a church, and James Earl Jones Sr. raised horses on a ranch nearby. In 1947, 18,000 people, mostly African American—which included my mom, uncle, grandmother, and grandfather—visited Val Verde for Labor Day.

The story begins in the early 1900s when black people could not play in most of Southern California's big-city parks. They were excluded from buying homes in many nice neighborhoods or renting rooms in most hotels. But there was one place where racially oppressive rules didn't apply: a town called Val Verde. The resort Haven nestled among rolling hills of the Santa Clarita Valley became known as the "Black Palm Springs." By the 1930s, the area was in full swing.

African-Americans threw parties year-round. They held coronation balls and pageants, put on sensational Fourth of July celebrations, and frolicked in Val Verde's park pool. Once a Mexican mining town, Val Verde was opened up to Los Angeles's black community in the early 1900s by a wealthy white woman from Pasadena, California. Angered by Jim Crow laws that segregated blacks and whites in public schools and on public transportation, in restrooms and restaurants, the woman whose name has been lost to history purchased Val Verde. The benevolence of that woman welcomed black residents there, according to Douglas Flamming, author of *Bound for Freedom: Black Los Angeles in Jim Crow America.*

In 1924, land was purchased by Sidney Dones and Joe Bass, both of whom were African American. The men wanted to turn Val Verde into a resort community for other blacks. By the 1930s, the area was wildly popular, mainly because it was one of only a handful of locations where blacks could go for recreation, according to Flamming. Harry Waterman, a white developer looking to make it rich, described Val Verde as a "sun-kissed valley with wooden hills... and becoming a veritable paradise of comfortable homes in an idyllic spot." Waterman donated fifty acres of land in 1937, which eventually became Val Verde County Park.

The enclave attracted celebrities and a who's who of black society, including film stars Louise Beavers and Hattie McDaniel. McDaniel was in the film *Gone with the Wind*, a 1939 American epic historical romance film adapted from Margaret Mitchell's 1936 novel of the same name. She was the first black person to win an Oscar for her role in the movie. The town boasted picnic tables, sports fields, barbeques, and theatres with all-black productions. Hundreds of people visited Val Verde, especially in the summer. Val Verde flourished as a retreat until the Civil Rights era brought long-overdue access to Los Angeles' housing, pools, and beaches. Many blacks moved back to the city and visited Val Verde on weekends, holidays, and vacations.

Since I was eight years of age, twice a year for several years, during my childhood on Memorial Day and Fourth of July holiday, my family took a seemingly exciting long trip to Val Verde Park. It was perhaps an hour's drive from our South Spaulding Avenue home in Los Angeles. After we had moved to Inglewood in 1965, we took the same trip from our Inglewood home on West 79th Street to Val Verde Park. As it was with thousands of black families from past decades, Val Verde Park was an amazing place to visit where we held our cultural traditions including recreation, picnics, barbeques, and we had incredible fun like no other.

Stepfather Dick who seemed to have fun himself, which was rare in my opinion, and with my mom and my grandmother, they would pile us into our family's VW bus. We'd pack food, blankets, ice coolers, picnic baskets, baseballs, gloves, and bats for some sports fun. When I was thirteen years of age, I remember on the Fourth of July 1969, my stepfather allowed me take my "Taco" minibike with us, and I had a blast riding it on the country roads along the edge of the park. Occasionally, we would invite a relative, friend, or neighbor to take the trip with us, and off we'd go to the oasis in the hidden valley.

Hiking on the surrounding mountain trails with my brothers and guest was an enjoyable adventure, up and down the rugged mountain terrain overlooking the valley far below us at the distant park where the picnickers and pool were located. While hiking on the mountain trails, sometimes we heard the rattling sound of a rattlesnake and watched as lizards scurried across the path in front of us. Also, we heard and saw a variety of other critters or varmints. My mountain hiking experience at the park, which was imaginative at times, was just like traveling with pioneers of the Old West; it was being watchful for bandits and Indians while searching for the new frontier.

As we hiked the mountain trails, the climate was almost always sunny bright with scorching dry heat, exceeding 100 degrees by midday. The extreme heat and physical exhaustion caused perspiration and thirst in all of us, so we would briefly squat under a sagging tree for shade and rest as we took a well-deserved swig of cold canteen water. After returning to the picnic site from our long journey on the mountain, we became excited about getting our swimming trunks and towels and then hurrying down to the park's swimming pool for a dip and swim in the refreshing cold water. Ah, the water felt great! Fond memories I have with my family, relatives, and guests and the joys we had at Val Verde Park throughout my childhood were indeed an experience I will always cherish.

21

LITTLE LEAGUE BASEBALL

My passion for baseball motivated me to play Little League Baseball in the mid-1960s and late 1960s when I was growing up in Los Angeles and Inglewood, California. Most of the boys who lived in my neighborhood, including my brothers, the twins and Vernon, a.k.a. Sputdoll, played Little League Baseball with me. Baseball dominated our lives in the late spring and early summer months. I started playing baseball and other sports (football and basketball) beginning in the third grade at Baldwin Hills Park in Los Angeles. I played in what we called the "Minor League" baseball. My uniform was a baseball cap, T-shirt, and my black rubber cleat baseball shoes with my favorite infielder's glove. After I grew older and more skillful, I tried out for and made it to the "big league," which was the Little League. Finally, I was issued a real baseball uniform (some were used of which had been worn by the team before us).

I wore my white and yellow baseball uniform proudly. I thought it was the coolest article of clothing I had possessed. The Darby Park Little League teams in Inglewood, California, were named after an organization of service clubs: The Women's Club, Kiwanis, Lions Club International, Rotary Club, Junior Chamber International, etcetera. I played shortstop position for the "Sertoma Club." My uniform shirt had my team's name written across the front. It was a perfect fit.

In baseball positions, shortstop is the best, and I was considered the best. There is no better position to play than shortstop which was the position I had always played. Shortstop is the infielder who plays close to and on the left side of second base. Shortstop is often considered the most important and demanding defensive position aside from pitcher and catcher. Like other infielders, to play the position of shortstop, I was and I had to be agile and able to start and stop running quickly.

In playing the position of shortstop, I had to cover a larger area of the infield than the third baseman and make longer throws than the second baseman. As a shortstop, I also often was the pivot man on ground ball double plays and I covered second base on stolen base attempts when the batter on the opposing team hit the ball toward the right side of the infield. The shortstop needs to have as much range as a second baseman and as strong a throwing arm as a third baseman, which is why the position is generally regarded as the most difficult infield position. I was the captain of the infield. The short-stop is often the captain of the infield and gives signals to the other infielders about how to position themselves.

Many second and third basemen are initially drafted as short-stops and moved to the other position, but it is rare for second or third basemen to be moved to shortstop. Often in Little League, the best player plays shortstop as the position demands athleticism and range. Incidentally, my brothers played on Sertoma Club with me. Renee, who was left-handed, played the first base position, Andree played the third base position, and Sputdoll played outfield in the right field position. The Woodman brothers—we were a team who played on a team. Wow! How wonderful that was!

Also, the league considered me to be a very good batter. As a player in Little League Baseball, my batting average was consistently and slightly above .300. However, there were only a couple of play-ers in the league whose names were Kenny Washington and Stanley Stewart, all-American. They both were ranked as high achievers in batting with averages that exceeded .300 during the season. In mod-ern times, a season batting average higher than .300 is considered to be excellent.

Even though it has been more than fifty years ago, I still have fond memories of playing Little League Baseball, especially when I played with my brothers the twins, Rene and Andree, and Vernon "Sputdoll" Woodman.

As a postscript to this, my motivation and passion for baseball intensified when I watched on television:

- The 1965 National League tie-breaker series between the Los Angeles Dodgers and the San Francisco Giants, and
- *Damn Yankees!* (1958) TV Movie Musical

Daddy's Home!

When you have a father whom you loved go away to prison, nothing can compare to the feeling when you get to finally welcome him back home after being away for a long time. I was so happy to see him. It was terrible to have my father away from us. However, my reality kicked in quickly. While he was incarcerated, my mother divorced him and remarried, which meant my father was not home to stay. It grieved me greatly because I was living with a stepfather whose ways I disliked, and I needed my real father back home with me. My little sister, Leslie, didn't recognize my father at all because she was two years old when he went away. Leslie only saw a strange man embracing our mother and us. The only father she knew was our stepfather Dick, whom she called dad.

After school during the early evening of 1964, when I was eight years old, my father came to see us at what used to be his home. His visit was the first time I had seen him since his incarceration in 1961. He had just been paroled and released from the California state penitentiary after serving three years of a five-year prison sentence for armed robbery. As a child growing up, I do not remember a time when my father wasn't incarcerated. He was in and out of prison from when I was five years old until I was sixteen, and he lived at a halfway house upon each prison release. After he was freed from the rules and restrictions of the halfway house, his sister, my Aunt Beverly, would give him a place to live at her home.

This happened each and every time. My father's recidivism rate was high; his life was like a revolving door for at least eleven years of my childhood and as a teenager. But I adjusted to not seeing him during his incarcerations. Even though my mother had remarried, my stepfather was a poor example of a role model and a man. While growing up, and throughout my entire life, I've had to deal with endless disappointments in my father. There were times when I became jealous seeing other boys interacting with their dads and enjoying the companionship of their fathers.

My father continued to be the disappointing weak link in the family never to rise again as a strong father figure. Memories of him throughout my life are so vague and remote that he's more a stranger to me than a stranger in the streets. He had become the daddy whom I did not know, showing up once a blue moon, bearing gifts and an uncertain smile. My grandmother, Needie, often described his smile as the grin like a Cheshire cat. My father's attempts at playing part-time Santa Claus and spreading good cheer failed to win me over. Although my father made me happy whenever he came for a visit, I also had ambivalent feelings about him. After each visit, he always left me wondering, "When will I see him again?"

Before my father went away, I only remembered some things about our specific relationship. Being the oldest of his five children, I had memories that my younger siblings didn't have. I would have to describe my parents' relationship as respectable and loving. Life as I had remembered it with my father was never the same again. For many years in the past to this day, my father and I haven't had any kind of relationship; and now, I neither see nor seldom speak to him.

Uncle Butch the Sailorman

Uncle Butch's real name was Clyde Carey, and he was my stepfather Dick's younger brother. Butch was on active duty in the US Navy when he took his vacation leave during the summer of 1964. We had met him that summer when I was eight years old. Butch resembled his brother, Dick, in some ways. He had a stocky muscular build with several tattoos on both his left and right arm, and he spoke in a raspy smoker's voice.

Butch reminded me of "Popeye the Sailorman" without the one eye, corn pipe, and can of spinach. He was the same age as my mother; they both were twenty-six years old at the time we met each other. He lodged in our home at Los Angeles on South Spaulding Avenue for one month while he was on annual leave from the US Navy. Even though Butch had retired from the navy as a Chief Petty Officer and is now deceased, I will always think of him as Uncle Butch the "sailorman" with all of his tattoos. Everybody who knew Butch, including the Dickerson's next door and the Williams, thought of him as fun-loving, crazy, and cursing like the sailor that he was.

He was always the life of any party, a popular and gregarious man. Butch was animated and bigger than life. He also had lots of stories to tell from his sea voyages around the world. When Butch talked, the cigarette and his words took turns on his lips. Sometimes he had problems keeping his cigarette lit because he talked so much, especially when he was drunk after drinking liquor.

Butch treated my siblings and me like we were his children. I remember him with great fondness. He was unlike any man I had ever met before him. Butch brought our family so much hope in a man, which was sadly lacking since my dad's incarceration. While Butch was staying with us on his vacation, at times he made me feel like I was his son.

Butch was kind and generous. I was so excited about him being a navy man that I kept asking him questions about himself, his tat-tooed jellied arms, life aboard a navy ship, and sailing the world's oceans, etcetera. When I asked Butch about his large white navy sea bag that he had carried with himself, he paused momentarily, then he opened it and took navy memorabilia from the bag. Among the many things that he brought with him from his ship were a half dozen brass geographic compasses, and he gave each of us, including my sister, Leslie, a compass. We had the most fun playing with the compasses because while we held them in the palm of our hands, we were able to see on the face of it the north, east, south, and west directions as we walked around our house and outside; it was a delight! Butch also gave us utility belts worn by the sailors in the navy, and he explained the purpose and uses of it. Utility belts are principally used to carry tools and other useful items around the waist.

We had lots of summer fun with Butch from camping outside in our backyard under the stars to swimming and roasting marshmallows over a bonfire at Playa Del Rey Beach to enjoying the amenities at Knott's Berry Farm and Disneyland. Finally, picnicking, barbeque, and hiking at Val Verde Park with Butch and our neighbors, the Dickerson family. We had a blast with him that summer. Butch, mechanically gifted, was the ship's engineman. As an engineman in the navy, his job was to maintain and keep the ship's enormous diesel engines running at all times. He served on an oil tanker navy ship.

One day, Butch surprised all of us when he came riding home on a used late 1950s Triumph Motorcycle. His motorcycle had a kick start with a crazy brutal sounding exhaust similar to the classic Harley Davidson sound. After the big surprise, Butch immediately using his mechanical skills, dismantled his motorcycle down to its frame, then he sanded it and painted it, using several cans of candy apple red spray paint. After he finished painting it, Butch started reassembling the motorcycle with one nut and one bolt at a time until it was completely reassembled. To make the package complete with style, Butch bought attire to wear while riding his motorcycle. He wore a classic men's black buffalo leather motorcycle jacket with the zippers and belt, leather boots, and gloves. For safety reasons, he also bought and wore a candy apple red-colored motorcycle helmet to match the color of his motorcycle.

This was one of my best summers. My friends and me had fun riding on the back of Butch's motorcycle. Since I had never ridden on the back of any motorcycle before, my ride for the first time was an awesome experience. I had felt a combination of exhilaration, fear, relaxation, and pleasure that changed me forever. It was physical and emotional pleasure with a layer of anxiety and adrenaline. Soon after, toward the end of that summer, I became sad and teary eyed because Butch had to return to his navy ship in San Diego; his vacation had officially ended. Thus, Butch packed his things on his motorcycle, wearing his dress white crackerjack navy uniform, motorcycle jacket, helmet, and gloves. He said his goodbyes, and off he rode on his candy apple red motorcycle into the wild blue yonder.

I could still hear the crazy brutal sound of his Triumph's exhaust pipe as he left our block and entered the eastbound onramp to the Santa Monica Freeway. Within minutes, the exhaust sound had muffled as he rode in the far distance toward the Harbor Freeway to San Diego. I would not see Butch again for several years because of the Vietnam War. He also spent the remaining part of his enlistment with the US Navy in Japan where he met and married a Japanese woman named Susie. When Butch had retired from the US Navy as an Engineman Chief Petty Officer in 1971, he returned to the United States and introduced us to his new wife.

Susie spoke little English. However, she was very friendly and warmhearted. While Butch was in the navy and stationed in Japan, he had learned enough of the Japanese language to communicate effectively with Susie. After their visit with us at Inglewood, California, they returned to Butch and Dick's hometown in the city of Youngstown, Ohio, and had a son named Michael. I would not see Butch and Susie again until more than a decade later.

Mrs. Feldon

Third grade at Saint Agatha Catholic School was a transition year for me. It also provided me with more challenges. While teacher supervision continued to be important, I was provided with many opportunities to learn about choices. I was given increased responsibility for my own work. This freedom of learning made me feel proud that I was growing and maturing.

From fall 1964 to spring 1965 was my last school semester attending Catholic School. It was my best school year too. For the first time, my teacher wasn't a Roman Catholic nun, but she was a young lay teacher. Her name was Mrs. Feldon who was an African American. She continued to direct my spiritual, educational, and personal development in her classroom. But this was only part of her qualifications as a Catholic school lay teacher; she was truly whole because her faith in the Holy Spirit empowered her to lead and teach her class with authority, compassion, Godly wisdom, and understanding.

As a result of Mrs. Feldon's efforts and particularly her compassion toward me to learn from her teachings, my grades improved tremendously. In prior classes, I had been a struggling C student or an average student. Delighted that I was learning something new and challenging in her classroom every day, I also rejoiced in the outstanding grades I began to receive for the first time in my educational experience. I harken back to receiving outstanding grades for perfectly memorizing Bible verses, prayer, and the Act of Faith, Act of Hope, Act of Love, and the Act of Contrition. Additionally, I received outstanding grades for my understanding and knowledge of the Roman Catholic religion as well as the following academic subjects: reading, writing, and arithmetic. Mrs. Feldon was indeed a blessing to me during my final year at Saint Agatha Catholic School.

"Cock of the Walk"

Whenever my grandmother's friend and friend of our family, Ernie Cruz, visited our home, he would often call me the "cock of the walk." I was five or six years old when I first heard Ernie dub me the "cock of the walk." But I also understood what he meant because I was the oldest of five children and therefore top of the pecking order.

Definition of Cock of the Walk: "the leader in a group, especially one with a conceited, domineering manner."

Surely, as the oldest brother of five siblings, most of the time, I fulfilled the definition of "cock of the walk" when I interacted with them. Laughing out loud, I was as proud as a peacock and grateful to have been the firstborn child in our family. Even at school, if a nun or teacher had a problem with one of my younger siblings, they would always summon me for help. "Get the Woodman boy," they'd say. I've always enjoyed my position of power and authority in our family hierarchy, and I always will.

An Awesome Bike Trail: The Pre-Santa Monica Freeway (I-10), 1964 to 1965

On Christmas morning in 1964, I received a wonderful Christmas gift leaning on a kickstand next to our white flocked Christmas tree; it was a new and beautiful blue 1964 Schwinn deluxe stingray bicycle. I was so excited and ready to go riding with my friends—Michael, Gregory, and Craig—on the raised earthen mound; it was just north of my home, and it was being used as a foundation for the preparation and construction of the new Santa

Monica Freeway. The raised earthen mound was put there by the California Department of Transportation (Caltrans). After using eminent domain for public use several years earlier, Caltrans took private properties for that stretch of freeway. I watched for several years as Caltrans demolished miles and square miles of private properties. The private properties included business properties, residential properties, and vacant properties.

Before demolition and removal, I often rode my new Stingray bicycle to the residential area where individual private properties had been condemned by Caltrans for construction of the Santa Monica Freeway. I'd go and play inside of the abandoned houses and liked playing upstairs and downstairs in the abandoned apartment buildings. Sometimes I'd pick up rocks and throw them at unbroken or partially broken glass windows inside the abandoned buildings. One time, when I was riding on my new bicycle in the condemned residential area, there was an attractive young woman who was wearing a white nurse's uniform sitting down on the front porch steps of an abandoned house. I think perhaps that house had belonged to her before Caltrans had condemned it for public use. When the young woman saw me cruising slowly on my bicycle, she smiled at me and said hi. Afterward, she offered me some candy, but I had remembered the TV commercials and warnings to children about kidnappers. "Never accept candy from a stranger." With that warning in my mind, I smiled back at her, then I began peddling my bicycle past her and I continued riding it quickly all the way to my home on South Spaulding Avenue, south of West Adams Boulevard.

After demolition, removal, and groundbreaking, construction of the Santa Monica Freeway started with the stretched raised mass of earth, which was within clear view from my front yard. For several months while construction was underway, I enjoyed riding on my new stingray bicycle for at least a couple of miles or more on that stretch of raised dirt. The new freeway was being constructed at La Cienega and Venice Boulevards, which was within bicycling distance from my home on South Spaulding Avenue. When I rode my bicycle on the raised dirt mound, the Caltrans crew had either left their work for that day or they didn't work that day, and the heavy construction machinery and equipment was left and set aside on both the north and south shoulders of the construction site. Caltran's work crew's occasional absence from the miles of construction site perfectly accommodated my use of it.

During the work crew's off-days, my friends and I had an awesome bike trail all to ourselves! The distance eastward starting from La Cienega Boulevard on that wide stretch of raised dirt seemed infinite, and none of us dared one another to ride our bicycles that far. The Santa Monica Freeway opened its corridor for motor vehicle traffic in 1966. However, I was the little pioneer who rode that stretch of the Santa Monica Freeway on my new Schwinn Stingray bicycle; that is, from the end of 1964 to the middle of 1965. Wow! What an historical accomplishment I had made for myself. For several months, 1964 to 1965, I rode my new Schwinn Stingray bicycle on the work-in-progress, Santa Monica Freeway, before any person driving a motor vehicle in California had driven on it.

22

THE HOME IN INGLEWOOD, CALIFORNIA

When I was nine years old, we moved into a new home at 2615 West 79th Street, Inglewood, California. The thick black smoke-filled easterly skies above Watts and South Central, Los Angeles, which is within nine miles east of Inglewood, had nearly dissipated. It was on August 16, 1965, when the Watts riots had winded down and came to an abrupt end just days before our family moved to Inglewood. My stepfather, Dick, had rented a medium sized moving truck, and my dad who was wearing a baseball cap—ready and willing—helped Dick facilitate the move to our new home. When the packing and moving was completed, I needed to settle into the new space.

> Inglewood is a city in southwestern Los Angeles County, California, in the Los Angeles metropolitan area. As of the 2010 US Census, the city had a population of 109,673. It was incorporated on February 14, 1908. The city is in the South Bay region of Los Angeles County. So Fi Stadium is under construction in the city and, when completed around 2020, will be the new home of both the National Football League's Los Angeles Rams and Los Angeles Chargers.

This was the hardest adjustment I had to make. Saying good-bye to my old friends, especially my best friend, Michael Williams, was difficult. But the excitement of moving to a new home, a new neighborhood, helped reduce the initial anxiety that I was feeling. However, I wasn't completely anxiety free because we had just moved from the westside of Los Angeles where I had felt safe from the dangers of the Watts riots to Inglewood, which was a short distance west of the South Los Angeles slum. Remembering more than a week ago, the Watts riots had raged for six days and nights, and recorded facts have it as the most violent, most destructive race riot in American history.

So I wasn't entirely at ease with the move to Inglewood at first because it was too close to Watts for my comfort zone, and our home was almost in view of the National Guard's front lines. Also, it was difficult and confusing for me to understand the concept of a race riot because I was a nine-year old boy who happened to be a Christian Cub Scout, and I had attended Catholic schools where skin color didn't matter. I knew nothing of the violence that had taken more than thirty lives. But I was excited by the sight of military trucks carrying troops of National Guardsmen and military jeeps rolling down South Van Ness Avenue, West Florence Avenue, South Crenshaw Boulevard, and West Manchester Avenue. The jeeps carried mounted machine guns manned by the National Guard. While Watts was still under Martial Law, there was a heavy presence of California National Guardsmen enforcing the law.

More often than not, dark-skinned black kids use to call me "light-skinned" or "yellow" because I looked more white than black, having physical characteristics or features similar to that of my European ancestry in contrast to that of my African ancestry; but my physical stature is more like my African ancestry. Not surprising, but until then, I didn't see myself as being black. I only saw myself as being God's child.

By September 1965, many black students and myself attended Daniel Freeman Elementary School at the beginning of the 1965 to 1966 school year. It also was "the very beginning of the integration process" in Inglewood Unified School District/IUSD. Daniel

Freeman Elementary was located directly across the street from my new family home on West 79th Street between 5th Avenue and 7th Avenue in the vicinities of West Manchester Avenue to the north, South Crenshaw Boulevard to the west, and South Van Ness Avenue to the east. Back then, the city of Inglewood was proudly and determinedly white. But over the next several years, the adverse side effects from the Watts riots would transform Inglewood as black families fleeing from South Los Angeles arrived in overwhelming numbers. New black residents needed access to better, less-crowded schools than the crowded ones they left behind in South Los Angeles. Black people who lived in Watts wanted the right and the freedom to live anywhere they desired. During that same time period, white flight quickly and steadily moved flocks of white people of various European ancestries from racially mixed Inglewood to more racially homogeneous cities, towns, and suburban or exurban regions.

According to the 1960 census record, only twenty-nine "Negroes" lived amongst Inglewood's 63,390 residents. There weren't any black students attending Inglewood city schools. Real estate agents refused to show homes to blacks. A rumored curfew kept blacks off the streets at night. My mom told me after we had moved into our Inglewood home in 1965, her real estate agent, a young Jewish woman, was discharged by her broker for selling the house to us. By 1970, 10 percent of Inglewood's residence were black, and white flight gradually accelerated after the Watts Riots and the court-ordered 1970 desegregation of Inglewood High School, which had adversely affected some if not all of my graduating classmates of 1974 in general; and even now, after a very long time, myself in particular.

New Neighbors

As we were moving into our new single-story Spanish-style home with the tile roof, it reminded me of a small medieval castle without the surrounding moat and drawbridge. The new neighbors were noticeably curious as they watched us from their yard, transferring our furniture from the truck into the house. While we were still moving in, they walked over to us and introduced themselves as the Taylor family. Their names were Charles and Barbara Taylor, and they had two children whose names were Alan, who was three months younger than me, and Sharon who was slightly younger than my sister, Leslie. But all of us were in the same school grade. The Taylors were one of four black residents who had lived on our new block. Charles and Barbara both were a little older than my mother. Charles was employed as a Teacher with the Los Angeles Unified School District, and Barbara was employed with Travelers Insurance Company as a claim processor/claim adjuster.

Then our other new neighbor was the Paulsons. They were a German family of five. Mr. and Mrs. Paulson had three children. Their oldest daughter's name was Nancy. She was two years older than me. And there was Julie who was next to the oldest child. She was approximately my age. And finally, there was William who was the Paulson's youngest child and their only son. William was my younger brother Vernon's age. Mr. Paulson was an older man who was up in age, and he seemed much older than his wife, Mrs. Paulson.

Finally, there was Bryant McCloud and his family. Bryant lived in the house next to the Taylor's residence on the right. His family was the second of four black families who lived on our new block. Bryant was approximately the same age as my twin brothers, Rene and Andree; they were all in the same school grade. Bryant's mother's name was Esther. She was much older than my mother and Alan's parents. Esther was married to Bryant's stepfather whose name was John Holland. Bryant had three other siblings; his oldest sister's name was Debra McCloud. She was four or five-years older than Bryant. His younger half-sister's name was Stephanie Tucker, and finally, his youngest half-brother's name was Keith Holland whom they called Ki-Ki. Except for his oldest sister, Debra, Bryant's younger half siblings, were given birth from the same mother, Esther, but they all had different fathers. Ki-Ki's father was Bryant's current stepfather, John Holland.

"Marcus David"

On September 22, 1967, Mom gave birth to my half-brother, Marcus David Carey. He looked like a white baby boy with blond hair and blue eyes. We adored Marcus and often held him, changed his diaper, and fed him with tender loving care. Marcus was the second child and son of my stepfather, Richard Dick Carey, and my mom's seventh and youngest child of whom she had given birth. Marcus was born nearly twelve years after my birth.

When Marcus was born, I became the proud and oldest brother of six siblings: the twins, Sputdoll, Gretchen, Pepper, and Marcus. My teenage friends, Shelton Scarborough, and his brother, Randy, they both dubbed Marcus "Baby Mar-Mar." Sadly, and once again, as it was with my brother, Pepper, there was no baptism for Marcus because of Dick's unbelief in Christianity. His faithlessness in Christ bitterly disappointed my mother. Due to his lack of understanding and stubbornness, and just like with everything else, it was impossible for my mother to reason with my stepfather about the Christian and spiritual significance of baptizing Marcus.

Centinela Park

What I liked most about moving to Inglewood was that I would be living nearby Centinela Park. My mom had taken us to this pleasant place many times during the past summers for good old-fashioned family fun, picnics, recreation, and swimming at the outdoor pool. I had always thought of Inglewood as a wonderful place to live. It also had reminded me of other nice places, like the ones that I had watched on TV shows, such as *Leave It to Beaver* and *My Three Sons*. I was over the moon!

Catechism Classes

As we were preparing to enroll in public school, my mother signed us up for catechism classes at Saint Anselm Catholic School. She had wanted us to transfer from Saint Agatha to Saint Anselm, which was close to our new home. However, my stepfather, who was the only family income earner, used the excuse that he could not afford the full-time tuition for the four of us. So my mom opted for catechism, in which the twins, Vernon, and myself would attend the classes. Her goal was for us to continue our Catholic catechesis while we attended public school in preparation for the Holy Sacrament of

Confirmation when we reached the age of twelve. After the 1965 fall enrollment, we attended catechism classes each Saturday at Saint Anselm Catholic School. Not ever wavering in my Christian faith, I continued with the Catholic customs, traditions, beliefs, and practices throughout my life from childhood to adulthood.

My Prayer Life

As a devout Catholic back then, and as a faithful, hopeful, and charitable Christian now, I continue to pray day and night as my Lord and Savior, Jesus Christ, had done then, now, and forever.

Daniel Freeman Elementary School: 1965 to 1968

Daniel Freeman Elementary School's principal's name was Ms. Jessamine Herbst, and her vice principal's name was Mr. Darryl Lawrence. I recall my mom taking us to meet Ms. Herbst before school began. She was a friendly woman, tall in stature, who gave us a warm welcome. Ms. Herbst was confident that we would perform well at her school because she understood that my siblings and I had just come from a parochial institution of learning, which had placed emphasis on respect for self and others, promoting well-disciplined environments that were conducive to quality learning. After our interview with the school principal, she helped make our transfer to public school a little easier.

My first day at Daniel Freeman Elementary began on Tuesday, September 6, 1965, the day after Labor Day holiday. I had just begun fourth grade in a major transition from Catholic school to public school. There were some significant issues facing our nation back then: the Vietnam War, antiestablishment movements, hippies, drugs, free love, and it seemed like everywhere was in racial turmoil—the world was a ball of confusion. Nevertheless, attending public school in the Inglewood Unified School District, always referred to as IUSD, was exciting, especially with my new neighbor, Alan, whom also was my classmate. We both were in Room 12, and Mrs. Resnick was our new teacher. She was a beautiful young Jewish woman with long straight black hair that fell down to her waist.

The weather was hot and sunny that day, so my mom dressed me in a short-sleeved striped polo shirt, blue denim bellbottoms, a pair of black sneakers, and I had always styled a short haircut called the Covatis or Quo Vadis. No more wearing parochial school uniforms, I thought to myself. Also, I carried a packed lunch as I did in Catholic school, but sometimes during the school years, my mom would let me eat lunch in the school cafeteria. Since we lived just across the street from my school, I'd occasionally eat lunch at home, and I walked to and from school. Walking to school every day was a good way for me to get exercise in the morning before school and in the afternoon after school. Some of the kids who lived farther away rode on school buses, bicycles, or traveled to school by car.

After a while, my new neighbor, Alan, and I became best friends and fierce competitors in almost everything we did as boys from academic to athletic achievements, model car building, and we even competed for the same girlfriends. During our fourth-grade year, and at the same time, we both rivaled for the affections of two girls. They were cute girls, and we liked them both. Also, there were a variety of attractive girls at Daniel Freeman as well. But slightly shy as it were with me, I became a secret admirer, treating all of the girls with respect and kindness. And most of the girls thought of me as a nice-acting, good-looking, and smart boy. The majority of them were either white or mixed race of different kinds, but some of the girls were Creole, dark and brown complexioned.

When I arrived at school, I saw lots of other kids on the playground. Then I noticed all of the teachers were opening their classroom doors when it was time to go in. After the bell rang, we walked in a single file from the playground to our classroom. After going into the classroom, everyone had to find their own cubby. I found my cubby with my name already printed on it. Daniel Freeman divided the school according to grade levels. The lower grades encompassed the younger kids, kindergarten to third grade, and the upper grades were the older kids from fourth grade to sixth grade. So I was an upper grader.

My teacher greeted us as we entered her classroom, then she checked that everyone was there by taking our attendance. Afterward, we pledged allegiance to the American flag which hung in the corner of the classroom. After putting my things away, we sat down at our assigned desks and our teacher introduced herself to us. While she reviewed her classroom rules with the class, she explained California's fourth-grade history requirement and curriculum.

After she finished going over the classroom rules, Mrs. Resnick asked us to stand up, one pupil at a time, and introduce ourselves to the class. When it was my turn, I stood up and introduced myself, saying, "Hi, my name is Davion Woodman." I also had to explain to her and my classmates that the A in Davion is the short vowel sound and it can be found in other words like apple, attitude, cat, actually, and can. I did this because of its French origin and uniqueness. My name had often been mispronounced. Most people had pronounced my name by using the long vowel sound, like in David. My classmates smiled and Mrs. Resnick thanked me for my introduction.

As I attended a new school with curiosity, it was important for me know my way around. So during recess and my lunch break, I embarked on a mission to know where the bathrooms were. I also needed to know the names of the other teachers and where their classrooms were. Even though I was shy, I wasn't afraid to ask for help when I wasn't sure about something. It was also exciting to know what would happen during the day at my new school. I enjoyed getting to know the other kids as we worked and played together. I looked forward to morning recess, lunchtime, and afternoon recess. Occasionally, there was a school assembly with the rest of the school or some other classes in the multipurpose room, which was the school cafeteria. These things that I just mentioned were only part of my new daily school routine.

When I started at Daniel Freeman for the first time, I felt nervous. There were other kids who felt the same as I did. I think Mrs. Resnick was empathetic toward us, and she said it was okay to be nervous. So she helped us make friends and find things we enjoyed doing while we were in her classroom. Her compassion comforted both my classmates and me.

At the end of the day, my class said goodbye. I collected all of my things before leaving the classroom. Some of the kids went home on a yellow school bus while others were picked up by their parents. Happy and excited about my first day at Daniel Freeman Elementary, I was anxious to share it with my mom. Then I quickly walked across the street to my new home. My mom was happy about my first day experience, and she was pleased with me for making it clear to my class how my name was properly pronounced. She believed "Davion" was a beautiful French name and it shouldn't be mispronounced.

Fourth grade was fun and exciting too. I remember taking at least two field trips on the yellow school bus with my fourth-grade classmates. The first trip took us to the San Fernando Valley Mission. While the mission field trip was interesting, it also served to fulfill part of California's fourth-grade history requirement. Later that year, our second field trip took us to the Griffith Park Observatory because in science, we were learning about the Milky Way, galaxies, stars, and the planets. My experience at the observatory was surreal. It made me feel as though I was traveling in space.

The last day of fourth grade at Daniel Freeman Elementary in June of 1966 came swiftly. We celebrated the end of the school year with summer fun and enjoyment at our new home. It had been a school year full of excitement and challenges. My mom was proud that I was growing up and moving on to the fifth grade, and within one week, I was enrolled in fifth-grade summer school (1966) at Oak Street Elementary in Inglewood. Mom thought summer school would be to our advantage because she believed that it offered enrichment and academic programs in which teachers repeated what we had not learned in the previous year. Enrollment was open to anyone who wanted to attend. Summer school also provided high-achieving kids academic classes to help them get further ahead and enrichment classes to motivate average kids and thus improve their grades. Nevertheless, I made outstanding progress in fifth-grade mathematics and language arts because of the caliber of teachers at Oak Street Summer School.

Integration at Inglewood schools was underway and gained momentum after 1965. It wasn't only black students integrating the school classrooms, but black teachers were integrating the school faculties. Mrs. Smith, my new fifth grade teacher, was petite, attractive, and a feminine woman who always wore a dark bob wig, black dress gloves, and carried a large brown rugged leather purse. She became the first black faculty member to teach at Daniel Freeman during the 1966 to 1967 school year. Mrs. Smith taught a newly mixed upper grade class of fifth and sixth-graders in which I was one among her fifth-grade students in Room 15. It was my second year of attendance at the new public school.

In previous years before Mrs. Smith's arrival at Daniel Freeman Elementary, the school employed their first black non-teacher staff person whose name was Ernie. He worked as the school's day janitor. Ernie was dark-complexioned and cockeyed. He wore a conk hairstyle which was popular among black men from the 1920s to the 1960s. Ernie kept the schoolgrounds, buildings, offices, classrooms, and bathrooms clean and safe. He also performed security for the school and he helped with the lunchtime athletic programs. Sometimes Ernie coached us in various athletic activities, and he was our official basketball referee.

Mrs. Smith's fifth-grade class was an interesting and enjoyable learning experience. Taking on the challenge, I competed successfully with all of the kids in my mixed class. Within the school year, I had excelled in all academic subjects, surpassing my classmates in both grades. Technically, my class was a self-contained combined fifth/sixth-grade class. My class had no more than thirteen students from either grade level (class maximum of twenty-six).

The curriculum was accelerated, at least one to two years, in all subject areas. The instruction was multidisciplinary and was given by Mrs. Smith. Projects and tasks involving higher order thinking skills were built in all units of study. We also participated in PE, music, and art. Starting at the fifth grade, band, orchestra, and choir were available too. My mom wanted me to play the violin, but I didn't because I thought learning how to play the violin was uncool. I was more interested in learning how to play the drums, but it wasn't available at the school. So I didn't learn how to play any musical instruments that school year; not until junior high school.

On the last day of the school year, we were mentally checked out. I thought Mrs. Smith probably wasn't far behind. There was no more time for long-term projects. But we still needed to fill the day with something productive in order to keep the natives from getting ridiculously restless and out of line. Being creative and resourceful, Mrs. Smith had already organized our last day of the school year in her classroom with a couple of fun and memorable ideas:

- First, we held a traditional spelling bee using all of the spelling words from the whole school year. This took quite a while, but it certainly was educational!
- Then we wrote thank you notes, recognizing and appreciating who helped make our school year successful. I wrote thank you notes to my teacher, Mrs. Smith, and Ernie, the janitor.
- Finally, we received our grade report cards from Mrs. Smith and went home to enjoy the summer.

I spent my first four weeks of the summer season in 1967 at La Tijera Elementary School. My mother always wanted my siblings and me to receive the benefits of public school summer programs. While in summer school, the focus time and time again was on the core subjects in mathematics and language arts where I continued to excel. Summer school gave me the distinct advantage. It prepared me tremendously for the sixth grade in the coming new school year.

23

FINAL DESTINATION: SYLMAR JUVENILE HALL—SUMMER 1967

After completing summer school at La Tijera Elementary during 1967, I and two other boys from my neighborhood named Rodney Baker and Carl Johnson (Carl's sister was Junie Johnson, my sixth-grade classmate and president of the student council at Daniel Freeman Elementary School during the 1967–1968 school year), on a warm summer day in August, went bicycle riding throughout the City of Inglewood where we stopped at two stores. The first stop was at an auto parts store on Manchester Boulevard just west of Prairie, and then the second stop was at Sears Department Store near Downtown Inglewood across the street from IHOP. While at Sears, we browsed around in the automotive section of the store when, momentarily, I was separated from them. Meanwhile, they both had been caught shoplifting cans of spray paint, and all three of us were detained by two Sear's security officers. After being detained, I adamantly protested not stealing anything from the store, but Sear's security explained to me that being in the company of them who had, they were compelled to detain me also.

Afterward, we were taken to individual private rooms in the store where an investigation report was written by the security officer. No criminal charges were alleged; however, later that evening, we

192

were transported in a station wagon by Inglewood PD with our bicycles in the back to the final destination—Sylmar Juvenile Hall. The facility was where we were further detained and then later released to the custody of our parents. The trip to juvey seemed long and quiet. I believed it served as a scare tactic and lesson to be learned—that it's wrong to be with anyone whose caught stealing or shoplifting.

This ordeal flustered me because I had never been in trouble with the law before. So my silent prayer for grace made me feel truly sorry for what had happened. Also, with the help of God's grace, I prayed that I would try not to sin again. It was after dark, and within two hours of being detained at Sylmar Juvenile Hall in San Fernando Valley, I was finally released to the custody of my mother and stepfather. They picked me up and drove me back to our home with my bicycle in the back of the VW. I had endured a long arduous day, and I was happy that I was going back to my comfortable home on West 79th Street at Inglewood, California. My mom was happy too.

School Year 1967–1968

Best School Year: Outstanding Student.

After beginning the new school year 1967 to 1968, I was a happy successful student, popular with my classmates, and appreciated by my sixth-grade teacher, Mrs. Orem. She was a young Caucasian woman, a strawberry blond from Minnesota who had readily acknowledged my abilities and attempted to respond with appropriate curriculum interventions. Now at age eleven, I had the reading abilities of a fourteen-year old and showed a definite talent for math problem solving. As a gifted speller, I was selected by my teacher to participate in the annual sixth-grade national spelling bee along with another classmate named Sherry Page. In that same year, I also was asked by the school principal, Ms. Herbst, to be a cross-age tutor for a second-grader named Brian. He needed help with word spelling, pronunciation, and dividing words into syllables. I happily accepted the task of tutoring him, and he soon learned how to pronounce and spell words correctly at his grade level.

Before graduation, our sixth-grade class took a field trip ride on the bus in 1968 to Albert Monroe Junior High School to help prepare us for the transition from elementary school to junior high school. Being in the sixth-grade was my best school year ever, not only because of my success as a student, but my mom was our Classroom Mother. When there was back to school night or open house, my mom assisted Mrs. Orem with classroom presentations for the parents. Mom was admired by my teacher and parents alike. They liked her very much. My classmates liked my mother too! My mom had a significant influence on my success in the sixth-grade. A friend and classmate named Aundre Williamson once said, "Davion, your mother is pretty!"

And I replied with a smile, "Thank you, Aundre." My mother always made me proud of her.

I graduated from the sixth grade with numerous accolades. At the end of each school year, Daniel Freeman Elementary held a sixth-grade graduation picnic and swimming party at the beautiful Children's Baptist Home in Inglewood on 12th Avenue. Also, the sixth-grade graduating class received blank autograph books for signing on the playground. It was interesting and fun to read the things that were written about me from my teacher, classmates, and other kids in the autograph book. During that time, I had become fully aware of the fact that I had gained many friends and admirers.

Here, I want to acknowledge two boys whom I had picked to play on my noon sports team during the school year because of their exceptional athletic abilities and who helped our team win first place: Reggie Theus, a talented fifth-grade basketball player, helped our team win all of the noontime basketball games; years later in 1978, after playing college basketball for the University of Nevada, Las Vegas, Reggie was drafted into the NBA as a point guard for the Chicago Bulls. Also, Jarvis Redwine, a talented athlete in the fourth grade, helped our team win all of the noontime baseball games. Years later in 1981, after playing college football for the University of Nebraska Cornhuskers, Jarvis was drafted into the NFL as a running back for the Minnesota Vikings. As their sixth-grade team captain, I knew back then both Reggie and Jarvis were destined for future professional athletic stardom and success.

The following list is some of the awards I received at the Year End Awards Ceremony:

- Team Captain of the Year Award
- Boy Athlete of the Year
- First Place Team—Noon Sports Award
- Perfect Attendance Award
- Student Council Award; my classmate, Junie Johnson, received the Student Council President Award
- Student Tutor Award
- Noon Equipment Monitor Award
- Straight "A" Student Award
- Almost Every Award

After I had graduated "with flying colors" from the sixth grade in June 1968 and attended the yearend awards ceremony, the school semester was finished. Proud as a peacock and a happy twelve-year-old boy, I walked across the street to my home on West 79th Street. Being very excited about my accomplishments, I could hardly wait to show my mother all of the awards and accolades I had received from Daniel Freeman Elementary. While we were sitting at the counter in the kitchen, relishing my moment of glory, I delighted in hearing her say to me, "Davion, you have everything going for you." When I heard mom say that to me, I became overjoyed because most of my life, I did my best to make her happy and proud of me. I loved my mother, and I truly honored her.

Bittersweet Love

Although I was happy most of the time during my sixth-grade year at Daniel Freeman Elementary School, it also was during those unhappy times when my mom drank that I felt sad too. After my twelfth birthday, the switch turned on my heart light, and suddenly, with some clarity, I began to understand important issues affecting me. A major one in particular was my mother's social drinking, especially on holidays. The social drinking started around the time my father went away. When my mother drank on those occasions, she often would drink shot glass after shot glass, on the rocks or straight up, Jim Beam Bourbon Whiskey as if it were going out of style and until she became fully inebriated.

After my mom had her drinks during those episodes, she would talk to me. While grieving all over again about her tragic past, sometimes she'd cry for my sympathy. My mom's tragic past was about her brother's death, my dad's incarceration, her divorce and excommunication from the Catholic church, our loss of Mama Dear, and Needie's nervous breakdown. In those heartfelt moments, she would always apologize to me by saying, "Davion, please excuse me for being morbid." Sometimes my mom's sorrow was so intense, she'd fallaciously tell me that she was dying from a malignant tumor. I knew it wasn't true, but it hurt me nonetheless.

Witnessing my mother's torment and suffering saddened me greatly. I didn't like seeing her unhappy. I wanted nothing more than to see my mom happy. So I always dreaded holidays and those times when my mother drank. When those moments of drinking and sadness occurred, we were either sitting down at the counter in the kitchen or sometimes in the living room on the sofa. While we conversed amicably, I would listen to my mother describe her lifetime feelings of grief with as much understanding and compassion as I had. I showed her the best of my love, although comfort for the both of us would only come with prayer and by the grace of God.

Whenever my mother drank and sadly talked about how she missed her late brother, she'd always listen to just one song over and over again on a 45-record entitled "Your Precious Love," which was a popular duet song that was a 1967 hit for Motown singers Marvin Gaye and Tammi Terrell. During those occasions, I often wondered what this song meant to my mother. Whenever I heard this song, it made me feel sad as I associated it with her alcohol drinking and unhappiness. But "Your Precious Love" lyrics describes perfectly what this song meant to my mom in her moments of sorrow and her love for her beloved brother, Vernon.

Your Precious Love

Marvin:
Everyday there's something new
Honey, to keep me lovin' you
And with every passin' minute
Ah baby, so much joy wrapped up in it

Chorus:
Tammi: Heaven must have sent you from above
Both: Wo, Heaven must have sent your precious love

Tammi:
And I, I've got a song to sing
Tellin' the world about the joy you bring
And you gave me a reason for livin'
And ooo, you taught me, you taught me the meaning of givin'
(chorus)
Marvin: To find a love like ours is rare these days
'Cause you've shown me happiness, yes, in so many
ways
Tammi: I look in the mirror, and I'm glad to see
Laughter in the eyes where tears used to be
"So be it"

Summer of 1968

By the summer of 1968, boys had begun to wear their hair longer: curly, straight, natural, or afro. But as with girls, they began wearing the controversial miniskirts with boots and long locks hairstyles. That summer, I was attending summer school at Monroe Junior High for four weeks and playing Little League Baseball at Darby Park. My mom consistently sent me to summer school every summer. I enrolled in an Arts and Crafts class and PE class. The art teacher's name was Mr. Krisslock who had a bald head and a prosthetic rubber left ear. He was a Korean War Veteran who had lost his left ear during a battle in Korea. He taught us how to become resourceful by using everyday things in our house to make other useful things. The Arts and Crafts class also taught me how to become more imaginative and creative that summer.

Taking PE in junior high summer school was new and challenging for me because for the first time, I had to wear a jock strap during gym class and shower afterwards. It was a communal shower, no separate stalls. Coach Capagna was a short bowlegged Italian man who'd spit when he spoke gave detentions to anyone who refused to wear a jock strap or shower. We had one kid, Sonny, who racked up detentions like crazy. He always refused. But generally, everybody, including myself, wore a jock strap and showered with little complaining about it. I had fun attending junior high summer school.

Junior High School Memories: 1968 to 1970

My seventh and eighth grade years of junior high school were the most exciting for me. I don't remember any bad experiences within these two years. I associated with a variety of kids back then. It seemed as though while I attended junior high school, I rarely worried about anything, and there never were any real pressures from the school. My favorite part of school was the friendships I had with my classmates and how close our class was. Everyone was friends with everyone, and we all hung out together.

Everyone still had their "best friends," small groups within our class. These kids were with each other more than with other friends; however, the class as a whole was still very close. We all went crazy when someone was about to have a birthday because that meant a house party at the end of the week. I don't know how we had so much fun at these parties, but we did. Slow drag dancing with the cute girls and sipping on the spiked punch seemed to be the best ingredients for a party that would be talked about at school on Monday.

I will always remember the seventh and eighth grade "White Cap" dances at Darby Park. Going to a dance in brand-new cuffed and creased Levi jeans and wearing a black leather jacket with a colorful Italian knit sweater to have fun with all of my closest friends was a delight. It usually started out with all the girls in a group or circle, eventually making the boys who were trying to be cool or hip around the park's gym dance with them. But I loved to dance, so a couple of my friends and me were usually the first one's dancing with or without the girls. Along with these dances came some early teen drama like a break up or a couple getting together at the dance. They would be the subject of conversation for that night.

At school, we were in our own world, and looking back, sometimes I wish it had never ended. I believe that all the good memories that came from junior high school are still with me. I haven't forgotten. Since I've attained middle age, and from time to time when I see people from my junior high school class or when I was on social media, they still talk about the memories of when we were younger. This subject never seems to get old. I feel truly blessed.

Fool's Hill

As a happy kid with a cheerful heart and winning smile, I often shunned bad situations; but my ascent upon what my mom called "fool's hill" was a long, challenging, confusing, difficult, rugged, and steep climb to the summit. As an adolescent baby boomer in the seventh grade, on September 3, 1968, I arrived on the school district's yellow bus at the base of "fool's hill" in junior high! It was a time when I was trying to transition from a sheltered school life in an all-day one classroom at Daniel Freeman Elementary to the larger Monroe Junior High School where I had to find my way through not only the struggles of early adolescence but also through six periods of different classrooms a day; and sometimes having to double time it from one end of the school to the other between periods as well as squeeze into the always smoke filled, noisy, kid packed, boys bathrooms to use the bathroom and the bathroom mirror to afro pick my afro hairstyle. As for public school, I believed it had caused me to gradually live a more secular life. Without daily prayer, worship, and catechesis I had been accustomed to in the Catholic school setting, the remaining years in public junior high and high school brought me confusion and worldly lessons that I didn't always understand.

To begin, I still had not noticed the black and white issue until the seventh grade. Even so, and without any choices, I had to endure the next several years of secular public school instruction. The black students at Monroe Junior High hung together, and the white students stuck with the whites. Black students who befriended white students were called "Uncle Tom" or "Tom," and they were despised by the more radical black students. Divided along racial lines, sometimes the students banded together and hurled insulting remarks at each other. This type of behavior amongst the races was frequent and more extreme at neighboring Morningside High School. There were fights on both campuses at lunchtime—"white versus black."

At that time, the riot-inspired Black Power movement was in full-force. In 1969, the King of Soul, James Brown, recorded the hit song "Say It Loud—I'm Black and I'm Proud." Also, "Black is Beautiful," a cultural movement that started in the late 1960s by African Americans. It aimed to dispel the racist notion that black people's natural features, such as skin color, facial features, and hair are inherently ugly. So a lot of black kids, including myself, wore their hair in naturals or afros which consisted of a full bushy hairstyle that stuck out all around the head. While I attended Monroe Junior High, there always seemed to be a constant feeling of fear or anger between the black students and the white students.

Vanity of youth took hold of me like a shadow as I continued my climb up "fool's hill." The biggest challenge and reoccurring issue presented to me came from being light-skinned in color with keen physical features. It is based on the general belief that light-skinned black people are deemed more attractive, more successful, and smarter than dark-skinned black people. Most of my life, the light-skinned black notion has put me into conflict with all races and genders of people, particularly with the black race. Clearly, this is a misconception; however, the effects of these false impressions are all too real. One misconception of being a light-skinned black and "good-looking" was that I was stuck-up or too good to associate with other blacks who were darker than me and whose physical features were less keen than mine, especially the black girls. It simply wasn't true. Another mistaken belief was I'm not "black enough;" therefore, being a Christian teenager, I often had wondered why colorism was an issue with everybody because I believed and I still believe according to the Bible in the Book of Genesis 1:27 that "God created man in His own image; male and female."

> Colorism is a practice of discrimination by which those with lighter skin are treated more favorably than those with darker skin. In the African American community, this traditionally played out via the paper bag test. Those lighter than the standard paper lunch bag were allowed entry into fraternities, sororities and other realms of black upper-class life, while dark skinned blacks were excluded. The Spike Lee film *School Daze* is an exploration of colorism. (About.com)

Despite racial disharmony, Monroe Junior High "White Cap" Dances were popularly given for all of the seventh and eighth grade students once a month at Darby Park in Inglewood, California. They played music sensations like the Delfonics "La La Means I Love You;" Sly and the Family Stone's "Dance to the Music;" the Beatles' "Hey Jude;" and Jose Feliciano's "Light My Fire." Other popular songs of the school year 1968–1969 were "If You Can Want" by Smokey Robinson and The Miracles; "I Heard It Through The Grapevine" by Marvin Gaye; "I'm Gonna Make You Love Me" by The Supremes and The Temptations; "There Was a Time" by James Brown; "I'm a Girl Watcher" by the O'kaysions; "Born to Be Wild" by Steppenwolf; and "Crystal Blue Persuasion" by Tommy James and the Shondells.

24

FIRST SEMESTER
1968 TO 1969

As the first semester of junior high school moved forward in the fall of 1968, I was assigned a homeroom teacher whose name was Mrs. Barnett. She was a popular and gregarious young woman who also was my seventh-grade English teacher. In Addition, I was assigned my own personal locker with a combination lock that I had to memorize for the safekeeping of textbooks, school materials, and my personal belongings. Since I had achieved high math scores from Daniel Freeman Elementary School in the sixth grade, I was placed in an advanced seventh grade mathematics class to learn about complex subjects such as algebra, geometry, and linear equations. It was a very challenging educational environment. My math teacher was Mr. Wiley, an African American. He was a brilliant math teacher who cared about his students learning and achieving high marks. While Mr. Wiley sported a well-manicured thick black mustache, he always looked very dapper in the suits he wore to class each day. At year end, I passed Mr. Wiley's advanced seventh-grade mathematics class with an A. Hooray!

Another new educational feature in my schedule of classes at junior high school was woodshop! This class was for beginners—seventh graders. I considered woodshop the most fun class of things to do; it was new and exciting. The teacher's name was Mr. Lampley. He was a large and jolly man who made us laugh with many jokes.

Mr. Lampley focused on safety using basic power tools like the drill press, band saw, scroll saw, table saw, and more. I also learned to use hand tools such as a hammer, hand plane, miter saw, and everyone's favorite—sandpaper! I recall making three or four great projects throughout that semester. There were three wood-making projects I created that I could be very proud of. I made a small wooden bookshelf, miniature park bench, and a varnished wooden plaque with the "Cub Scouts Honor" written on it using the letters from the alphabet soup. My final grade in woodshop at the end of the school semester was a whopping A. And I felt deep satisfaction as a result of my achievements.

I also participated in the annual Monroe Junior High School talent show contest with four other classmates. For the talent show, we portrayed a singing group called The Temptations. That was exciting! The Temptations were a popular R and B American vocal group who released a series of successful singles and albums with Motown Records during the 1960s and 1970s. Our Temptations group wore matching black long-sleeved turtleneck shirts with beige-colored bell-bottom trousers. We lip sung a rendition of the Temptation's top hit single "Cloud Nine" in September 1968. Being slightly shy, I was still chosen by our group to portray David Ruffin, the lead singer of the Temptations. The other four backup singers of our group were my classmates Bruce Casey, and his brother, Tony Casey, with Herbert Davis and Sonny Curry.

They portrayed Otis Williams, Eddie Kendricks, Paul Williams, and Melvin Franklin of the Temptations respectively. The rendition of the Temptation's "Cloud Nine" was sensational, and I recall that we won first place in the talent contest. My peers loved it! Afterward, our popularity at Monroe Junior High skyrocketed with the girls and boys alike. And I was over the moon!

School Christmas Break 1968

During the school Christmas break, 1968, on Christmas day, I received the best gift ever under our Christmas tree. My grandmother, Needie, had bought me a present that I had been wanting since I was eleven years old. It was a purple 1968 Taco 22 motorized minibike. My mother said this was a special gift to me for being such a good son. And I jumped up and down for joy!

I had tons of fun riding on it. My stepfather, Dick, would pile us into the VW bus and take us to this vacant hilly area of undeveloped land called "Devil's Dip," where my brothers and me could safely ride my Taco minibike off road. This area was located just southeast of Imperial Highway and Western Avenue behind Southwest College in South Los Angeles. Since then, that land in recent years became part of a major redevelopment which is now the 105 LAX Freeway. For the first and only time, my neighbor, Jarvis Redwine, whose father had bought him a blue Bonanza minibike for Christmas, went with us and rode his bike at "Devil's Dip" too. Sadly, two young thugs assaulted Jarvis. After knocking him off of his minibike and hijacking it, they rode away on it. Despite a subsequent police report, Jarvis's minibike was never recovered nor replaced.

Unfortunately for me, several months later after the incident with Jarvis's minibike, a thief burglarized the toolshed in our backyard and stole my Taco minibike. Days later, while I was at school, some of my classmates who lived on the opposite side of Inglewood witnessed a so-called mutual friend named Michael Brown riding on my minibike and apparently enjoying himself. But I couldn't prove he had stolen my minibike. Soon after, he got rid of it. And it was never recovered nor replaced neither. This incident was heartbreaking. However, by the power of the Holy Spirit, I moved forward and forgave Michael. Afterward, when I saw Michael at school or elsewhere, I treated him like he was my best friend, and I never questioned him about the theft of my minibike. Although he never expressed it nor admitted it, I believe Michael felt guilty and remorseful toward me for what he had done.

Second Semester 1968 to 1969

Second semester of 1969 began with a blast. I involved myself with the Monroe Mariners Junior High School Marching Band, intramural sports, and I played competitive flag football in both the seventh and eighth grades. Monroe Junior High School competed in flag football against our only crosstown rival, Crozier Junior High

School. We always defeated them. Also, with some distractions, I became a girl watcher as the lyrics sang by the O'kaysions. When it came to girls, I was always happy because not being serious or going steady with any one girl, I played the field with many girls.

School Semester 1969 to 1970

When I returned to school for the eighth grade on September 2, 1969, everybody was talking about a remarkable cultural event that had happened over a three-day period during the summer of August 15 to August 18 on a dairy farm in Bethel, New York, near the town of Woodstock. This event came to be known as the Woodstock Festival—three days of rock bands, R and B bands, and vocalists entertaining an estimated half a million people. It was a crucial moment in popular music history. Make love, not war; flower children; and youth rebellion against the Vietnam War and the American establishment.

Monroe Junior High's dress codes had changed. By 1969, the girls were allowed to wear miniskirts to school. And by 1970, they could wear pants. The restrictions on boys' hair had also relaxed. Many boys, particularly the Caucasian boys, could be seen with hair down to their shoulders.

During the school year, there were many references to peace and love. The slang words *groovy* spoken by the white kids and *hip* spoken by the black kids was everywhere. I often used the word *hip* in my vocabulary and dialogue. Our English teacher, Mrs. Barnett, didn't seem to mind the use of these words. But as long as we insisted on using them, she insisted on the correct spelling, proper usage, and context.

Mrs. Barnett was a good English teacher who loved learning, and she worked hard at giving her students meaningful tests and realistic grades. She didn't compose tests that required simple regurgitation on what we had studied because for us who were good at memorizing, tests would be easy; and she believed that wasn't learning. Learning meant you could apply a concept to something you hadn't seen before. So if it were a test on English usage, the sentences on the test were different from the ones studied in class.

As often as she could, Mrs. Barnett put the sentences in context rather than in isolation. In literature, we were given a short story we'd never seen before and asked to identify elements such as character development, foreshadowing clues, examples of irony, or whatever concepts we had studied in other pieces of literature. According to her, she always hoped that if students realized they could apply what they learned to something new, the reward would be greater than memorizing something for the moment.

During the school year 1969 to 1970, The Jackson 5 were very popular. Their first hit single, "I Want You Back," was released in late 1969 and was number one on the charts as of January 1970. As did "Ain't It Funky Now," Pt. 1, Pt.2 by James Brown, and "Call Me" by Aretha Franklin. The English rock band, the Beatles, made a splash on the popular music scene in 1969 with "Come Together." It reached the top of the charts in the United States and peaked at number four in the United Kingdom. "Do the Funky Chicken" by Rufus Thomas became his biggest hit in early 1970.

Daunting News

As the 1969–1970 school year came to an end, it marked a huge change in the Inglewood Unified School District. Before the summer of 1970 began and soon after my junior high school graduation, my mother received an official letter from the Inglewood Unified School District Board of Education, stating: "Brown versus Board of Education declared it unconstitutional to segregate children in schools. The decision overturned Plessy versus Ferguson which declared state-sponsored segregation acceptable in 1896. Brown passed unanimously and was ruled a violation to the equal protection clause of the 14th Amendment." Inglewood Unified School District (IUSD) would have to be forced by court order to desegregate in 1970.

For me, the Inglewood School District letter was daunting news because it shattered my plans of attending Morningside High School! This meant that my class would be Inglewood High's first integrated graduating class of 1974 and the first integrated class to desegregate Inglewood High School in the 1970–1971 school year. I would soon become a product of the district's court-ordered desegregation in 1970 that delivered hundreds of black students to a campus that had been virtually all white for half a century.

This all began early in 1970 when I was in the eighth-grade at Monroe Junior High School. That year, parents of nineteen black students sued, accusing the district of fostering racial polarization. A federal judge agreed and ordered the immediate desegregation of city schools. Crosstown busing began in the fall of 1970 as my class of 1974 entered the ninth grade. During the fall of 1970, we would arrive at Inglewood High, and our divisions would unsettle—then remake—that campus.

My Eighth-Grade Graduation Ceremony

Moving from junior high school to high school was a big transition for me. I felt excited, anxious, unsure, and everything in between. For me, eighth-grade graduation marked the end of an era. My high school years at Morningside High now drew much nearer. I had looked forward to the excitement of attending Morningside High School since the fourth grade. As a Monroe Junior High eighth-grader, I ruled my old school; but in high school, I'd be little fish in a much bigger pool. However, my faith didn't allow me to worry because I knew I would adjust. And the older kids probably wouldn't bother me that much. Just remembering each year that I'd move up the ladder what happened the year before would hardly even matter. So I celebrated my achievement on that special day, and I remembered bigger milestones were still on the way.

My eighth-grade graduation from Monroe Junior High School was fifty years ago—June 18, 1970. Amazingly, it has been a half century since that day. This special occasion represented a milestone in my life. The ceremony was held on a sunny morning weekday in an outdoor auditorium theatre at Centinela Park in Inglewood, California. Disappointingly, my parents couldn't be there, so I was by myself. My mother had to stay at home and take care of my two-year-old brother, Marcus, and my grandmother, Needie.

Meanwhile, my father, who unfortunately had been incarcerated again, couldn't possibly attend. However, all of my eighth-grade classmates and friends were there. And to my surprise, Bruce and Tony Casey's stepfather, Reverend Glover, was the Master of Ceremony. I'll never forget his commencement speech, which was spiritually inspiring.

When young people graduate, they're often told to follow their dreams. Change the world. After all, the sky's the limit. But what if you don't know what you want to be when you grow up or lack the required social positioning to achieve it? There are always limits to following self-centered dreams. But I've postured myself as a "living sacrifice" seeking God's dreams and God's will; the possibilities really are endless.

David Brooks, a columnist for the New York Times, several years ago described how graduating students are often told to discover their passion, then pursue their dreams. Yet, Brooks says, "Most successful young people don't look inside and then plan a life. They look outside and find a problem, which summons their life." It's true! As I have applied my God-given spiritual gifts to the needs of the world, I've begun to discover my vocation. It's also true that an outward-focused posture of humble servant leadership is more commendable than a life of egotistic achievement.

I believe serving God and others rather than seeking money and social status has shaped the pattern of my achievement. For this has required humility, a scarce commodity in a culture of self-importance. Being humble, the Holy Spirit has directed my own desires toward God's purposes. The Apostle Paul describes an orientation toward God's will.

> Do not be conformed to this world, but be transformed by the renewing of your minds, so that you may discern what is the will of God—what is good and acceptable and perfect. (Romans 12:2)

Indeed, God promises to be our guide and has supplied us with abundance for knowing his will. I can now pray for wisdom and strength, study Scripture, seek counsel from mentors, and take note of others' experiences.

Being filled with the Holy Spirit, Reverend Glover's commencement speech was like Jesus was the commencement speaker that day. And the life advice he gave our graduating class went something like this: Love the Lord your God with all your heart, with all your soul, and with all your mind. And love your neighbor as yourself. Jesus teaches me each day to live with an outward-focused spirit. A humble posture of service to God and each other runs counter to individualistic egotism and American exceptionalism. Living into my calling is a journey that bends toward bringing God's reign on earth as it is in heaven.

When the graduation ceremony ended, I received my Monroe Junior High School Diploma of Graduation from the eighth grade and admission to high school. Then my classmates, Mark Jordan, Dwight "Sonny" Curry, and myself left Centinela Park and walked home together. It was a joyful and exciting spirit-filled day. While we were walking home, we talked about the graduation ceremony. Back then, junior high school graduation was a big thing; that is, it was a big June thing. We also talked about the eighth-grade graduation dance. The dances and graduation parties were huge. Finally, we discussed our plans for the summer of 1970 and high school for the 1970–71 school year. After arriving in the neighborhood, we went our separate ways to our respective homes.

A Joyriding Thrill on Graduation Night

After our eighth-grade graduation dance in Monroe Junior High's auditorium, the yellow school bus arrived at 10:00 p.m. in front of the school to pick up the graduates and take us back to our homes on the other side of town. By then, I was still over the moon and cooler than ice. I had become very popular in junior high school with both the boys and girls and some of the teachers as well. So just prior to the school bus arriving, a Morningside High School student named Billy Harris, who was in the tenth grade, came driving up at the front of the school in a brown 1964 VW bug. Billy offered a fellow graduate, Michael Watkins, and me a lift home. Thinking of myself as being a cool dude, I chose not to ride on the authorized yellow school bus with my fellow graduates for transportation back home, but I hopped in the front seat of Billy's unauthorized VW bug instead; and with Michael in the backseat, Billy sped away.

Joyriding is a term used by people to refer to thieving incidents where thieves steal a vehicle, most commonly a car, and drive it with no particular goal other than the pleasure or thrill of doing so, which is exactly what happened on my graduation night. Billy, whom we didn't know was a thief, had been driving a stolen car. Meanwhile, Michael and I innocently rode with him as passengers for the thrill of it. As Billy was driving dangerously at a high rate of speed, north-bound on Crenshaw Boulevard, approaching Manchester Boulevard, an Inglewood Police patrol car with red lights flashing and siren sounding off pursued us. It wasn't until the police began chasing us that Billy admitted he was driving a stolen a car. Realizing at that moment what was unfolding before us, the thrill of joyriding quickly turned to a surge of anxiety.

With the police in hot pursuit, Billy panicked. Attempting to evade the pursuing patrol car, Billy turned left on Manchester Boulevard and made a sharp right turn into an alley next to the Academy Theatre. Then Billy stopped the car, and while it was slowly rolling, he bailed out. Abandoning the stolen car with us in it, Billy fled the scene on foot with a police officer in close pursuit. Billy being a fat kid was too slow, and he quickly was overtaken, captured, and apprehended by the speed and power of the pursuing policeman.

All three of us were arrested at the scene and taken into custody to the Inglewood Police Department where multiple charges were filed against Billy for felony grand theft auto, misdemeanor joyrid-ing, and felony evading a police officer and/or arrest. While I was sitting in a jail cell, waiting for my parents to pick me up from the police station, I was very sorry that I had used bad judgment against God; that is, making the wrong decision to ride with Billy in a stolen car in relation to not making the right decision to ride on the autho-rized school bus with my fellow graduates. So I prayed the "Act of Contrition" and "Hail, Mary" asking the Lord for his mercy. Soon after praying, I felt the comforting power of the Holy Spirit who brought calm over me.

Initially, both Michael and myself were booked and charged with misdemeanor joyriding; however, without court action and subsequently found innocent, the charge against us was immediately dismissed by the Inglewood Police Department. And by power of the Holy Spirit, we were exonerated from the allegation of misdemeanor joyriding and having a criminal record.

25

SUMMER OF 1970

In 1970, I began ninth grade at Inglewood High Summer School. Being part of the first black minority class of 1974, integration of all white majority Inglewood High had been thrust on me. I would have gone to Morningside High had it not been for the federal court order to desegregate Inglewood High. Changing demographics had also brought unrest to Inglewood schools. A busing program to alter the racial mix went into effect in 1970. With other minority students in my class, I suddenly became part of Inglewood High School's long and sometimes turbulent history. For me, the transition to Inglewood High was a sudden rude awakening, but I came through my first two years as a freshman and sophomore, 1970–1972, safe and sound, without suffering any injury, damage, or harm. Meanwhile, for the others, the transition was abrupt and rocky, resulting in racial turmoil, which fueled prejudices, fears, and resentment lasting approximately three decades.

After four weeks of attending the summer school program at Inglewood High, it came to an end, and that was the first summer I didn't play organized baseball. However, I still enjoyed my passion for swimming at the local beaches and swimming pools. But most of all, I spent the remainder of that summer with my girlfriend, Tamara Edmonds. Tamara and I had met at Monroe Junior High during the first semester of 1969. When we became boyfriend and girlfriend, she was twelve years old in the seventh grade, and I was fourteen years old in the eighth grade. Back then, she was my first and only girlfriend.

As a very young couple, we had a crazy, loving, and wonderful friendship/relationship. Like those couples who are mad about each other, we thought we were madly in love with one another. And together, we did just about everything under the sun. During our seemingly long-term relationship, I never thought of our love as only "puppy love" until one late evening in 1970 when Tamara's mother, Irene, caught us slumbering in Tamara's bedroom. Remember, we were baby boomers who were part of the counterculture of the 1960s and 1970s that demanded peace while indulging in the act of "free love."

Apparently surprised, Tamara's mother urged me to leave their home immediately before her stepfather, Willie, awoke from his sleep. Willie was a large black man who owned an auto mechanic business. So she said, "Do you not understand what Willie would do if he sees you here?"

I thought, *Only God knew.*

Before leaving, Irene, who was whispering in a low voice, chastised us both, saying, "You two shouldn't be doing this thing, it's only puppy love!" But I didn't believe her. I only believed our love was real.

Afterward, feeling scared and ashamed, I hightailed it out, and we never rendezvoused there again. While walking back to my home later that night, and being thankful to God, I prayed the "Hail, Mary" for forgiveness. After nearly fifty years, Tamara and I are blessed friends to this day.

Inglewood High School Daze: 1970–1972

When we arrived on the bus at Inglewood High School, home of the Sentinels, in the fall of 1970, I didn't see much or sometimes any of my classmates from Daniel Freeman Elementary or Monroe Junior High School. My ninth-grade class had approximately seventeen black students, which was disproportionately less in comparison with the number of white and Jewish students while the tenth, eleventh and twelfth grades were predominantly all white and Jewish. However, I remained that same God-fearing kid with a winning smile who only wanted to do good for myself and make my mother proud. For high school, my plan was to become valedictorian by having the highest academic achievements of my 1974 graduating class and deliver the valedictory at our graduation ceremony. My other plan was to earn varsity letters from the sports I loved in swimming, baseball, and football and scholarships to major universities such as Loyola Marymount University, UCLA and USC. I also wanted to become either an architect, CPA, dentist, commercial airline pilot, or get drafted by Major League Baseball and play shortstop for the

San Francisco Giants. And finally, graduating from high school—as my mom used to say, "with flying colors"—was a very important goal that I wanted to accomplish.

Unlike some of my black classmates who complained about the "rude reception" from the beginning and those who followed in subsequent years, most of the white students and teachers respectively welcomed me with open arms. Including the Dean of Boys, Mr. "Bob" Hoffman, who encouraged me to keep up the good academic work, and Coach Peters, track and football head coach, asked me to try out for freshman football and cross-country track because of my speed and athleticism. They both were wooing me. So there were no problems from day one after I got off the bus.

I shared this phenomenon with my mother who said, "Davion, they see you in a good light as a young person who happens to be pleasant, talented, and good-looking and whose neither hostile nor intimidating. And they're really curious to know who you are."

After all of the confusion with integration and my issues with the races, both black and white, it really was comforting to hear my mom say that to me, and I was filled with joy.

From then on, and in a daze, I tried very hard to fit in with virtually everybody. However, my efforts were fruitless, but as popular as I was, and never antisocial, I began separating myself from the other kids along religious lines during my freshman year in high school, going on about my business as an individual but always honoring my mother and fearing the Lord. Spiritually, I've understood that "I'm in this world but not of this world." I had become a unique kid and a leader; and for many years to come, even to this day, most of my acquaintances have either referred to me as a mystery, legend, or OG, understandably.

After finishing my sophomore year at Inglewood High School in June of 1972, my father had just been paroled again from a California state prison. By that time, I had enough of both the chaos at Inglewood High and the diabolic cunningness of my stepfather. When my father was released from prison, he moved in with my Aunt Beverly at Windsor Hills, which is an unincorporated residential community in Los Angeles County. Afterward, and by my father's noncustodial right, I left Inglewood High and began spending more time with him, and he enrolled me at the virtu-ally all-black Crenshaw High for my junior year. By transferring to the "sanitized" campus of Crenshaw High, I avoided "the long and messy process of integration" at Inglewood High; nevertheless, I'm glad that I had experienced the beginning of Inglewood's radical transformative history.

Dealing with the Youth Street Gang Problem: 1971–1972

In addition to dealing with the desegregation problem in the Inglewood schools, another problem had suddenly erupted onto the streets of Inglewood. A new peril had made their way to Inglewood from South Central, Los Angeles. They were a cowardly violent youth street gang of young black hoodlums and thugs who noto-riously became known as the "Westside Crips." When I was fifteen years old, the Westside Crips began bullying only the black com-munities of Inglewood in 1971. Shortly after the beginning of their lunacy, black on black crime in Inglewood rose.

Before their notoriety, I had become aware of them from an acquaintance named Philip "The Lizard" McCain who was a Westside Crip gang member. Philip invited me to join their gang, so out of curiosity, I contemplated on it until I met up with them. It happened on a warm Southern California summer night in August 1971 at the Inglewood Forum where James Brown, the King of Soul, was performing his hit songs "Hot Pants," "Sho Is Funky Down Here," "Escapism," and many more soulful songs. Early that night, Philip and I had walked westward on Manchester Boulevard down to the Inglewood Forum at South Prairie Avenue with the intention of me meeting the ringleader and joining the gang.

When we arrived, there in the Forum parking lot and along the circular outside corridor of the Forum were approximately fifty to seventy-five rowdy street punks (low-class hooligans) synergized together, and their ringleader was committing a variety of felonious and misdemeanor crimes.

I also witnessed a lot of them who didn't have concert tickets nor money stampeding through the side doors of the Forum and pouring inside while others attempted to rush the main entrance door of the Forum. But suddenly, they were beaten back by the swift reactions of the Forum security guards who were wielding batons at them. One of the ruffians, a large six-foot four-inch, 240-pound, twenty-year-old whom the Crips called "Big Bob" and "Knock 'em out Bob" had been severely beaten about his forehead, and blood was gushing out from the front of his head down to his face, which soaked the front of his shirt. I'm almost certain he sustained a concussion with a bad gash just above his eyebrow.

After his beating, several gang associates began hurling profanities and threats at the security guards, but they slammed the doors closed. I knew the injured gang member was in need of medical attention and probably stiches to close the long deep cut on his head. Within moments after that violent incident, I noticed the ringleader who quickly came to the aid of his underling. By using a Crip-colored blue handkerchief, he applied pressure to the wounded warrior's head, hoping that he could to stop the bleeding.

The ringleader wore a dark-colored afro hairstyle and had a medium to dark-brown complexion. He was muscular and approximately five-foot-eleven in height with a stocky build. His face was somewhat scarred. He donned a waist-length black leather jacket with a black nylon wifebeater t-shirt underneath it, a pair of tanned khaki pants, a wide brimmed black Stetson hat with one gold-looped earring in his pierced left earlobe. With his attire, he also wore a shiny pair of boot-length black biscuits, and he walked with a confident strut and swagger, like a peacock strutting through the grounds. Occasionally throughout the night, the ringleader would take off his black waistline leather jacket and flex his large biceps, chest, and upper back muscles as if he were exhibiting his physique at a bodybuilding competition where there were no competitors. He prided himself with infamy that preceded him and intimidation that defined him.

Up to this time in my life, I had become the "Fool on the Hill," a song written by Paul McCartney of the Beatles. It's about a man who is considered a fool by others but whose foolish demeanor is actually an indication of wisdom. Furthermore, I had thought of myself as being "Crazy like a fox," which is appearing foolish or strange but actually very clever. I was young but smart. However, remaining prayerful, and never wavering in my faith, I had become less religious and more worldly. But unlike the Prodigal Son, a character in a parable Jesus told who left home for a far country, I had not squandered my family heritage nor compromised with riotous living the good values my mother instilled in me.

After a short night of spectating curiosity, I came up against the ringleader of the Westside Crips. His name was Stanley "Tookie" Williams. He was a rough-looking seventeen-year-old street tuff and bully who had come to South Central, Los Angeles, from the bayous of New Orleans, Louisiana. Tookie had intervened on my behalf after a dozen or more of his gang, clearly outnumbering me, turned and attempted to beat the living daylights out of me. At that moment, Tookie pulled me out of the fray with his muscular arms, and by the grace of God, he protected me from a deadly encounter. He demanded respect from his gang of bullies, and he had complete control and authority over them. Thank God I wasn't seriously hurt. Nonetheless, I faked pain and suffering anyway to win their sympathy.

Afterward, Tookie released me from his clutches, and he gave me safe passage from his rowdies while they looked on in amazement. But different from Custer's last stand of courage, for me, a quick run was better. So with tremendous speed, I hightailed out of the Forum's parking lot, running across Manchester Boulevard, and with a single bound, I leaped over the Inglewood Cemetery wall. Slightly rattled, but cool, calm, and collected, I ran through the dark cemetery park to the other end on Florence Avenue. And without stopping or resting, I ran all the way home. Oh, what a night it was for me! Thus, moving forward, I had a lot of thinking and planning to do.

Convinced that I had a resolve with Tookie and the Westside Crips, it came one day by chance. When I met this large muscular dude whom they called, "Tank," he was eighteen years old, and his larger more muscular brother, Huey, who was twenty-one years old. We became acquainted in late 1971 at a mutual friend's home whose name was Eric Cotton. He lived on West 76th Street between 5th

Avenue and 3rd Avenue in Inglewood. Both brothers were former gang members of an old 1960s street gang from Dorsey High School in Los Angeles known as the Chain Gang. The Chain Gang had been around before the formation of the Crips along with a Los Angeles street gang called The Brims.

When I found the solution to deal with Tookie and the Crips gang problem in Inglewood, I unwittingly adopted the Chain Gang to stand up against them. So near the end of the summer in 1971, the new Chain Gang originated in the northeast section of Inglewood, California, under the tutelage of Tank and his brother, Huey. The neighborhood of the Chain Gang stretched from Crenshaw Boulevard to Van Ness Avenue, around 76th Street to 94th Street. Soon after the Chain Gang was set into motion, it immediately began feuding with the formidable Tookie and his Westside Crips. The Chain Gang occupied this area of Inglewood for a short time (1971–1972) and was one of the first rivals of the Westside Crips.

I walked away less than one year after my initial involvement with the Inglewood Chain Gang and rivalries with the Westside Crips. I had quite enough of the foolishness that ended in two separate tragedies of two teenage boys. They both were brutally murdered by the Crips. And I grieved for them because of their youth and their innocence. Robert Brooks Ballou was sixteen, and Douglas Green was fifteen years old.

The first tragedy occurred on April 20, 1972. As reported by the local news stations and newspapers, "the night the Crips became infamous." His name was Robert Brooks Ballou Jr., sixteen, Los Angeles High School student, football player, and son of a lawyer had just left the Hollywood Palladium after a concert. When he ran to the aid of his friend who was being beaten and robbed by the Westside Crips for his long black leather coat, called a Maxi coat; but another faction of the Crips called the Compton Crips intervened, and the kid, Ballou, ran into them instead (at that time, there were three Crip Gangs: The original Crips of Raymond Washington who were by then known as the Eastside Crips, the Westside Crips who included Stanley "Tookie" Williams, and the Compton Crips, headed by Mack Thomas).

The beating, stomping, and kicking of Robert Ballou began. Witness accounts of the violent incident, who were just feet away, state that it was a shocking scene. According to one eyewitness: "Robert Ballou didn't have on a leather jacket. He had on a beige suit. But anyway, he runs right past his friend right into a bunch of the Compton Crips. They started in on him. He went down. They got in some kicks on him. I was watching, and I'm thinking, *Whoa. They knocked him out.*" But Robert Ballou Jr. was not knocked out. He was dead.

According to an article published on December 23, 2015, Krikorian writes: "The Hollywood Leather Jacket Murder, Part 2."

Bob Souza was the first LAPD detective on the scene. It was his first homicide: "I got there around midnight," Souza recalled a few years back. "The body was out there in full public view. He was stomped and beaten and when I got there, he was kind of half on his side and half on his back, kind of curled up. I don't remember a lot of blood, but I remember it was a horrendous crime scene. It was a mess because of the crowd. There were just throngs of people and I knew I needed to protect the crime scene," said Souza, who consults on police-related television shows and wrote the Harrison Ford movie *Hollywood Homicide*. "It's a distant memory, but I remember it. How could I not?"

Souza gave the officers on the scene "field interview" cards to get potential witnesses but had little success. "I remember nobody was volunteering much information even though there were hundreds of people out there and some of them had to had seen what happened. As it turned out, the whole point was the leather jacket," Souza said. "That was the whole thing that started this."

After the Ballou tragedy at the Hollywood Palladium on April 20, 1972, the second tragedy occurred exactly one month later on a cool Saturday night on May 20, 1972. Most of the partygoers were kids from Inglewood. We were finger-popping and dancing to hit Rhythm and Blues songs at a house party in "South Los Angeles" on West 81st Street and South Gramercy Place, which is to the east of Van Ness Avenue (former Westside Crips territory) that borders Inglewood to the west (former Chain Gang territory). The party was given by Markie Washington who was the boyfriend of my childhood friend, Fay Jackson. If I recall correctly, this party was given by Markie to celebrate Fay's fifteenth birthday.

After hearing about our party from a canary, the Westside Crips, absent of Tookie but with his approval, wanted to teach us a lesson. So they swiftly emerged on the scene later that night. As we partied, they surrounded the house. Three of them suddenly kicked in the front door and rushed inside with their other homeboys. The house exploded, and the Westside Crips rumbled with the Inglewood Chain Gang inside of the house and outside of the house, from the front yard to the backyard. Both rival gangs ran into the swinging fists and hand-to-hand fights amongst each another. The happy birthday party had quickly turned into a violent scuffle, and several people from both sides were injured.

One of the Crip gang members who they called Pookie was a tall, thin, dark-skinned, barefoot (he wore no shoes nor socks) big mouth who had a disheveled dark afro and donned a blue stingy brim hat over it; he repeatedly ranted and raved like a lunatic the words, "Westside Crips, Cuz!" While we stood in the living room face-to-face and toe to toe, he brandished a .32 caliber revolver, and then he pointed it at me. I froze with fear as I looked down the barrel of this big mouthed kid's gun. Then suddenly, by the amazing grace of God, a comforting feeling came over me, and with confident gentleness, I asked Pookie, "Is it necessary to point a loaded gun at me?" Meanwhile, I pretended my partner, Ronald Starling, who was standing next to me was also packing a gun. Then bluffing Pookie, I calmly said to my partner: "Hey, Ronald, hand me the roscoe;" meaning hand me the gun. But I knew neither of us had a gun, and Pookie was scared stiff of believing we had one too.

The bluff worked! And the barefoot kid nervously and quickly put the revolver back into his waistband, and he scurried outside to the front yard of the house where a large number of his hooligans had gathered, including the treacherous Philip "The Lizard" McCain.

Meanwhile, Markie urged me to protect myself from the Crips by ducking into his parents' bedroom where his father kept an unloaded 12-gauge shotgun. He said the Crips would soon return to attack me. After they had surrounded Markie's house, I had no escape, so I took his advice. Following Markie, we both hurried into his parents' bedroom where I found some degree of cover. Minutes afterward, at least three of the Crips brazenly came creeping in the hallway with murderous intent toward the bedroom where Markie and I were. So to protect us as best as he could, Markie picked up his father's unloaded shotgun. And faking as though it was loaded, Markie aimed his father's shotgun down the hallway in the direction of the approaching and hostile Crip gang members. He merely wanted to protect us and scare the hell out of them.

The bluff worked! When they perceived what they thought was going to happen to them after facing the barrel of the shotgun, the Crips reacted as though they had seen a ghost, and the trio suddenly stopped in their tracks, then they quickly turned around in the hallway and bailed out of the house.

However, the fighting hadn't ended yet. Throughout the entire skirmish, and moments after my encounter with the three thugs in the hallway leading to the bedroom, one gunshot rang out. A kid named Douglas Green, who had no gang affiliations and a classmate of mine since the fourth-grade, had unexpectedly and unwittingly walked to the party and right into the midst of the Westside Crips who had completely surrounded the house. According to the horror of one eyewitness who had attended the party, she said as soon as Douglas stepped up on the front porch, he was confronted by the mob. And within moments, one of them pulled out a gun, pointed it at Douglas, and pulled the trigger. Meanwhile, I was still in the bedroom when I heard a loud pop followed by a bloodcurdling scream. Then I heard cries, "The Crips shot Douglas!"

After Douglas was shot, he screamed from apparent shock, then he stumbled forward from the front porch through the front door and collapsed a few feet away on the living room floor in front of the fireplace. Afterward, pandemonium broke out, and it seemed like everybody panicked and fled from the party, including the Crips. When I entered the living room, I saw Douglas lying on his back with eyes half open. Then I walked over to Douglas in shocking disbelief, and leaning over him, I called his name, but he didn't respond to me because he was already dead from a fatal gunshot wound to his neck. I immediately felt emotionally shattered by what had happened to him and I could hardly move.

According to the LAPD 77th Street Division homicide report, Douglas Green was killed by a .32 caliber revolver; it was the same handgun that Pookie had pointed at me several minutes prior to the shooting of Douglas.

When the dust settled, only a few of us remained at the house where earlier that Saturday night, it was a fun-filled party, full of laughter, dancing, finger-popping, and good R and B music that had spread through the living room and dining room permeated with marijuana and tobacco smoke. Then, just past midnight, two LAPD black and white squad cars with flashing red lights, one unmarked car with a homicide detective, and a meat wagon from the Los Angeles County Coroner's office rolled up. That night had suddenly turned from a lively house party to a violent conflict that resulted in a horrendous crime scene. The homicide detective and lead investigator who supervised the crime scene was an African American man and a lieutenant from the Los Angeles Police Department's 77th Street Division. Shortly after his arrival, the police detective took a witness report from me and others who remained at the house, and then they took Douglas away in the meat wagon to the Los Angeles County Morgue.

Later that night, after I had walked several blocks with my buddy, Ronald Starling, from the party, I arrived at my home distraught, cold, and exhausted. And seeing my mother, I told her what had happened. And the first words she uttered were, "Davion, you look white as a ghost!" Then looking at me with compassion in her sparkling green eyes, she gave me a warm hug and told me everything will work together for the good and not to worry. Right away, my mother's love, understanding, and consolation made me feel much better. And it was at that precious moment in her arms I knew in my heart everything was going to be okay.

Finally, after being awake until the wee hours of Sunday morning, I said my nightly prayers, then I crashed and fell fast asleep.

Following Douglas Green's death, three Westside Crip gang members were arrested shortly afterward by LAPD's 77ᵗʰ Street Division. They were Louis Angelo White, a.k.a. "Pookie," Michael Concepcion, and Lavell Frierson whom were all charged with his felony murder. After their arrests, they would spend the next thirty days of their lives in lockup while awaiting trial at Eastlake Juvenile Hall (formerly known as the Central Juvenile Hall); it's the first juvenile detention facility in Los Angeles County. Subsequently, the State of California subpoenaed me to appear in the Eastlake Juvenile Court at their trial as a witness for the plaintiff/state. When the matter ended, only defendant Lavell Frierson was convicted of Douglas's murder, and he was sentenced to the California Youth Authority where he became a ward of the state. The other two cases in the matter of codefendant's, Louis White, a.k.a. "Pookie," and Michael Concepcion were dismissed by the juvenile court judge, and they both were released forthwith from Eastlake Juvenile Hall's custody.

When I attended Douglas's funeral, I extended my condolences to his family. His funeral service and interment took place at the Inglewood Park Cemetery in Inglewood, California. Unlike most funerals, Douglas's funeral was very sad because he was only a fifteen-year-old kid who had died senselessly and prematurely. While I was at his funeral, I grieved his loss and wept quietly to myself. At the end of his funeral service, I prayed to God that I would not let Douglas's death be in vain; and henceforth, I would live the rest of my life worthy of the Lord's abundant blessing.

Unbeknownst to me, up to then, I had unwittingly established a reputation of being a cool bold dude and leader of the Inglewood Chain Gang. Philip "The Lizard" McCain who betrayed me at the Forum on that warm August summer night in 1971 referred to me as "Little Bold Day-vi-awn." And the Westside Crips, without cause, made me their number one target in Inglewood; but ironically, I had done nothing gang-worthy to get that kind of notoriety. And according to his book, *Blue Rage, Black Redemption*, even Tookie himself unjustifiably regarded me as a force to be reckoned with to the point that he mistakenly identifies Huey, the twenty-one-year-old cofounder of the original Chain Gang for me, and Tookie also misspells my name as Daven, instead of the correct spelling, Davion, on page 81 in the second paragraph of his book (refer to Tookie's book, *Blue Rage, Black Redemption* for his perspective on the Westside Crips versus the Inglewood Chain Gang rivalry).

Tookie wrote, "One evening at a dance held at the Saint Andrews Park gymnasium (Crip turf), the Chain Gang caught a few of us off guard. The guy who approached me was Daven (not me but Huey), a twentysomething loudmouth who wouldn't bust a grape with cleats on (I was sixteen, cool, calm, and collected) but surrounded by a mob of other grown men posing as his backup. Daven (not me, but Huey) was bold enough to thrust a finger in my chest and ask, 'Are you Tookie?'" Blah blah blah.

Then Tookie writes, "I lunged at Daven (not me but Huey), causing both of us to fall to the ground. The darkness in the gym enabled me to crawl out of the scuffle while Daven's (not me, but Huey's) homeboys continued to punch and kick him, thinking that it was me they were beating. Meanwhile, Bub, in the gymnasium kitchen, held other Chain Gang members at bay with a starter pistol, until they realized it was fake. But like me, he managed to escape a serious beatdown."

After the tragic, senseless, and premature deaths of both Robert Brooks Ballou and Douglas Green in 1972 (for me, a year that will live in infamy) by the hands of the Compton Crips and the Westside Crips respectively, I reached a turning point; it was time to dust myself off and start fresh. So in the beginning of the following summer, I renounced and denounced my affiliation with any and all gangs. Blessedly, I came through those perilous times unscathed. When I left it behind me, I never looked back nor went back (still, some folks to this day unfairly refer to me as "OG"). However, no sooner had I cut all ties with the Inglewood Chain Gang than the gang eradicated itself, and a few of its members blended into a new and more hostile gang, calling themselves the Inglewood Family.

26

McDonald's: 1971–1974

Beginning in the spring of 1971, I landed my first real job at McDonald's while I was a fifteen-year-old high school student. I had practically dreamed of making money and buying everything I needed and wanted, including perhaps saving for a car because I needed transportation in lieu of riding on the RTD city buses, and I wanted to low-ride my car for enjoyment while impressing my girlfriends at the same time. So this job would help me save lots of money to do these things.

It all began while I was attending Inglewood High School as a freshman in the ninth grade. A woman named Mary Chambers who had two young daughters, whom my mom provided daycare for, knew the owner of the McDonald's on La Brea Avenue, just south of Pico Boulevard in Los Angeles. My mom understood that I really wanted to work and earn some money while I attended high school. So Mary, who loved my mother for her kindness and generosity, got me my first job flipping hamburgers, mixing milkshakes, and cooking French fries at the fast-food restaurant. Man, I was elated and thankful for both of them.

McDonald's was a great first job. It helped me grow in so many ways. I worked at McDonald's part-time for the entire three years (1971–1974) because of my full-time studies in high school, and being under eighteen, legally, I was not allowed to work more than four hours at a time. I worked with a variety of people who attended the local area high schools such as LA High, Dorsey High, Hamilton

High and, of course, Crenshaw High. Other McDonald employees attended various colleges, and some of the adult workers, eighteen and older, just worked full-time. The people that worked there were relatively decent and some willing to help.

Back then, and even now for most college students, holidays are a great time to sleep in, catch up with your family, and eat delicious homecooked meals. For me back then, holidays consisted of coming home and working my high school job, McDonald's. But I learned many things over the years when I worked at McDonald's. While I was in high school, one of the best things about being employed with this company was their willingness to work with my busy high school schedule. In the beginning, at fifteen years old, taking orders wasn't exactly the most comfortable thing in the world. From angry customers to sassy teenagers, I had learned how to deal with a variety of people. Although I was already an outgoing kid, working fast-food had taught me how to deal with people in both a friendly and professional environment.

With this job, I learned valuable time management skills. My availability for work was a couple of evenings during the week and anytime on weekends. So I had to force myself to wake up early in the morning on Saturday to get to work on time. Also, having a weekend job would cut into my study time, which meant although some of my few friends, especially girlfriends, were either hanging out at the shopping centers or parks on Saturdays, I had to learn to prioritize both my school and work schedule. On the upside, I almost never lacked in extra spending money to meet my buying needs!

It was amusing back then to think there were leadership opportunities at McDonald's, but there were a few. Although I was fifteen, I started thinking early about moving my way up the ladder. When I first got hired, I was considered a "Crew Member." However, over the course of my employment with McDonald's, I received good job performance evaluations. And based on my eligibility, I eventually was promoted to "Lead Crew Member," which wasn't bad pay for a struggling teen in high school.

I harken back to when some of my friends and foes alike made fun of me because I worked at McDonald's. But I didn't care as I was a teenager making extra money, paying into social security, building on my resume, and getting lots of work experience. Working at McDonald's in high school was one of the reasons why it was so easy for me to find my next good job at Thrifty Drug Store (now called Rite Aid) while I attended West Los Angeles College. So as a kid, it was part of the fun getting out there and earning extra cash! And dreaming perhaps one day, I could own my own McDonald's franchise!

Crenshaw High School Was a Welcome Reprieve: 1972 to 1974

After successfully completing my sophomore year at Inglewood High School in the spring of 1972, I had to attend summer school at Crenshaw High, home of the Mighty Cougars (located on 11th Avenue in the Crenshaw district of Los Angeles, California) where I planned and prepared myself for the upcoming school year: 1972–1973. After four weeks of accelerated study, the summer school program came to an end. Happy as could be, I had passed both Trigonometry and American Literature with good grades. Afterward, I looked forward to enjoying the rest of my summer and attending Crenshaw High in the fall. This was exciting to me as I would be attending a newly built high school which first opened in 1968. And Crenshaw High was absent the chaos I had left behind at Inglewood High because it consisted predominantly of African American students. Plus, the high school was known for its winning sports programs, ROTC program, and a whole host of other educational programs as well as its high enrollment of very cute/pretty girls. Hooray!

Being the "new student" in the fall of 1972 was a joyful and peaceful deliverance. It occurred during my junior year. While transferring from Inglewood High School, an educational environment hardly conducive to learning because of its racial tension, Crenshaw High School was a welcome reprieve. However, I had to adjust and transition myself from a familiar place to a new place with all new rules. Not only did I have to adjust to my new high school, but I also had to meet new people who were already firmly established in their friendships and lifestyles.

Finding my niche at Crenshaw High School where everyone else had already found theirs was challenging. It was virtually like starting a race when the rest of your competitors were halfway to the finish line. When you get right down to it, the beginning of my junior year of high school felt like I had to put forth a determined effort to get to the finish line. But being a gentle, sensitive, and somewhat shy kid, I got to the finish line lacking nothing. Surprisingly, my new classmates had begun treating me like a prince on a throne, both girls and boys alike.

They would continuously flatter me throughout my next two years at Crenshaw High to say the least. Most of the flattery came from the girls. Some girls gawked at me while others flirted with me, some girls would even groom themselves in front of me, and others swarmed me like ticks on a hound. This kind of behavior from the girls happened to me in and out of the classrooms and everywhere on campus, including off-campus before and after school. I have to admit, the attention the girls gave me was delightful, and I generally would react to most of them with a warm smile, charming compliment, or an occasional wink of the eye. I harken back to when this very pretty girl, whose name I don't remember, who walked over to me in the quad during lunchtime, and acting as though she was the messenger and representative for all of the girls at Crenshaw High, she had the good courage to say to me, "A lot of girls at this school really like you." This is just a few examples of many on how favorable I was regarded by most of the girls who attended Crenshaw High School.

But the transition to an urban campus in the Los Angeles Unified School District was an eye-opener. I had attended a very large public high school with about 350 students in my junior class, and I realized on the very first day that things were not going to click for me the way they always had in the past. Many of these students had grown up together. We were all much older, in our mid-teens, and more wary of new people, so attempting to fit myself into my new classmates' lives and friendships was no simple feat. I had a good few poignant revelations of loneliness to some of my close friends in

Inglewood and more than a few prayers with my Lord about my then current situations and future endeavors.

With time, however, things got better; I stopped feeling like an outsider, and I found people whose company I truly enjoyed. But my junior year was mixed with both ambivalent feelings of needing to fit in and humdrum school days. Although I lived in my own fantasy world, I had found my niche, which was to be the coolest and the most cultured African American kid at Crenshaw High; but with that, I had abandoned all my goals of graduating with flying colors, becoming class valedictorian, and earning varsity letters in baseball, football, and swimming. Instead, I had emerged on this all black campus as the "cock of the walk." Even though there was a stark difference in my skin color, physical features, and characteristics compared to most of my classmates.

To begin my school day, almost every morning before I left from home, I would pump myself up by listening and dancing to the music of James Brown, the King of Soul. For the first time in my life as a student attending an all-black school, I became aware of the need to understand as much as I could about my African American culture. This included memorizing the lyrics to all hit R and B songs, striving to be the best dancer with the latest dance moves, wearing the most current African American fashions in shoes, clothing, and head gear from wide-brimmed Stetson hats to Ace Deuce stingy brims. While at school, between class periods, nutrition, and lunch breaks, I would strut (bowlegged and slue-footed) like the "cock of the walk" all over the campus with a swag that no other student could imitate. At times during my junior year, I really thought I was on top of the world at seventeen.

While I continued to live a more secular life as an older teen, my high school academic and athletic goals soon became a past dream instead of a present reality. And my two years of attendance at Crenshaw High School was fleeting. To cure the occasional restlessness I experienced at Crenshaw, it was during the second semester when I elected to take an army JROTC class. I also took a music class elective where I learned how to play the flute, hoping that I would become a member of the "Crenshaw Cougars Marching Band" in my senior year. I also understood by learning to play the flute, it was a great opportunity for me to continue the family legacy of jazz musicians handed down from one generation to the next, and as a fourth-generation Woodman, I could follow in my musical family's footsteps. After I signed up for the music class, my father bought me a used nickel-plated flute at a pawnshop in Los Angeles, and I was ready to blow. So inspired by my father and the Woodman musical legacy, I practiced playing the flute until the end of my senior year. It was then I realized I had musical potential.

Also at the beginning of the second semester of my junior year in 1973, I was bused to LAUSD's public high school, Alexander Hamilton High School. The high school is located in the Castle Heights neighborhood within the westside of Los Angeles, California, where I took the army JROTC elective class along with a state-required US History class. This was a fun and exciting adventure for me as I looked forward to departing from Crenshaw High a few hours each day and arriving at the predominantly Jewish High School.

On the way to Hamilton High, the bus driver would also stop at Dorsey High School to pick up students and take them to Hamilton High as well. The students and teachers were both friendly and welcoming toward me. And many girls of various ethnicities who attended Hamilton High were very cute. I enjoyed watching and interacting with them. They were the highlight of my day.

So the monotony of being at Crenshaw High all day quickly evaporated from me. By the end of my junior year in 1973, I had been promoted to the military rank of corporal. Hooray! Although across the street at Daniel Freeman Elementary School, Ms. Herbst, the school's principal, saw me from her office window wearing my army JROTC uniform one day. And she said to my mother when she later saw her, "Your son, Davion, looked very handsome in his army uniform. Is he not a four-star general?" Mrs. Herbst had only said this to my mother because I was an outstanding student when I attended her school. She paid me an enormous compliment, and I was grateful for it.

My high school junior prom basically completed my junior year at Crenshaw High. It happened on May 18, 1973, at the luxurious Los Angeles Biltmore Hotel (now named the Millennium Biltmore Hotel) located opposite Pershing Square in downtown Los Angeles, California. No limo, but I drove my 1967 Chevelle Malibu to the prom. I had a wonderful time; dancing was awesome, food was delicious, took nice prom pics, and my date, Karen Freeney, looked pretty. I will always remember this special occasion for the rest of my life.

After the first semester of my senior year (1973–1974) ended in late January 1974, I had fulfilled the California state requirements for my high school diploma; therefore, I had graduated one semester sooner than my class. By then, I was eighteen and eager to move on beyond Crenshaw High School. So at the beginning of the second semester in February 1974, I applied for admission, got accepted, and enrolled at West Los Angeles City College in Culver City, California. However, there were two more things that I wanted to do at Crenshaw High, and that was to go to either my senior prom or high school graduation ceremony, but not both. So I opted to attend my senior prom instead, and I skipped the graduation ceremony.

My senior prom was an event I had looked forward to for my entire four years of high school. Like it was with my junior prom, there was no limo to ride in for my senior prom, but my dad gave me permission to drive his beautiful black on black 1972 Pontiac Grand Prix, and driving it to my senior prom was much better than riding as a passenger in a limo. On May 17, 1974, my senior prom night happened aboard the elegant and classic legendary *Queen Mary* ship located in Long Beach Harbor, which was and still is the most unique and distinct prom venue in Southern California. I have to admit it, getting dressed up was fun, but it was painstaking when I had to tie the perfect bowtie. Now when I think about it, that moment when I looked in the mirror before I left and saw how all that hard work paid off, nothing felt better than knowing I was a solid twelve out of ten.

Crenshaw High School was full of cliques. Everyone was not friends with everyone, contrary to popular belief. But one or more of my friends, and a few people that I was friendly with, came to the prom. Also, my prom night allowed me the experience to bond with people I wasn't very close to before. I asked a beautiful girl named

Michelle to be my date and go with me. Wow! She gladly accepted my invitation and willingly took on this adventure with me. Like a fairy tale, Michelle was the princess who accompanied me, the prince, to the ball.

Certainly, there were still some sports games and, of course, graduation, but senior prom was the last chance my class had to all be together in a totally fun setting. Although I didn't know the majority of the people in my graduating class, there was still some sentimental value there. After that night, I never saw those people again. But seriously, looking back on my life, I'm glad I had gone. Along the same lines as the previous reason, this was the last dance of my high school career.

My prom, unlike homecoming or other things, was much more than just dancing. There was good food and beverages, and there were fun things to do like posing with my date for photographs and touring the *Queen Mary*; her history was very interesting. We enjoyed walking around, looking at pictures of people, including famous passengers and former crew members over the past thirty-eight years. The *Queen Mary* was the biggest luxury liner ever built at that time, and it was just fun to walk through and see it all. Being a hotel, you could even lodge in it overnight and tour the alleged haunted sections of the ship.

Both Michelle's parents and my mom were good friends, and my dad loved seeing us go to the prom together. They all thought she was pretty and that I was handsome. This special occasion was as big of deal to them as it was to Michelle and myself. And the thought of me soon going away to college was also a big deal to my mother. She was going to miss me more than anything, and getting this last chance to see me get dressed up and go out made her very excited. So I didn't go to the prom only for me, but I did it for my mom too.

For Michelle, I believe my prom was like a fairy tale. She dressed up like a princess, and I showed up and whisked her away to as close to a ball as we would ever get. Prom queen is the dream of almost every little girl. For me, it was like a white-collar gala, walking around the *Queen Mary* ship, socializing, looking fresh and slick. Everyone knows guys look their best when they clean up and wear a suit. It seems simplistic, but prom is iconic. It's not high school without prom.

As recent as 7/20/2019, I chatted with my prom date, Michelle, on Facebook Messenger regarding our prom picture that I had sent her:

Me: Hey, Cuz, remember this picture of us at my Crenshaw High Senior Prom, 1974, aboard the *Queen Mary*?

Michelle: Always…it is one of my fondest memories…had a real nice evening…will remember it always.

Me: I was looking through my old photo album when to my surprise, I stumbled on this wonderful picture. You looked beautiful, and I was proud to be with you on that very special occasion.

Michelle: Thank you…ditto

Michelle: Brings back very nice memories…awww

Me: I loved being with you. The most beautiful and smartest girl accompanied me to my prom aboard the *Queen Mary*.

Michelle: You have always been my greatest supporter…even when I didn't know how to support myself…I always love you for that and always will…muah

Michelle: Your words and thoughts are always so special and uplift-
     ing...thank you for always loving me
Michelle: Love you back...muah

To sum up, I had a good time at my senior prom. There were
many reasons to go, a lot of things to do there. I gained a lot from
going. It wasn't just another dance; this was the last time to celebrate
with my class. So I got out there, danced, took pictures, and made
memories that have lasted me the rest of my life.

They Hurt My Brother, Vernon
     The shooting of my brother, Vernon, whom we affectionately
called Sputdoll, occurred in late March of 1973 when he was a fifteen-year-old freshman at Inglewood High (I was seventeen years
old in the second semester of my junior year at Crenshaw High).
Fortunately, he survived the .22 caliber bullet wound to his abdomen. Vernon's friend, whose name was Anthony Nolan, told me on
the same day of the shooting that they were walking together when
it occurred. He said he heard one gunshot ring out from a drive-by
which looked like a carload of Crip gang members. Unfortunately,
the shooter(s) were never identified, charged, or brought to justice by
the Inglewood Police Department.
     Anthony went on to say that the shooting happened after
school while they were walking northbound on 2nd Avenue toward
his house near West 83rd Street in Inglewood. After Vernon's discharge from Daniel Freeman Hospital in Inglewood, California, one
month later, he confirmed with me Anthony's version of the shooting, but he believed the shooter was actually Philip "The Lizard"
McCain. Ironically, more than four years later, after they hurt my
brother, Philip himself was shot and paralyzed by LAPD's 77th Street
Division Precinct after he attempted to shoot a police officer. He
allegedly used the same .22 caliber revolver in that shooting which
critically wounded Vernon in 1973.
     Was justice served for both Vernon and our family when Philip
was shot by the Los Angeles Police Department several years later?
Or, was the shooting of him which resulted in his paralysis retribu-

tion for all of his wrongs and criminal acts? Only God knows. By faith, however, I never sought vengeance against Philip for allegedly shooting my brother. I forgave him instead, and I asked the Lord for his mercy. I believe God answered my prayer on this matter, and throughout the entire ordeal, I felt peace, guidance, and comfort from the Holy Spirit.

Thrifty's Drug Store

In need of more money to help support myself financially, it was during the spring of 1974 while I attended West Los Angeles College that I was hired as a part-time stock clerk at Thrifty Drug Store (now Rite Aid Pharmacy). The new job location was at the shopping center on Crenshaw Boulevard and Imperial Highway in Inglewood, California. This was my second and best job at that time. Also, I had considered myself gainfully employed, earning $2.35 per hour. Thrifty's hourly wage exceeded MacDonald's $1.65 minimum hourly wage.

I had fun working at Thrifty's, even at its busiest times. Management started me in the ice-cream/liquor department and slowly moved me up to the photo counter. After those initial jobs, I became a stock clerk and learned how to do inventory, price merchandise, cashier, and helped in the pharmacy. A typical day at Thrifty's went by fast because I kept busy working all facets of the store. This was the first job where I learned how to multitask. I also enjoyed helping customers and I got to know some of them, especially the cute girls who enjoyed eating our delicious ice-cream on hot summer days. My employment with Thrifty Drug Store was a short duration as I only worked there for six months from February 1974 to August 1974 because in the following month, September 30, 1974, I enlisted in the United States Navy.

27

WEST LOS ANGELES COLLEGE

After graduating from Crenshaw High School at the end of January 1974, I enrolled at West Los Angeles College during February 1974 and began my first semester of college studies. It marked an important milestone in my higher educational career. What I had expected in terms of classes and student life in my first year of community college was twofold. First, I had expected to build on my academic accomplishments and technical skills to create a springboard for my future working endeavors; and secondly, I had expected to engage myself in an exciting element of community college which was the social interaction. With a plethora of clubs and organizations, I easily found friends who shared my interests. When I treated my social events in college like my work at Thrifty's Drug Store and my academic responsibilities in the classroom—meaning that I carefully planned my time based upon those commitments—it allowed me to thoroughly enjoy a well-rounded first semester college experience. As I had imagined, my first semester in college was both fun and engaging.

The Apple, Occasionally, Doesn't Fall Far from the Tree at Los Angeles County Men's Central Jail (Like Father, Like Son)

What is the likelihood of a son and his father unexpectedly meeting each other while they both are inmates at the same jail and at the same time?

Well, strangely enough, this event happened to both my father and myself back in July of 1974. At that time, my father was thirty-seven and I was eighteen years old. The drama began when I was told that two Inglewood Police detectives were looking for me with an arrest warrant at my home and at my place of employment. Then I immediately became concerned. The warrant was a written order issued by a judge, authorizing the policeman to arrest me for failing to appear in the Inglewood Municipal Court to answer for a minor traffic ticket. The reason for missing my scheduled court date was that I had plum forgotten about it. But as soon as I discovered the warrant out for my arrest, I told my mother what was happening, and it was within that same afternoon when I grudgingly and unwittingly hurried downtown and turned myself in at the Inglewood Police Station, County of Los Angeles. With both civility and diligence, I had attempted to resolve this matter beforehand to avoid being arrested and placed into police custody.

However, when I surrendered to the warrant at the Inglewood Police Station, two Inglewood peace officers took me into custody, and I was booked and fingerprinted. Soon afterward, I realized I should have probably first contacted a lawyer and sought free legal advice instead of turning myself in. At this point, I was allowed to make one ten-minute phone call from a black Pacific Bell rotary telephone which was mounted on the wall in the booking area. So I placed a dime in the coin slot of the telephone, and then I called my mother, telling her how much I loved her and not to worry about me because I was going to be okay. After the phone call ended, I was taken to a small cell block and placed into a jail cell where I was held until my court appearance the next morning.

When I stood before the judge the next morning in court, I pleaded no contest to the traffic violation, and consequently, he sentenced me to ten days in the Los Angeles County Jail; in addition to my jail sentence, I had to pay a failure-to-appear penalty and a fine in excess of $300. That was a large sum of money back then! Anyhow, I paid it on the spot, and then I prepared myself for the ten-day county jail sentence.

It was shortly after dark when the deputy sheriffs removed me along with other prisoners from the court's holding cells and lined us up. Then we were handcuffed, chained in groups of four, and marched to an awaiting Los Angeles County Sheriff's black-and-white bus. It had just pulled up in the parking lot behind the Inglewood Courthouse. The sheriff's bus was heading toward the County Central Jail in downtown Los Angeles. When I boarded the bus, there were more than a dozen sleepy prisoners accused of crimes ranging from petty theft and trespassing to child molestation and murder.

"Hey, put out that cigarette!" yelled the deputy as he pounded on the glass partition that separated him from us.

A startled woman inmate obliged, stomping it out on the floor.

"Sit down and shut your mouth!" snapped another deputy to a male prisoner who had stood up to exchange a few words with another prisoner as the bus was leaving the parking lot. Two deputies were assigned to the bus. One drove while the other one watched over us and handled the paperwork.

The policy for inmates who were considered especially dangerous, involved in controversial or newsworthy cases or deemed high escape risks were often handled separately and sometimes taken to the courthouse in smaller vans or sedans. Gang members were kept apart from members of other gangs. Women prisoners, who were transported to the Central Jail earlier from Sybil Brand Institute were handled separately from the men. Most male prisoners, regardless of the crime they had been charged with, had to sit together on the bus. Women had to sit together, segregated from the male prisoners. "Snitches," prisoners who had turned informers or witnesses for the state, also were seated separately. On the average, thousands of prisoners each weekday morning were transported from county jails, sheriff's substation, and Los Angeles police stations to dozens and dozens of courts located throughout Los Angeles County.

Within an hour of leaving the Inglewood courthouse, we arrived on the sheriff's black-and-white bus at the LA County Jail-Inmate Reception Center (IRC). This facility was for adult male inmates who were eighteen years and older. It was a medium-security detention center located at 450 Bauchet Street, Los Angeles, California. The LA County Jail-Inmate Reception Center was operated by the Los Angeles County Sheriff's Department, and the prison was operated by the California State Department of Corrections. This jail held inmates awaiting trial, sentencing, or who had been sentenced to less than a year. Prison was only available for people who had been sentenced to more than a year on any one charge.

Los Angeles County IRC's custody and security level took in new arrests and detainees who were delivered daily. Law enforcement and police booked offenders from Los Angeles County and nearby cities and towns. Some offenders may have stayed less than one day or only for a few days until they were released in a court proceeding, some after putting up a bond and then were released to a pretrial services caseload under supervision by the court or were released on their own recognizance with an agreement to appear in court. The jail was divided into "pods," each of which included individual cells, common areas, and an outside recreation court—a space bound by towering concrete walls. All of the meals were approved by a dietician. The common area tables were made of solid steel with attached four seats. Inmates would crowd around the tables playing cards or board games, like chess and checkers.

Inside the cells, there were only a sliver of a window allowing inmates to peer out. There were two to three inmates per cell. When I was an inmate in July of 1974, the jail had recently been built, and they called it the New County Jail. Back then, the jail was at less than 50 percent capacity, and this population varied from day-to-day, never overcrowding (in contrast to recent years, overcrowding is at about 90 percent capacity and sometimes higher on any given day). There were a number of people who arrived at the jail actively or recently drunk or high or arrived with injuries from fights/assaults that led to their arrest, and/or were mentally ill with no other place for law enforcement to deliver them. This made the intake process challenging for the jail's staff and its medical personnel.

When I was incarcerated at the Los Angeles County Jail during July of 1974, "Peter J. Pitchess had been the twenty-eighth sheriff of Los Angeles County, California, serving from 1958 to 1981. He was credited with modernizing the Los Angeles County Sheriff's Department, turning the department into the sixth-largest police department, and the largest sheriff's department, in the United States."

During my ordeal, I reaped one minor benefit. Because I had surrendered to the warrant, both Inglewood police and the court judge looked upon it favorably. It was apparent to them that I took responsibility for my actions rather than fleeing from the police. This meant the difference between being sentenced to ten days in the Los Angeles County Jail versus thirty days. So with leniency from the judge, I received the former sentence of only ten days in custody.

After being sentenced to county jail time, and having proved myself to be trustworthy, I became a jail trustee. A jail trustee is usually an inmate who, because they are not in jail for anything really serious and they are close to being released and don't want to mess it up, will behave and assist in the operation of the jail. I was given a little trust, hence the term *trustee*. As a trustee, I was allowed a little more freedom and privileges than the mainline inmates. For example, I got time out of my cell, I had access to more recreational activities, and had longer visits from visitors, etc. I also worked long hours, making and serving food to the inmates.

So it happened during my seventh day in custody at the Los Angeles County Jail, when I was allowed to go to the chow hall with the other trustees to see a musical group performance. While I was enjoying the entertainment, I saw a familiar face amongst the group who was playing the saxophone. Sure enough, he was my father! Like father, like son. We both were behind bars at the same jail! And he was also a trustee! When I was certain it was him, I signaled to a deputy and told him so.

Afterward, the surprised deputy summoned the jail's warden who also was surprised, and the warden arranged a brief meeting between my father and me. I could tell just by looking at my father, he was in a very awkward situation. Upon seeing me, he was as surprised as I was when I saw him and somewhat embarrassed too. Nevertheless, we gave each other warm hugs and made small talk. And then quickly, we departed from one another and returned to our separate cell blocks.

Having mixed feelings about my dad after that very touching scene with him in the jail's chow hall, I pondered many thoughts of him as I made way back to my jail cell. Some of my thoughts were these: *It is a small world after all. Wow! I don't believe this! Like father, like son?*

When I was released from jail a few days later, I returned home and gave my mother a warm hug. Then the first thing I said to her was, "Mom, guess who I saw while I was in the sheriff's custody."

And she answered me with a question, "Who did you see, Davion?"

Then I answered her with an exclamation. "I saw Billy!"

And Mom casually replied to me, saying, "I'm not surprised."

Overcoming My Dysfunctional Family

> Family dysfunction rolls down from generation to generation, like a fire in the woods, taking down everything in its path until one person in one generation has the courage to turn and face the flames. That person brings peace to their ancestors and spares the children that follow.
>
> —Terry Real

"I Had Nothing to Lose"

After finishing high school and one semester of college, it happened during the summer of 1974 when I came to a major crossroad in my life. As an eighteen-and-a-half-year-old young adult, I was terribly confused and began stressing out because I needed and wanted to go to college to fulfill my short-term goal of earning a college degree while making my mother proud of me. But by not having a job nor an academic or athletic scholarship, I didn't know how I was going to pay for a college education. Meanwhile, it seemed like I came to a standstill. It felt as though I had hit rock-bottom. So believing "I had nothing to lose" but "everything to gain," joining the military was a good idea and one way to help me pay for college and perhaps build my resume.

After carefully considering joining the US Air Force or the US Navy to become an "air traffic controller" serving in a squadron or onboard an aircraft carrier, I decided to join the US Navy. My choice for joining the navy was made in part because of Uncle Butch's influence as well as the Vietnam-era peacetime TV recruitment slogans such as "Join the Navy, See the World;" "Heritage;" "Be Cool and Join the Navy;" and "US Navy: See the World! Save Your Money! Serve Your Country!"

Additionally, my decision to join the US Navy in general was made because I understood they would pay for my college education and provide me with many benefits such as health care. So within one month after making my inquiries about the Armed Forces of the United States, it happened on Monday, September 30, 1974, when I enlisted in the US Navy.

From 1974 until 1977, I spent most of my naval service in Virginia Beach, Virginia, at the Little Creek Naval Amphibious Base located just thirteen miles from the Naval Operations Base in Norfolk, Virginia.

Active Duty Military Service in the United States Navy: September 30, 1974–September 29, 1977

Recruitment and Enlistment.

At the beginning of September 1974, a childhood friend and former neighbor from South Spaulding Avenue, Michael Williams, and myself decided to enlist in the US Navy together under the "Buddy Program" (we were also buddies in the Cub Scouts). Upon meeting the Navy recruiter on Regent Street in Downtown Inglewood, California, we found in the Navy, you could join with up to four of your friends (same gender). This was very appealing. Because in the Navy's "Buddy Program," friends could go through recruit training together and even get assigned to the same station after training. To get assigned to the same duty station, we had to sign up for the same job/category. The recruiter also mentioned getting assigned to the same station was not that important as we would make plenty of friends wherever we'd go. Deciding to join the Navy under this program was perfect for my friend and me.

Afterward, we began the Navy recruitment process. The recruiter was a Boatswain's Mate 2nd Class Petty Officer. I cannot recall his name, but I can recall that he was a chubby African American of short stature who spoke fast in Ebonics, or simply, "black speech." This navy man also appeared to be a boozer. He would assist Michael and me with the preparation of all the paperwork that was necessary for us to join the US Navy.

Once we gave the go ahead to him that we wished to enlist, he had us take an Armed Forces Entrance Exam practice test in his office. Based on our passing scores, he set it up for us to take the real test. So the next morning, we were back in his office testing. When we finished, the outcomes of the test scores were very high because Michael and I both passed with flying colors. According to the recruiter, our scores exceeded fifty which was significantly higher than the Navy's minimum passing score of thirty-five. This delighted us, and we were eager to move to the next step in the Navy recruitment process.

After I scored well on the test (now called ASVAB) and cleared the initial background check, the navy recruiter safely assumed that I was also healthy and motivated to proceed forward in the recruitment process. I had kept my nose clean for the last eighteen years, and life was pretty good. However, when we had reached this point, my childhood buddy, Michael, dropped a bomb. He bailed on me after all we had been through together since childhood. His sudden change of heart was both unexpected and disappointing. I asked Michael, "Why are you doing this?"

He said because he failed the background check and it made him ineligible for enlistment. Then I encouraged him to stay the course and straighten it out because the Navy would probably waive it! But with feelings of frustration and discouragement, Michael said to me, "Nah, that's okay, I'm going to continue with school instead."

Then I thought to myself, *Oh well, that's life.* So even after being abandoned by Michael and alone, I was undaunted by it; but having had a strong desire and enthusiasm for enlisting in the Navy, I continued the venture without him.

28

ARMED FORCES ENTRANCE EXAMINATION STATION (AFEES)

For my efforts of passing the test and background check, I was given a date to go to the nearest AFEES site on Wilshire Boulevard at Crenshaw Boulevard in Los Angeles, California, where I would be poked and prodded and asked a lot of questions and sign a lot of paperwork and do a lot of waiting. At this point in the process, I distinctly remember my recruiter saying to me, "You're in the game now, baby." Then he briefed me and expected me to bring to the AFEES appointment my social security card, birth certificate, driver's license, etc., and he also told me to get a good night's sleep.

The next morning, I left the Inglewood recruiter's office on Regent Street with my recruiter, and he drove me in a white four door sedan to the AFEES station where I had to spend the entire day processing in preparation for entrance into the Armed Forces of the United States. I soon found out that everything I wanted to do in the US Navy started right there. The AFEES determined on that day I had met the physical, mental, and moral standards established by the US Navy and decided that me and the navy were compatible, and therefore, we both made a good fit.

My day inside of the single-story AFEES on Wilshire Boulevard began at 8:00 a.m., and the first words I heard uttered from the midst of the large group of potential recruits for the various branches of the US armed forces were, "Hurry up and wait (Believed to have originated in the American military, "hurry up and wait" is a humorous phrase used to refer to the situation in which one is forced to hurry in order to complete a certain task or arrive at a certain destination by a specified time, only for nothing to happen at that time often because other required tasks are still awaiting completion)!"

They were baby boomers of whom half were Caucasian males, and the other half were made up of various ethnic groups including African American, Latin American, and Asian American. The majority of us back then wore long hairstyles which was typical of that era. The Caucasians, Mexicans, and Asians wore long various hairstyles while most of the African Americans, including myself, wore long bushy Afros. For me, this later would prove to be an interesting scenario at the Navy Recruit Training Command's barbershop.

After arriving inside the building, I sat in a chair. We had to fill in the seats sequentially, starting with row 1, seat 1. They sectioned us off by military branch—myself with the Navy—to get an index fingerprint via touch inkpad (now, touch pad scanners are used) and name/ID sticker, which I wore the entire time I was at the AFEES. Next, I recall picking up a colored folder with all the paperwork I needed for my physical. Afterward, I sat in a waiting room and then got briefed about the busy day ahead of me. There was also an indoctrination slideshow and film we had to watch. Then I began my physical in a separate unit inside of the AFEES.

It was about 8:45 a.m. when they began the full physical examination process. First thing was blood and heart rate; mine were normal. Next room, they looked over my paperwork, asking me to verify the information was correct. "Check it," they said, and I verified everything was correct. Then they sent me to vision testing. Vision testing was different for each branch of service. But I did the Navy's near/far vision testing and passed it with 20/20 vision. They didn't test me for color-blindness, but the last vision test I took was the depth perception test, and upon their advice, I took my time and passed it without difficulty.

Being that it was an all-day process, we were given a one-hour break at noon, and the government handed out free ham and cheese sandwiches, chips, and cold beverages for lunch. After finishing my lunch break, I continued with the physical examination process, which included a hearing test, urine and blood test, and briefing. Then I stripped down to just my underwear and got height and weight measured to see if I was within Navy standards. Next, I did range of motion testing; these included range of motion exercises and the dreaded duck walk. My test results were favorable. I had passed all of them within their respective normal ranges. Lastly, I had a physical with a doctor. He asked me questions about my medical history, marijuana, and alcohol usage. I answered him truthfully and honestly; yes, I had experimented with marijuana and drank alcohol in high school, but very little. But overall, I was in excellent health.

Then it was done. I had successfully completed the Navy's recruitment and enlistment process. On Monday morning, September 30, 1974, after a warm hug and emotional goodbye, my mother dropped me off at the Inglewood recruiter's office. Afterward, the recruiter and I returned to the AFEES for the last time where I took my "Oath of Enlistment." It would be the first of many, many successes I'd experience in the United States Navy. There, I signed off on my enlistment contract and was ready for the next step in my new life: boot camp!

Boot Camp

After I had taken my oath of enlistment at the AFEES, it was within a few hours later just before sunset when me and dozens of other enlisted Navy/Marine recruits boarded military buses and were transported to the Naval Training Center/Recruit Training Command for basic training or more commonly known as boot camp at San Diego, California. This was my first official military assignment as a Seaman Recruit in the US Navy. The trip from AFEES in Los Angeles to the San Diego Naval Training Center was 120 miles on I-5 South or approximately a two-and-a-half-hour ride on the bus. When I arrived at my destination, it was after dark. First, the bus driver stopped at the Marine Corps Recruit Depot (MCRD), San Diego, to drop off the Marine enlistees. Then about several hundred yards further ahead, and adjacent to the Marine Corps Recruit Depot (MCRD) was the Recruit Training Command (RTC) where fellow navy enlistees and I got off the bus.

Recruit Training Command was where I transitioned from civilian to military life, and indeed, it was culture shock. I would learn the history, traditions, customs, and regulations of my chosen service, and I would also receive instruction in naval skills and subjects which became basic information to guide me throughout my period of naval service. On the following morning, me and my fellow navy recruits were rudely awakened at approximately 4:00 a.m. from the noisy sound of a metal garbage can. It rattled and rolled on the surface of the floor at the center of the barracks where we were sleeping. The metal garbage can was tossed unto the barracks floor by a Chief Petty Officer and his assistant, a First Class Petty Officer.

While they scowled and yelled a barrage of obscenities and profanities at us, they gave us five minutes, ordering us to immediately fall outside on the grinder and stand at attention on our assigned billet numbers. While our group stood anxiously at attention during that early morning hour, it was still dark and cold with a thick fog drifting just over and about us. The fog had come directly from the San Diego Bay area.

From there, we marched to the chow hall in our civilian clothes where I ate my first breakfast at RTC. After we finished eating our breakfast meal, we mustered back outside to the grinder and stood on our billets where we waited for further orders. And I thought, *What's next?*

Next, we were ordered to march to the RTC's barbershop where I got my first haircut! Although I felt clean-cut for the first time in a long time, I liked my new military look. Unlike some of the recruits who worried their girlfriends wouldn't like the haircut, I didn't have a girlfriend to think about.

After getting my navy regulation haircut at the RTC barbershop, I marched with my group to the Receiving and Outfitting Unit, better known as "R and O," where I received my first introduction to recruit training. Here I was, given a thorough medical and dental examination, including various mental tests, and I was issued my outfit of Navy uniforms and clothing. Soon afterward, me and other fellow recruits were also issued the Navy's Blue Jacket's Manual and assigned to our recruit company. The Bluejacket's Manual is the basic handbook for the United States Navy personnel. It was first issued in 1902 to teach the new recruit or Bluejacket on arrival at boot camp about naval procedures and life and offers a reference for active sailors. It has become the "bible" for Navy personnel, providing information about a wide range of Navy topics.

As a newly formed company, we were "welcomed aboard" by an officer representative of the Commanding Officer, and we were placed under the charge of an experienced senior petty officer who was our company commander throughout our period of recruit training. As a platoon, we became known as Company 288. In Forming the Company, the verbal scripts or commands went like this:

"Shall we get started men?"

"When I call your name, answer up."

"Next, you will stencil in your name."

"Fall in."

"Move out smartly."

And the Company verbal Commissioning scripts went like this:

"Good morning men, I am Lieutenant _____, your Division Officer."

"Post the Company Flag."

"Good luck."

"Company Commander Dalby, take charge of your company."

Afterward, we marched away as Company 288 with me leading my squad of seven young (men) recruits amongst six other squad leaders of seven recruits each as well.

The Company Commander was a US Navy Submarine Quarter Master (QM) First Class Petty Officer whose name was Dalby. Carefully selected to become our commanding officer, QM1 Dalby was a thoroughly experienced career Navy petty officer of demonstrated leadership ability who had received special training in working with recruits. He was tall, lean, and mean, clean as a whistle, and he had a razor-sharp mind. During my recruit training, Dalby made me feel proud and confident to be under his leadership and command.

During the formation of our company, QM1 Dalby selected me to be a squad leader. The company was a large platoon or principal subdivision which consisted of approximately forty-nine seaman recruits organized into seven squads of seven men each.

As a new recruit and squad leader in my new company, I met young men from all walks of life and sections of the country. These men became my shipmates for the coming nine weeks. Unfortunately, some of the recruits took longer than nine weeks because they did not pass certain tests such as water survival, etc. Shortly after the formation of our company, one of the most important steps in the "in processing" stage was the administration of the Navy's General Classification Test. The results of those tests together with a later meeting with a trained classification interviewer led to the selection of my career pattern in the Navy giving me the option of attending a seaman apprenticeship training program or special schooling after my graduation from boot camp.

For choosing the former in which upon successfully completing basic training and an additional two weeks of apprenticeship training, I received a specified rating and entered the fleet with a general designation of seaman apprentice. The other sailors who chose the latter received a specified rating and were sent to various apprenticeship or "A schools" located across the United States for training in their occupational specialty or ratings. After General Classification Testing and Interviewing and having donned my new Navy uniform and my civilian clothes shipped home, I was ready to move to Primary Training. The Primary Training Regiment was where my company had actually gone on schedule. To "go on schedule" meant to officially prepare our company for graduation after successfully completing nine weeks of the Navy recruit training program.

To be of maximum effective use to myself and to the Navy, I had to be in top physical condition. I was obliged to know how to care for my body and be able to survive in the water at sea. To the end that all navy men could possibly meet these demands of naval service, our company participated in a physical training program that involved strenuous physical training and physical exertion, instruction in swimming and sea survival, and instruction in first aid, life-saving, and personal hygiene. Often when young navy recruits report for duty, some of them are soft, some are overweight, and some are underweight. To build some up and trim others down, and to condition all for the rigors of life at sea, the Naval Training Center (NTC) had a well-planned physical training program integrated with other phases of training: military drill, an active outdoor life, good food, and good living habits.

These physical training activities emphasized correct posture and muscular coordination. It strived to develop our respect for authority and habits of instantaneous response to commands. Because our lives as sailors would be spent at sea, we had to know how to swim, how to use life jackets, and if no jackets were available, how to use our clothing as flotation devices. I spent many hours with my fellow recruits in the swimming pool. The Abandon Ship Drill at the swimming pool gave us an opportunity to use our clothing as flotation devices.

I recall moments before jumping from the edge of the pool into the water, "Will this really work?" and "I hope so!" Then with my shirt over my head upon splashing into the pool water, I brought it underneath my chest, and to my surprise, I found myself floating on top of the water and reflecting, "It sure does work." But to advance to the second week of training, we also had to pass the Swim Test. The swim test involved jumping from a tower into the deep end of the swimming pool, tread water, swim, walk, or crawl around the pool. Non-swimmers (recruits who failed their swim test) were held back a week, formed a non-swim company, and were taught how to swim. Qualified swimmers like myself improved their ability and advanced to the second week of primary training. All recruits learned sea survival and water safety.

For us who'd go down to the sea in the ships, a knowledge of basic seamanship was fundamental. Although some seamanship skills could be mastered only from long experience at sea, the foundations upon which these skills were based formed an important part of my recruit training. Emphasis in my training was placed upon teaching me and my fellow recruits the language of the sea and the names and uses of the tools of our new trade. Among the subjects taught to us were marlinspike seamanship and knot-tying, steering and sounding, anchoring and mooring, and the recognition of various ships, their characteristics and structures. Additionally, I learned the principles of shipboard organization and something of the role I'd later play as a member of my ship's company. I also received instruction in the use of the sound-powered telephones by which sailors stationed in various parts of a ship could communicate with each other.

To facilitate practical demonstrations of these subjects, the *Recruit*, a scale model of a destroyer escort was constructed on shore for use by us, the recruits. Onboard this landlocked ship, practical exercises were held in stationing personnel. The *Recruit* was also used for getting underway and anchoring to the handling of mooring lines and the manning of watch and battle stations. By the time I completed recruit training, I had learned many of the fundamentals of seamanship. This would stand me in good stead on board ship in the fleet.

The pages of history of World War II are filled with instances where brave men, given the proper equipment and the necessary "know-how," were able to save their ships from apparently certain loss, following severe battle damage. Fires were extinguished, flooded compartments plugged and dewatered, and the wounded cared for to the end that the ship survived and returned to fight other battles. Damage Control instruction for me and my fellow recruits taught me the fundamental principles of firefighting and a working knowledge of the equipment which would save our ship and our own lives. Probably one of the longest remembered days of recruit training is the one I spent at the Firefighting Center. Here I learned the chemistry of fire, basic principles of combating fire, and then I spent nearly an entire day extinguishing actual fires!

However, under the watchful supervision of trained firefighters, I was able to put out serious fires under simulated shipboard conditions. After receiving this valuable practical experience, I lost most of my fear of fire and gained confidence in my ability to combat serious fires. My fellow recruits and myself also received practical instruction in the use of the gas masks, oxygen-breathing apparatuses, and other equipment designed for our personal protection. In the teargas chamber, I had the opportunity to test the effectiveness of my gas mask. Basic instruction was also given to each of my fellow recruits and myself in the probable effects of an atomic explosion and the measures taken to ensure our personal safety and survival. I recall leading my squad of seven recruits while we held a heavy fire hose during fire drill, and the words of the script amongst us went something like this:

"Go."

"It don't fit."

"Got it."

"Turn it on."

"Quick, turn it off."

"Now it's right."

The military drill, watch standing and inspections that were all a part of my recruit military training, was a new experience to me. The marching, the facing, the manual of arms at first seemed difficult beyond all reason, but after a week's practice, confidence began to appear, and by the end of primary training my company had become a sharp appearing unit. Even though the navy man seldom carries a rifle or marches in a military unit after completing recruit training, I understood that there was a definite and important place in naval recruit training for military drill. The military control of our company was gained and maintained through constant drilling. Leaders such as myself were discovered and developed, and others learned instantaneous response to command.

All of us developed coordination of mind and body, and an "esprit de corps" grew within our company. Together with physical training, military drill was a part of the physical conditioning or "hardening up" process for me and my fellow recruit. But most of all, military drill taught me the importance of implicit obedience to orders and the importance of the individual in a military group whether he be in a marching unit, on a gun crew, in the fire room, or on the bridge. Inspections will always be an important matter in the life of a man in the Navy. In recruit training, the vigorous competition maintained between the recruit companies was based largely on a series of regular inspections, which served the double purpose of teaching me and my fellow recruit the requirements of military life while comparing my performance and that of my unit with the performance of others in training with me.

Afloat or ashore, each naval unit was generally a self-sustaining unit. The messing of the crew, all the housekeeping chores, and the watch standing had to be performed by those assigned to the unit. Throughout an enlistment or naval career, regardless of rate or rating, each man is in some way concerned with these service duties to which I was introduced during service week. In any unit, men in the lower rates usually performed the "chores," and those in the higher rates would supervise them; all had to stand watches, and all had to live together in the same ship. The fourth week of my recruit training was devoted to instruction and practical experience in Ship's Work Training.

For six weeks of my training period, I was waited upon in the mess hall by other recruits, and for one week, I took my turn in performing these important tasks for my shipmates in recruit training. Although the fourth week was specifically designated for training in these duties, much of my training continued throughout the entire training period. Every messenger or sentry watch and every cleaning detail was a part of my training in the problems of community living. In the Recruit Training Command, I believed that the things I had to learn in ship's work training was best taught by actually doing them. For experience was my greatest teacher of all.

Chow Line Word Script:

"Company 288 reporting for chow."

Food Serving Word Script:

"Is that all?"

"Sure, it's good."

"Spoons on the left, forks in the middle."

Scullery Word Script:

"That's enough."

"Clean the tip."

"Move them out."

"Why me?"

Probably the most important thing that I had to learn during recruit training was how to live with others in a military organization. Life and living conditions in the Navy differed so greatly from anything I had known in civilian life that teaching me to live in close quarters as a member of this military group became one of the major missions of recruit training. At the Training Center, my barracks was my "home." It was in my barracks that I spent an appreciable portion of my time in training. Here I established myself—in a sense, dropped my anchor—for the weeks in which I experienced the transition from civilian to military life.

The barracks was not only a place for me as a recruit to sleep, but it was my most important classroom. Here I "learned by doing." I learned to live with others and to take care of myself and my belongings. The scrubbing of my clothing, the cleaning of my barracks, and the constant inspections all served but one purpose—to prepare me for a successful life during the remainder of my tour in the Navy. And it was not all work. For me, I had to also learn the need of a Navy man for the companionship of my fellows, for mail from home, and for amusement and relaxation. I also had to develop the habits of writing letters and budgeting my spare time. These things I learned in my barracks life at the Training Center.

"God, we pray to thee; For those in peril on the sea."

In making the change from civilian to military life, I didn't leave behind the religious beliefs which I learned at home. Instead, I was given every opportunity and encouragement to maintain and strengthen my religious interests. Soon after my arrival, I was given an opportunity to talk to a chaplain of my own faith, Roman Catholic, who acquainted me with his role in the command and explained the religious programs, which would be available to me during recruit training. Regular divine services were conducted by chaplains of all faiths, thus giving each recruit an opportunity to worship in accordance with his religious background.

Voluntary classes of religious instruction were held regularly for the benefit of recruits who desired to prepare themselves for church membership. The chaplains cooperated closely with the local churches to facilitate membership or attendance at services in those churches.

Character guidance talks given by the chaplains were an integral part of recruit training. These were designed to foster the growth of moral responsibility, spiritual values, and strong self-discipline within us. As recruits, we were encouraged to participate in the religious life of the station by joining the choir or providing musical accompaniment at divine services. In time of distress or personal emergency, the chaplains stood ready to give advice and counsel, and we were encouraged to take our personal problems to a chaplain of our choice at any time. The chaplains also maintained close contact with the Navy Relief Society and The American Red Cross in obtaining financial and other assistance in need.

Recreation played an important part in my training at the Naval Training Center. But during my first weeks of training, I had little or no time to spare from my daily routine for recreation. In order to bring me through the loneliness and sharp readjustment to life in my new environment, a special effort was made to keep me and fellow recruits fully occupied throughout each day of primary training, and I therefore had little time or inclination for the recreational opportunities which lay ahead of me. Liberty to visit San Diego was not granted until after the final week of training. The recreational facilities of the Training Center were many and varied. An attended telephone exchange made it easy for me to call any place in an emergency or just to hear familiar voices from home.

Intercompany softball, baseball, and volleyball games afforded a diversion from the daily routine, and spectator interest in varsity athletics was often keen. During my off hours, I could have also used one of the swimming pools or played golf, tennis, or handball. However, I didn't use any of these facilities for my personal pleasure. Recruit boxing and wrestling bouts and impromptu entertainment acts afforded interest at periodic Recruit Smokers. Just the same, I neither indulged in these activities nor was a spectator at these events until my participation in the two-week Seaman Apprenticeship Program that followed graduation from boot camp. In total, I spent eleven weeks at the San Diego, California Naval Training Center (NTC)/Recruit Training Command (RTC); thus, nine weeks in training at RTC or boot camp, and two additional weeks of Seaman Apprenticeship training or on-the-job training.

Commencing my final week of training, me and fellow recruits who earned the privilege were granted liberty on two days after our graduation parade. During my liberty hours, I was "on my own" to select my own form of recreation, but by group indoctrination, I was reminded that I had an obligation to the uniform I was wearing to conduct myself in a manner which would bring credit to myself, my organization, and the Navy.

Navy Graduation Review

Since the beginning of recruit training, I had looked forward to graduation day. This was the big day our company had spent nine weeks working, preparing, and diligently practicing the military drills for which we would have to perform as a sharp marching military unit in the upcoming graduation parade before high ranking naval officers, dignitaries, family and friends of the recruit, and the general public. For long hours each day, and through constant drilling, we learned how to march together as a company to the national music of "The Stars and Stripes Forever" while carrying the rifle on our shoulders and practicing the passing in review. We also learned the facing and the sixteen-count manual of arms. And on top of all this, we were ordered to memorize and learn the Navy's eleven general orders, and so on and so forth. After my final week of intense recruit training, it culminated on Monday, December 2, 1974, when me and Company 288 took our place in history at the Naval Training

Center (NTC) and marched for the Navy's recruit graduation review, on that day, I believed God blessed me, and I was proud to be an American and a US Navy man.

29

MY FIRST LIBERTY
IN THE NAVY

After the graduation review was over and earning the privilege, I was granted liberty to leave the Naval Training Center (NTC) and enjoy some personal time and recreation in the great city of San Diego, California. However, I had the pleasure of being in the company of my mother and her dear friend, Norma Smith, who had driven to San Diego to be present at my graduation ceremony. They both met and visited with me at the reception center where we were afforded a convenient, relaxing, and attractive surrounding. This was one of the most memorable and joyful days of my life thus far. So with beaming smiles, my mom and I both embraced, holding each other tightly, and Norma and I also embraced each other.

They both were very proud to see me wearing my new dress white Navy uniform. While my mother and Norma enjoyed all the pomp and circumstance fitting the occasion, they also enjoyed the recruit graduation parade as well. Then, my mother who had called me by my childhood nickname, O'Toole, said: "I've closed my eyes for but a moment, and suddenly, a man stands where a boy used to be. I may not carry you now in my arms, but I will always carry you in my heart. You have given me so many reasons to be proud of the man you have become, but the proudest moment for me is telling others that you are my son. I love you now and forever."

After hearing my mother's expressions of love for and pride in me, I reacted with great pleasure and warmly embraced her again.

Man, I was over the moon about everything that had just happened to me up to my graduation day! This included becoming nineteen years old on Friday, November 22, 1974, at the end of my seventh week in boot camp. Although not surprised, I was somewhat disappointed with my father and stepfather for not showing up. I was especially disappointed with my father while I stood talking to my mother and Norma at the reception center. It had been several months since we had spoken or even acknowledged each other's existence. I watched other fellow Navy men interact with their proud fathers and wished that I could have had what they had; I had tried all my young life to build a relationship with my father, but it always seemed that there were more important things that mattered to him than a relationship with me. This sadly had been a recurring theme in my life; all my father and stepfather both had done was disappoint me. But in fairness to them and honestly speaking, it was not entirely their fault as to why our relationships didn't exist; they were never taught how to be a father or a husband which, in the end, left me longing for a relationship that they couldn't give me anyway.

Be that as it may, my meeting at the Recruit Training Reception Center with my mother and Norma was brief. Afterward, we left the Navy base for a couple of hours while I enjoyed my first liberty in the Navy and visited with Norma's parents at their home in San Diego, California. This was my first time meeting them, and they were very friendly and hospitable. Norma's father also shared his story with me of being a WWII Navy Veteran. When we finished our visit, Norma took me back to the Naval Training Center and my mother, and she returned home to Inglewood, California.

On my own during the second day of liberty, I left the training center wearing my dress blue Navy crackerjack uniform to enjoy some of the many worthwhile attractions in San Diego, California. Changing into my swimming trunks, I began my liberty by relaxing on the sand and swimming the surf at San Diego's first-rate local beach resort, Coronado Beach. Next, I visited Balboa Park with its excellent zoo and other scenic and recreational attractions, which had always been popular with recruits and men-of-war alike. The shopping and amusement facilities of downtown San Diego also attracted me while I was on liberty. Finally, because of my curiosity, I sought out the USO and Armed Services YMCA who did their part to help me enjoy the rest of my liberty in San Diego, and I had a blast!

The Seaman Apprenticeship Training Program, My Orders, and My Departure from San Diego NTC/RTC

My training as a Navy Seaman Recruit started immediately after I had completed nine weeks of basic training/boot camp at the San Diego Naval Training Center (NTC)/Recruit Training Command (RTC). And it was at this place where I would spend an additional two weeks attending the Seaman Apprenticeship Training Program. The training course provided me with knowledge on basic theory in shipboard operations and evolution. After I had completed the program and was promoted to Seaman Apprentice, I was assigned to shipboard duty where the Navy needed me the most.

My first duty station assignment was with a Navy construction and battle unit called Amphibious Construction Battalion Two. It was located in a strange and unknown place called Little Creek at Virginia Beach, Virginia, just thirteen miles from the Naval Operations Base (NOB) at Norfolk, Virginia. When I read my orders, I thought, *Where in the heck is the Navy sending me?* because I was expecting to report for duty aboard a large US Navy ship where I would sail the seven seas. Honestly, after I reviewed my orders, I felt somewhat anxious about reporting for duty at Little Creek!

Anyhow, my departure from NTC/RTC occurred in mid-December 1974 after I had finished the Seaman Apprenticeship Training program. The Navy granted me five days of leave; everyone in the military earns 2.5 days of leave (vacation time) for every month of active duty. After I left RTC for the last time, wearing my dress blue Navy uniform with orders in hand and Navy sea bag harnessed on my shoulders, I caught a taxi cab headed to the San Diego Airport. Using the transportation voucher paid for by the Navy, I boarded a United Airlines commercial jet at the San Diego Airport destined for the Los Angeles International Airport (LAX). After my departure from San Diego, I arrived at Los Angeles LAX and caught a taxi cab ride home where I enjoyed the Christmas Holiday with my mother, grandmother, brothers, and sister at Inglewood, California.

Journey to My First Duty Station at Little Creek, Norfolk, Virginia

When my five days leave and Christmas vacation was over on December 26, 1974, I said goodbye to my family. And then I rode with my stepfather and mother to LAX, wearing my dress blue Navy crackerjacks. After they dropped me off at the airport's curbside, I said my goodbyes and gave my mother a warm hug. Next, smiling and feeling excited, I entered the building with my sea bag harnessed to my back and duffel bag gripped in my hand; then I checked-in my luggage at the United Airline's counter. Afterward, I entered the airline terminal, and moments later, boarded a United Airline commercial jet destined for Denver International Airport in Colorado. After Denver, it was onto Chicago O'Hare International Airport where I incurred a one-hour layover. Afterward, I boarded an unfamiliar airline at O'Hare called Piedmont Airlines for my final destination to Norfolk International Airport in Norfolk, Virginia.

When I arrived at Norfolk, it was dark, and I was feeling tired and sleepy, so I caught a cab from the airport to a motel where I lodged overnight. At sunrise the next morning, after I got ready and ate a continental breakfast, I caught a taxicab and arrived at my new duty station, Amphibious Construction Battalion Two at Little Creek Naval Amphibious Base.

Reporting for Duty

After reporting for duty in December of 1974 as a seaman apprentice, the second lowest enlisted rank in the US Navy, I was assigned to Amphibious Construction Battalion Two. It was the home of the historic Seabees. To my surprise and delight, I suddenly became part of its meritorious naval history. The Seabees were and still are highly esteemed by all branches of the US Armed Forces. Upon my arrival at Main Gate 5 of Little Creek Naval Amphibious Base, I realized that it was substantially different from the Navy base I had envisioned from reading my orders at the San Diego NTC. Also,

I had realized that this Navy base wasn't just an ordinary naval base located at Little Creek, but it was a large Navy base of great historical significance located next to the Chesapeake Bay. Chesapeake Bay at Little Creek, Virginia, is a large inlet of the North Atlantic Ocean on the US coast that extends north 200 miles (320 kilometers) through the states of Virginia and Maryland.

When I arrived at Little Creek Naval Amphibious Base, the next thing that I did after checking in at my duty station and barracks was go to the Navy Disbursing Office and set up a military allotment. An allotment was used to distribute money from one-third of my Navy paycheck. These discretionary allotment checks were voluntary payments mailed to my mother once a month. During boot camp, however, at the San Diego Naval Training Center, I sent my mother 100 percent of my military pay in the form of a cash money order. While in basic training, the most humbling deed until then was sending to Mom with my love this much-needed money every two weeks, and it made me feel very good about myself.

Seabee

When I transitioned to the new duty station, I found not only was I a sailor, but to my surprise, I had become a Seabee and a member of the United States Navy Construction Battalion (CB) as well. The word *Seabee* comes from initials "CB." The Seabee motto is "Seabees Can Do." The Seabees are an elite cadre of construction battalion sailors who have a history of building bases, bulldozing and paving thousands of miles of roadway and airstrips, and accomplishing a myriad of other construction projects in a wide variety of military theaters dating back to World War II.

Naval Amphibious Base Little Creek, Virginia History

Naval Amphibious Base Little Creek began in World War Two as a training and practice center for developing the then radical concept of massive shore landings, known then and now as amphibious assaults. An early example of joint operations training, four facilities were developed on the site, Camp Bradford and Camp Shelton (named for the former landowners) and Frontier Base and Amphibious Training Base.

Prior to World War Two there was little concept of an amphibious assault; troops could land, but they either docked or were carried ashore by boat. The British had developed combined force operations as far back as the Napoleon wars, and the union had launched a massive landing against the Confederacy during the Civil War, but nothing quite like what the US of World War Two had in mind. The amphibious concept involved a much more closely coordinated operation of Navy launched amphibious tracked landing vehicles, with close shore bombardment support and Marine or Army troops storming beaches. Nothing quite like this had ever been done; the Imperial Japanese landed in motorized boats; Nazi Germany had conducted an air and sea assault on Crete, but the new US concept was to use water-to-land trucked vehicles.

Thanks to practice and training at Navy bases, especially what would later be called Little Creek, the US made this a specialty, successfully conducted at Morocco and Algeria, Sicily, Salerno, and Anzio, and the largest amphibious assault ever, the Normandy landings. In the Pacific Theater, the Marine Corps honed amphibious assault to a fine edge, making dozens of island beach assaults during the Pacific Theatre.

Camp Bradford, at Little Creek, originally focused on training Seabees (Construction Battalions) and later trained LSTs (Landing Ship, Tanks) for the Normandy Landings. Camp Shelton, also at Little Creek, trained bluejackets for gunnery on merchant ships. The Frontier Base served as training and housing center for troops destined for Europe.

The Amphibious Training Base was where the real development was happening; all kinds of landing craft were tested and adapted; tactics were developed from principles, tested, and revised. This went on in primitive conditions, as base housing and other facilities were at first non-existent, and then very basic. In time, the base developed, and trained over 200,000 Naval and over 160,000 Army and Marine personnel.

All of these bases were partially inactivated at the end of World War Two, after being used for service separation, but the need for superior amphibious assault training was recognized, and a permanent base, Naval Amphibious Base Little Creek was established in 1946. Here, thousands of military personnel, Navy, Marine, Army, and members of allied foreign militaries have trained in modern amphibious assault (www.littlecreek-housing.com/history).

Amphibious Construction Battalion Two, History

Abbreviated as ACB 2, or PHIBCB 2, it is an amphibious construction battalion in the United States Navy based in Little Creek, Virginia. Amphibious Construction Battalion ONE is its sister unit based in Coronado, California.

Mission: "PHIBCB TWO combines the small craft expertise of the surface navy with the construction capabilities of the Naval Construction force. We support Commander, Naval Beach Group TWO in amphibious force projection with fully trained, combat ready forces."

Motto: "We build, we fight."

History:

Amphibious Construction Battalion TWO traces its roots to the pontoon operation battalions of World War II that participated in every major amphibious assault, beginning with the invasion of Sicily. By the use of pontoon causeways, barge-mounted cranes and pontoon ferries, these battalions gave the amphibious forces the ability to quickly off-load the large quantities of troops and cargo needed to assure victory.

Since its commissioning as the 105th Naval Construction Battalion on 14 July 1942, under the operational control of Commander Amphibious Training Command, US Atlantic Fleet, the command has continually participated in major amphibious operations and exercises.

When Naval Beach Group TWO was established in 1948, the 105th NCB became a component of that command and was re-designated Amphibious Construction Battalion TWO (PHIBCB TWO) in 1950. Between December 1972 and 1975, PHIBCB TWO was a component of Naval Inshore Warfare Command following the disestablishment of Naval Beach Group TWO. However, PHIBCB TWO once again became a component of Naval Beach Group TWO when it was re-commissioned in 1975.

PHIBCB TWO has distinguished itself in a myriad of operations since World War II including:

- The 1958 crisis in Lebanon
- The Multi-National Peacekeeping Force in Lebanon from August 1982 to February 1984
- The October 1983 rescue of American citizens in Grenada

- Operation Sharp Edge in Liberia in 1991
- Operations Desert Shield and Desert Storm in 1990-1991
- Operation Uphold Democracy in Haiti in 1994
- Disaster recovery efforts for TWA Flight 800 and Egypt Air Flight 990
- More recently Operation IRAQI FREEDOM
- And Operation Unified Response providing much needed relief after the 2010 Haiti earthquake.

PHIBCB TWO has earned several unit awards, including two Navy Unit Commendations and two Meritorious Unit Commendations, and was the first Naval Construction Force command to receive the Department of Defense Joint Meritorious Unit Award. The Battalion also qualified for the Golden Anchor Award for retention excellence in FY 01 and FY 03.

With over 1,100 active duty and reserve men and women, Amphibious Construction Battalion TWO provides the US Atlantic Fleet with the ship-to-shore link so vital to success in amphibious operations.

My Tour of Duty at Amphibious Construction Battalion Two: December 26, 1974–September 29, 1977

I spent my tour of duty and most of my naval service in Virginia Beach, Virginia, at the Little Creek Naval Amphibious Base: Amphibious Construction Battalion Two, also called PHIBCB TWO or ACB 2. During my first ninety days on board as a Navy seaman apprentice (SA), I was assigned to typical shipboard duties which included standing security watches at the PHIBCB TWO Command and the adjacent waterfront. I was also responsible for repairing, maintaining, and stowing equipment in preparation for scheduled future detachments and underway operations aboard the Navy's Landing Tank Ships (LSTs) destined for the Mediterranean and Caribbean Seas.

After ninety days at PHIBCB TWO's waterfront performing basic shipboard duties, I requested and received on-the-job training in the Navy yeoman enlisted rating. During this period, I was assigned as "C" Company (steelworker and welder unit) yeoman and performed typing, filing, and various other clerical and administrative tasks. I also continued to work on the waterfront and on causeway operations performing deck seaman duties. I stood roving sentry watches as well.

On my first Report of Enlisted Performance Evaluation dated 21 August 1975 covering the period of April 01, 1975 to July 31, 1975, the Executive Officer, LCDR Olson, USN, wrote the following evaluation:

> SA Woodman is a good worker and is eager to learn more about his assigned tasks. (Highly effective and reliable. Needs only limited supervision.) He has shown much initiative in practicing

and training to become a better typist and office clerk. On the waterfront operations he has also shown a desire to become a well-rounded seaman. He accepts orders readily and always shows the proper respect. (Willingly follows commands and regulations.) He maintains a neat well-kept military appearance. (Smart. Neat and correct in appearance.) He has a pleasant smile and manner that makes him well-liked and readily accepted by all those he works with. (Gets along exceptionally well. Promotes good morale.)

For me, this first report of my performance evaluation was very humbling and motivating.

Nine months after my enlistment and shortly after I had received the foregoing enlisted performance evaluation, I submitted a promotion request to the Commanding Officer who granted my request and promoted me to seaman (SN). Hooray! As a Seaman, I became third ranked in the United States Navy, ranking above Seaman Apprentice and directly below Petty Officer Third Class. Seaman is a Junior Enlisted at Department of Defense paygrade E-3. Three white stripes instead of two white stripes (seaman apprentice) were worn on my uniform sleeve (below the shoulder) indicative of my higher rank of "Seaman." After my promotion to seaman, I was addressed by my shipmates and ranking officers alike as Seaman (SN) Woodman. Prior to my promotion to seaman, I was addressed in the former lower rank as Seaman Apprentice (SA) Woodman. Informally, though, most of my shipmates called me Woody, although some called me by my last name, Woodman.

While attached to Amphibious Construction Battalion TWO as a Seaman (SN), I continued to work on the C Company waterfront working in the area and taking part in local operations. While I was attached to the Mediterranean Amphibious Ready Group (MARG) 1-76, I worked on the causeway team and performed routine maintenance on the rig and causeways. I also served as the team yeoman and stood causeway security watches while the tank landing ship, *USS*

Barnstable County (LST-1197) was underway. This was my first antic-ipated deployment aboard a ship bound for the Mediterranean. As the famous quote goes: "Sailors belong on ships, and ships belong at sea."

MARG 1-76 of the United States Navy Atlantic 6th Fleet con-sisted of a naval element—a group of warships known as an amphib-ious task force (ATF)—and a landing force (LF) of US Marines, in total about 5,000 people. Together, with these elements and support-ing units, we trained, organized, and equipped ourselves to perform amphibious operations on various beaches of the Mediterranean.

My performance evaluation while deployed on MARG 1-76 had improved since my last evaluation at PHIBCB TWO. Dated 31 July 1976, after returning to Little Creek, Virginia from Med Cruise 1-76; Executive Officer H. M. Olson, LCDR, USN wrote:

> SN Woodman can be relied upon to perform the tasks assigned to him in an above average manner. He completes his tasks correctly and on time. He is working on YN3 and with a little more progress in this area he will be a fine yeo-man. His appearance is well above average with the exception that his Petty Officers have to occa-sionally remind him about his hair. Ratee associ-ates very well with both his seniors and peers. He is an asset to the detachment and to the Navy. SN Woodman is highly recommended for advance-ment and reenlistment.

After reading my performance evaluation, I was humbled, motivated, and over the moon.

30

ORDNANCE AND GUNNERY AT PHIBCB TWO

To be an effective fighting unit, a Seabee Battalion must be capable of inflicting maximum damage upon the enemy; to survive, it must be able to defend itself against hostile attack. In Ordnance Training, I learned some of the duties performed in my construction battalion by *The Man Behind the Gun*. While at PHIBCB TWO, Ordnance and Gunnery Training began with instruction in the use of small arms (.45 caliber semi-automatic handgun). Under the guidance of the command's Gunnery Chief, I learned how to load, sight, and how to fire the weapon. Later, I would fire the weapon at the battalion's outdoor range on the beach at Chesapeake Bay.

Throughout, the safe use of weapons was stressed in instruction and rigidly enforced on the firing line. I also received an introduction and instruction in the use of the larger weapons (M-16 automatic rifle with a twenty-round magazine) after my tour of PHIBCB TWO's Armory where I learned some of the principles of its operation. During my tour of the battalion's armory, I was shown the various types of ammunition I would encounter and handle at the battalion or onboard ship, and I learned the necessity for strictly observing the safety precautions which were necessary for my own safety and that of my fellow Seabees/shipmates. As a small group, we went to the outdoor rifle range where the area provided fifty-foot targets for the firing of the .45 handgun and 100-foot targets for the firing of the M-16 rifle. Then I heard the commands from our Gunnery Chief:

"Take your positions."

"Ready on the Left."

"Ready on the Right."

"Fire."

"Fire."

On that day, and to my delight at the M-16 rifle range, I shot bull's-eye after bull's-eye and qualified for the Navy Rifle Expert Award (Expert M-16), thereafter proudly wearing the award ribbon on my uniform.

My CB (Seabee) Embarkment Aboard the USS Barnstable County (LST-1197): Tank Landing Ship

Following are excerpts from the Mediterranean Amphibious Ready Group (MARG) 1-76 Cruise Book, *There and Back Again*:

Sailors Belong on Ships, and Ships Belong at Sea

For the USS BARNSTABLE COUNTY, Med Cruise 1-76 represented the opportunity to test the fiber of this often-repeated adage. Protracted periods at sea, including one stretch of 68 days provided ample opportunity to try the mettle of every man while constant preparations for and the conduct of a variety of evolutions kept people ever alert.

The cruise had its good moments and bad, times of excitement and days of tedious waiting, intense drama and sadness. Who will soon forget the extraordinary efforts of the engineers in effecting repairs to the boilers when the only alternative was cold showers. On the other hand, the good times such as liberty Rome or sightseeing in Ville France were infrequent but all the more memorable as a result. Drama in the form of unexpected touchdown of a disabled helicopter at Brindisi and the surveillance of Soviet ships kept people on their toes while the tragedy of a heli crash on the LPH served as a reminder to all that safety is indeed of paramount importance. The poignancy of a change of command at sea midway through the cruise reawakened in all the realization that men come and go but there can be no lapse in the vital task of maintaining peace.

Med Cruise 1-76 may not be remembered with joy but is should be remembered, if only for the tireless efforts of so many in accomplishing day to day tasks involved in maintaining a ready ship. It is to these fine men and their CB and Marine compatriots who rode the ship that this is dedicated.

Mediterranean Cruise 1-76: Chronology of My Voyage Aboard the USS Barnstable County (LST-1197)

The tank landing ship, *Barnstable County* (LST-1197) left Norfolk on 5 January 1976 and steamed to Morehead City, N.C., in company with the four other units of PHIBRON 8: Spiegel Grove (LSD-32), Raleigh (LPD-1), Guadalcanal (LPH-7), and Charleston (LKA-113). Arriving at Morehead City on the 6th, the ships loaded the 34th Marine Amphibious Unit (34th MAU) for rehearsal landings at Onslow Beach. After completing the weather-delayed exercises, Barnstable County finally got underway for Rota, Spain, on 10 January. The Atlantic crossing proved difficult and took longer than anticipated because engineering problems plagued several ships of the squadron. Upon arrival in Rota turnover formalities proceeded quickly, and Barnstable County officially joined the 6ᵗʰ fleet. Plans for a landing exercise on Spain's Atlantic coast had to be canceled as a result of civil war in Lebanon, and the squadron passed through the Straights of Gibraltar instead on its way to Augusta Bay, Sicily. The civil unrest in Lebanon dominated the ship's schedule for the remainder of the cruise.

During the first stop in the Mediterranean, Barnstable County anchored with the squadron at Sicily for a few days. In the course of the training anchorage visit there, a violent storm broke with winds exceeding 50 knots. Upon departing Augusta Bay after the storm subsided the ship headed for its first liberty port, Reggio di Calobia, on the Italian Rivera. The ship arrived on 1 February and stayed until 6 February. Departing Reggio on a Friday the ship arrived at Brindisi, Italy, the following day for a seven-day training anchorage visit. The ship then proceeded to Ville France arriving on 16 February. Barnstable County left Ville France on 23 February and proceeded to Monte Romano, Italy, where she carried out more amphibious training late in February. Early in March, the ship made a four-day port call at Naples, putting to sea again on the 5ᵗʰ bound for Sardinia to participate in NATO Exercise "Sardinia '76." After conducting a simulated opposed passage to Sardinia, Barnstable County sent her marines ashore in the first wave and then took little further part in the evolution. At the mission's conclusion, she reembarked the marines on 18 March and headed for Syracuse, Sicily, where her crew enjoyed a week of liberty.

On 26 March, urgent orders interrupted her deployment schedule once again and sent her to a holding area just east of Crete in response to an intensification of the situation in Lebanon. For the first few weeks she steamed squares in the ocean while rehearsing contingency plans for a possible evacuation of Americans from Beirut. Despite the passage of time, the Lebanese political scene remained volatile; so, the squadron moved to a deep-water anchorage outside Crete's territorial waters. April and May came and went without any real change, except that, late in May, the squadron got underway and steamed closer to Lebanon. Finally, after 69 days at sea, a lull in the fighting coupled with negotiations in progress allowed Barnstable County to proceed to Naples for a scheduled port call. The visit lasted from 1 to 4 June, and, then the squadron left for an amphibious exercise conducted at Carboneras, Spain. At its end, the squadron returned to the eastern Mediterranean and resumed station off Lebanon.

This time, the squadron moved to within 30 miles of the Lebanese coast. Spiegel Grove closed to within 25 miles of the shore and dispatched an LCU to the beach while Barnstable County and the other ships stood by on station. After Spiegel Grove evacuated several hundred civilians, the squadron moved back near the coast of Crete, where its relief soon arrived. The turnover process, during which the new squadron assumed stand-by-duties, lasted two days; and then Barnstable County shaped a westerly course for Rota. She reached Rota on 30 June and stayed there until 5 July when she embarked on a northerly passage home. Barnstable County arrived back in Little Creek on 15 July. Post-deployment leave and upkeep took up the rest of July and most of August.

31

NAVY LIFE BACK AT THE GATOR, LITTLE CREEK

Meanwhile, after I returned to my duty station at Amphibious Construction Battalion Two in Little Creek, Virginia, with my CB unit, I was assigned as a deck seaman and continued working with watercraft at the waterfront. Then more than four months later on 16 November 1976, I was promoted to Yeoman Petty Officer 3rd Class (E-4), and the Navy reassigned me to the Administrative Department at PHIBCB TWO where I began performing routine office duties. My tasks also included writing business and personal letters, notices, directives, forms, and reports. I had stood Quarterdeck and Sentry watches as a Seaman, and subsequently, Duty Yeoman as a Yeoman 3rd Class.

After my promotion to Yeoman Petty Officer Third Class, I had less than ten months remaining on active duty. At this juncture of my enlistment, the routine office duties of being a Navy yeoman was similar to that of a nine to five civilian clerical job, which gave me more time for recreation and leisure activities. Liberty from my military duties was just what the doctor had ordered. While on base, I made the best and most worthwhile use of the many and varied recreation facilities and opportunities that were available to me. This personal time of leisure also played a vital role in the support of my morale because I had become weary and disappointed in the penny-ante divisions of office politics I encountered in the course of my work as a yeoman.

While on base, I took delight in its excellent library, which contained a collection of interesting books, periodicals, and sometimes films and recorded music for me to read, borrow, or refer to. There were television lounges on base where I would often go to relax and watch TV. Occasionally, I would play various competitive games of pool with my shipmates in the billiards room. Oftentimes, during liberty, a few of us would delight ourselves in playing the sport of bowling at the base bowling alley. In fact, I had so much fun bowling there that I decided to purchase my own personal bowling ball, shoes, gloves, and bag to carry them in, instead of renting.

The base movie theatre called the Little Creek Gator offered reasonably priced tickets and concessions which made it, by far, the most cost-effective theatre to watch the latest blockbuster movies in Little Creek such as *Jaws* and *The Texas Chainsaw Massacre*. The facilities of the Navy Exchange store, Thirty-One Flavors-Baskins Robbins Ice-Cream, and the base grocery store, to name a few, afforded me opportunities to purchase my needs conveniently and at reasonable cost. On my off hours, especially during those hot and humid Virginia summer days, I would take a dip in the base swimming pool. How relaxing and refreshing that was; and I loved to swim anyway.

The base Education Office facility is where I took the Yeoman 3rd Class Petty Officer Correspondence Course. I studied the course independently in preparation for the Yeoman 3rd Class Petty Officer Examination. Shortly after passing it, I was promoted to YN3. My decision to join the US Navy was made in general because I understood they would pay for my college education, and with less than one year remaining of my enlistment, I decided to attend a college preparatory course using the base Education Office. It was my short-term objective to prepare myself for transitioning to civilian life and success in college.

The State of Virginia Community College System facilitated by the Navy Education Office made available a community service program that I attended on-base during the fall quarter 1976.

Having completed satisfactorily the preparatory education program through the Tidewater Community College of the Virginia Community College System, I was awarded an "Award of Completion" on 10 December 1976.

While off-base, I enjoyed my liberty at the Armed Services YMCA. And it was at the YMCA where I learned how to SCUBA dive. SCUBA diving lessons was the most exciting and interesting activity I had ever undertaken at that time. After four weeks of classroom training with pool sessions and a local open-water lake checkout dive, I successfully passed the YMCA SCUBA diving course, and I received my Certified US Divers License. Hooray! I could hardly wait to call my mother and share the good news that her oldest son was a Certified US SCUBA diver. When I told my mother about this venture, she reacted with ambivalent feelings of excitement for the activity, while at the same time afraid of the perils associated with it. Nevertheless, she was proud of this unique accomplishment (SCUBA is the acronym for Self-Contained Underwater Breathing Apparatus).

During the Fourth of July 1976 Bicentennial Holiday weekend, while on liberty, I caught the Greyhound Bus from Norfolk, Virginia, and traveled a short distance northeast to Washington DC for the celebration. The United States Bicentennial was a series of celebrations and observations during the mid-1970s that paid tribute to historical events leading up to the creation of the United States of America as an independent republic. It was a central event in the memory of the American Revolution. The Bicentennial culminated on Sunday, July 4, 1976, with the 200th anniversary of the adoption of the Declaration of Independence. While visiting the DC area on that Fourth of July weekend in 1976, I enjoyed the spectacular fireworks display and hundreds of thousands of other happy faces who emerged on Washington for the festivities.

During the two days I was in Washington DC, I also saw the White House, and I toured many of the amazing national monuments and memorials. I topped off my weekend in DC with a live musical performance starring one of my favorite singer/musicians, Johnny Guitar Watson. He performed his top songs: "A Real Mother for Ya," "Ain't that a Bitch" and "Superman Lover." When my patriotic weekend in Washington DC was over, I returned on the Greyhound Bus to Little Creek, Virginia, for duty.

In addition to having enjoyed all of my liberty benefits while I was on-base or off-base, I also had fun in the company of my shipmate, Theodis Springer, who I called "Springer." He was from Stuart, Florida. It was either at the end of 1976 or the beginning of 1977 while we were stationed at Little Creek, Virginia, that he and I actually became friends. Springer, who had been with Med Cruise 2-76, relieved us (Med Cruise 1-76) from Rota Spain in early July 1976. After he returned to Little Creek from his six-month voyage during December 1976, I noticed immediately that the previously quiet spoken sailor had morphed into a socially out-going Navy SEAL. Before his cruise to the Mediterranean, Springer had successfully completed over a year of hard work and training to become a US Navy SEAL. For his tremendous accomplishment, he was awarded the Special Warfare Operator Naval Rating. Man, I was proud of him!

As a Navy SEAL and Yeoman Third-Class Petty Officer earning good pay, Springer was able to purchase, among many nice things, a new burgundy-colored 1976 Chevy Camaro. During off hours, and throughout the remainder of my enlistment at Little Creek in 1977, Springer and I would continue to enjoy most of the amenities on-base as well as the scenery and places in Virginia off-base. While rolling on the streets of Virginia in his new Chevy Camaro, I saw some stunningly beautiful places to visit like Virginia Beach, Virginia.

Virginia, nicknamed Old Dominion, Mother of Presidents, Mother of States and the Commonwealth, is a state with lots of natural beauty. We also had fun going to musical concerts off-base accompanied by a few of the local girls in the Norfolk area for the enjoyment of music and songs from such entertainers as the Commodores at the Hampton Coliseum in Hampton, Virginia, and Parliament at Norfolk Scope in Norfolk, Virginia. Then suddenly, after waking up one morning in late August 1977, I came to the realization that my enlistment was short; only thirty days from separation of duty on 29 September 1977. Serving my country in the Navy made me truly believe in the old saying that "time flies when you're having fun," and with a slight twist, time flies when you're having goal-motivated fun.

My three years on active duty in the US Navy flew by indeed, and it was one of the best life decisions I had ever made.

My last Report of Enlisted Performance Evaluation was written by Executive Officer W. R. Mitchum, LCDR, USN, and is as follows:

> Yeoman Woodman was assigned to PHIBCB TWO in a sea duty status until 1 May 1977. At that time his billet was converted to shore duty. By Bureau of Naval Personnel/BUPERS direction he is now serving in a neutral duty status. He performs routine typing projects, also typing and filing of route slips. Files messages and types

Plan of the Day. Stands Duty Yeoman watches. Yeoman Woodman continues to perform his tasks in an above average manner, requiring little or no supervision. His appearance is above average with exception of him occasionally having to be reminded about his hair. Yeoman Woodman gets along well with his shipmates. He is an asset to the Navy and is recommended for re-enlistment and advancement.

Hooray! This final written report covering the period 1 February 1977 to 31 July 1977 was just as humbling and encouraging as all of my other ones. And once again, I was over the moon.

32

A Farewell Speech
to My Shipmates

While Personnel Specialists and Navy Yeomans of Amphibious Construction Battalion Two were securing from their assigned duties after a morning of administrative work at the office on 29 September 1977, I was preparing to debark for good. That's right, as a Yeoman, I had served my last administrative duty the day before, and I was separating from the US Navy after three years of dedicated service. During a farewell speech to the Executive Officer LCDR Mitchum, USN, Yeoman Chief Petty Officer Castano, USN, and my shipmates from a humbled heart, I expressed hope and good success in their future endeavors. And I thanked those who I worked with, served with, and those who mentored me while on my tour of duty at PHIBCB TWO. My farewell party courtesy of the Navy was given off-base at a local Pizza Hut in Virginia Beach, Virginia.

Veteran of the Vietnam Era: September 29, 1977
    Veteran of the Vietnam era means "a person who:

> (1)   Served on active duty for a period of more than 180 days, and was discharged or released therefrom with other than a dishonorable discharge, if any part of such active duty occurred:

(i)   In the Republic of Vietnam between February 28, 1961, and May 7, 1975; or

(ii)   Between August 5, 1964, and May 7, 1975, in all other cases; or

(2)   Was discharged or released from active duty for a service-connected disability if any part of such active duty was performed:

(i)   In the Republic of Vietnam between February 28, 1961, and May 7, 1975; or

(ii)   Between August 5, 1964, and May 7, 1975, in all other cases."

Type of Separation

I was released from active duty and transferred to the Naval Reserve on September 29, 1977. It was on this occasion that I became a Veteran of the Vietnam era after three years of service which began on September 30, 1974. The character of my military service was *honorable*. As a service member, I received ratings from good to excellent for my naval service. And by meeting and exceeding the required standards of duty performance and personal conduct and completing my tour of duty, I thereby received an honorable discharge. Getting an honorable discharge meant that as a veteran, I was relieved from having to participate in any military service obligations in the future, though being discharged from the military was not the same as being retired. Also, receiving an honorable was the only discharge that didn't have a negative impact on my veteran benefits. A veteran's discharge from military service can be in one of five categories: Honorable, General, Other than Honorable, Bad Conduct and Dishonorable.

Transitioning from Military to Civilian Life

After my separation from the Navy, I realized that I had to make the most of it. Returning to civilian life was a subtle change; but like most things, planning helped me make the adjustment.

From Despair to Hope, I Survived a Traumatic Motorcycle Accident

After my discharge from the US Navy, I faced a bright future, but nine months later during June of 1978, a motorcycle accident almost took that away from me. And then I began my long journey from despair to hope. Then, when I was just twenty-two years old,

I was living the life of many people that age—planning to move away from home, spending time with friends, and enjoying a bit of a party lifestyle during the discotheque era. That is, until a devastating motorcycle accident changed everything.

I had returned to my home in Inglewood, California, from the Navy and was working full-time as a landscaper under the Federal anti-recessionary CETA program (Comprehensive Employment and Training Act) for the City of Inglewood. Like many veterans on their own after separation from active duty, I would go out drinking and partying with my female friends and occasionally with my childhood friend, Michael Williams.

On one late afternoon, just before evening in June 1978 after dropping off Michael at his home in Windsor Hills, California, who had been riding on the back of my new 750k Honda motorcycle. I started heading toward home. Legally, I wasn't wearing a motorcycle helmet nor boots, and without the constrictions of the protective gear on me, my bike ride along the way home was more enjoyable, exhilarating, and relaxing. But in an instant, everything changed.

While I was traveling at about thirty miles per hour on east-bound 54th Street, I approached the Hyde Park Boulevard inter-section and collided into a middle-aged black woman's car who was making a left turn onto southbound Hyde Park Boulevard. The woman didn't see me approaching the intersection, and not having enough time to avoid her, I pressed on the rear brake with my right foot.

This caused my motorcycle to fishtail, and on impact with her car, I was thrown up in the air on top of her car, then I rolled off the roof of her car and landed hard on my back in the street where my body came to rest. Afterward, I immediately began to check myself for injuries, and everything seemed to be intact until I looked down at my feet (I was wearing a pair of white Adidas sneakers) and observed something terribly wrong. My left foot was in its normal upright position, but my right foot was distortedly, lying flat on the street as though it had been detached from my right leg. I was horri-fied, thinking to myself, *Damn, I've lost my right foot!*

Then suddenly, as I lay on my back in the middle of West 54th Street at South Hyde Park Boulevard in the Windsor Hills section of Los Angeles, I felt my whole body go into a state of shock. When I looked up to the left of me, I observed that the woman who was still sitting in her car had leaned forward with her arms and head on the steering wheel; and then adding to my distress, I saw that she was trembling too.

And having seen me helplessly lying on the street, the woman was moved with compassion, and she quickly exited her car and stood over me to protect me from the oncoming vehicle traffic while we waited for the Los Angeles County paramedics to arrive. During those crucial moments, she was calm but clearly upset about what had just happened; and as minutes were passing by, the onlookers who gathered around me from their nearby homes were shocked by the accident.

The emergency response to my motorcycle accident was swift, which was within five minutes of the occurrence. Both the Los Angeles County Paramedics and the California Highway Patrol (CHP) arrived at the scene and immediately attended to my needs. The paramedics who rendered emergency first aid applied a splint for preventing movement of my right ankle joint, and the CHP officer who arrived in a black and white patrol car, secured the accident scene and took a brief traffic accident report from the witnesses and myself. Finally, I was placed inside the ambulance and whisked away with red flashing warning lights and prolonged sound of the siren to Daniel Freeman Memorial Hospital in Inglewood, California, where I was taken on a gurney into the emergency room for medical attention.

By the time I arrived in the emergency department, the broken bone had caused my right foot and ankle to swell significantly, and I remember still being in shock. While experiencing constant pain, the attending physician told me that when I hurt my foot, the swelling occurred as a result of my blood rushing to the affected area. Despite the seriousness of my injury, Daniel Freeman Hospital could not provide medical treatment because I didn't have medical insurance from my CETA job yet. So they made me feel comfortable until I was picked up and transported by a Los Angeles County ambulance to Los Angeles County USC. Medical Center, formerly named Los Angeles County General in the Boyle Heights neighborhood of Los Angeles, California. When I arrived at USC Medical Center, I found out later that I had sustained an open fracture of the talus bone:

Talus Bone

> The talus is an important bone of the ankle joint that is located between the calcaneus (heel bone) and the fibula and tibia in the lower leg. The shape of the bone is irregular, somewhat comparable to a turtle's hump. The key function of this bone is to form a connection between the leg and the foot so that body weight may be transferred from the ankle to the leg, enabling a person to walk while maintaining balance. The bone also helps in the movements of ankle, and together with the calcaneus it facilitates the movements of the foot. Any injury to this critical bone may hamper the movements of the ankle and foot. A major fracture in the bone can cause serious impediment to a person's ability to walk or stand. Compared to most other bones, the talus is deficient in its supply of oxygenated blood. As a result, it takes a long time to repair following a serious injury.

Talus Fractures

> A talus fracture is a break in one of the bones that forms the ankle. This type of fracture often occurs during a high-energy event, such as car collision or a high velocity fall. 'In my case, a motorcycle collision.' Because the talus is important for ankle movement, a fracture often

results in significant loss of motion and function. In addition, a talus fracture that does not heal properly can lead to serious complications, including chronic pain. For this reason, many talus fractures require surgery.

Open Fracture

> When broken bones break through the skin, they are called open or compound fractures. Open fractures often involve much more damage to the surrounding muscles, tendons and ligaments. In addition, open fractures expose the fracture site to the environment. They have a higher risk for complications and infection and take a longer time to heal.

In June of 1978, I went into emergency surgery for repair of damage. I had screws placed on the right talus. When I woke up from surgery, I was told that everything went great. Then that night, I started to run a fever. The fever continued over the next few days. I was told that was normal, and maybe I was coming down with a cold. On the fourth day of a 103-degree fever, the doctors ordered Tylenol #2 with Codeine every four hours, and the minute the fever went down, they discharged me.

My fevers continued at home. My cast was on for only one week, and within that first week period, I continued to run a fever off and on. The next week, I continued to have extreme pain, swelling, and fevers. During this stage of my ordeal, I fell into a serious state of delirium. Then I was rushed back to the ER at USC. Medical Center by ambulance.

After my arrival, the first thing the emergency room physician did was order X-rays. When we saw the new X-rays, we were all shocked to see a three-inch section of my ankle (talus bone) was gone, and the screws were hanging by a thread. I was then sent for a battery of scans, X-rays, and tests. Afterward, I was told I had osteomyelitis, an infection of the bone which had eaten away at the talus (my ankle bone). Then I grieved over the fact that if there had not been a delay in emergency treatment between hospitals, and if my doctor would have run a simple CBC blood test, and if I had been treated with antibiotics after my initial discharge while I was at home, I believe I would have been fine.

It was at this juncture that the hospital administration asked me if I would be filing a lawsuit against Los Angeles County USC Medical Center for medical malpractice. I said, "If you can save my foot from amputation, then I will not file a lawsuit against the attending physician and hospital for medical malpractice." And I didn't sue them as I still have my former lowly and humbled foot (no prosthesis) in which it came to prominence over my other body members during the decades of attention and care it received and continues to receive up until this day.

A Prayer for Healing (With faith, I prayed this prayer daily and throughout my ordeal)

Lord,
You invite all who are burdened to come to You.
Allow Your healing hand to heal me.
Touch my soul with Your compassion for others.
Touch my heart with Your courage and infinite love for all.
Touch my mind with Your wisdom, that my mouth may always proclaim Your praise.
Teach me to reach out to You in my need, and help me to lead others to You by my example.
Most loving Heart of Jesus, bring me health in body and spirit that I may serve You with all my strength.
Touch gently this life which You have created, now and forever.
Amen.

Osteomyelitis

Osteomyelitis results from infection of the bone by bacteria or fungi. Symptoms noted include pain in the infected part of bone, and swelling or redness over the infected area. Treatments include surgery to remove the infected part of bone and antibiotics.

Symptoms

Osteomyelitis, in some cases, may not present with any signs or symptoms.

The signs and symptoms are sometimes similar to other medical conditions.

- Swelling, warmth, and/or redness over the area of infection
- Pain in the infected part of bone, which worsens with movement
- High fever and/or chills
- Irritability or lethargy, often reported in young children

Treatments

Treatment options for osteomyelitis include surgery to remove the infected bone and antibiotics to control infection.

Medication

- Antibiotics: Generally administered through a vein to kill the bacteria; in severe cases, oral antibiotics may also be prescribed: Penicillin, Amoxicillin, Cefotaxime, Erythromycin

- Antifungals: Drugs prescribed to kill the fungus: Clotrimazole, Econazole, Miconazole, Terbinafine

Self-care

- Complete the entire course of antibiotics prescribed.
- Do not skip your follow-up visits.

Medical procedures

Drainage—Debridement—Bone or tissue grafting—Amputation

Causes

- Osteomyelitis is the result of infection by bacteria or fungi
- Staphylococcus bacterial infection is the most common cause
- Bone infection can develop due to:
  - Bacteria or fungus in the bloodstream
  - Injuries that cause damage to deep tissues
  - Open deep wounds
  - Severe bone fractures
  - Bone surgeries, including bone implants
  - Blocked blood vessels disrupting normal blood circulation
  - Insertion of intravenous (IV) lines or catheters such as dialysis machine tubing and urinary catheters
  - Weakened immune system as in case of cancer treatment

I'd like to reiterate that it all started in June of 1978 when I was twenty-two years old and just nine months after my tour of duty in the Navy. While I was riding a motorcycle on my way home, I was involved in a serious accident. I'll never be able to erase that day from my memory. I still remember every minute detail of what happened afterwards. It was a horrific high velocity impact which almost severed my right foot. Although the impact caused me to sustain a severe compound fracture to my right ankle as it was slammed like a tennis ball and sandwiched between the motorcycle and the car's passenger front door, this occurred moments before I was ejected upwards on top of the roof of the car.

My horrendous ordeal initiated an eight-year long struggle that included twelve surgeries before the nightmare ended when I found, by the grace of God, old-fashioned Orthopedic Surgeon Dr. John Rieder of Los Angeles Orthopedic Hospital in 1986. All of the surgeries throughout those years were painful, arduous, long, and kept me out of a normal life for months at time and would forever hinder my range of motion even to this day. I had to have screws, pins, staples, physical therapy, an ankle brace, the works. And I was told by my initial doctor, Dr. Green, of USC Medical Center in June of 1978 I would be disappointed because the range of motion in my right ankle would never return. He was right, I was disappointed because it never did.

In the beginning and along the way during this most difficult time of my life, hope in God sustained me. But my confidence in the medical profession fell into almost utter despair until I saw Dr. Rieder. I had my first real understanding about Osteomyelitis, which you now know is a potentially life-threatening infection of the bone that is not that well studied by most orthopedic surgeons or at least most of them are unable or unaware of the effective methods of treating Osteomyelitis.

I was given the textbook treatment by the lead orthopedic surgeon, Dr. Green, at Los Angeles County USC Medical Center with the application of IV antibiotics after a surgery that consisted of debridement, some removal of dead ankle bone, and a split-thickness skin graft (STSG) which was unsuccessfully used in an attempt to cover the complex open wound on the inside of my right ankle (it was Dr. Rieder who enlightened me to the heart stopping fact that most Orthopedic Surgeons don't have the slightest clue as to the characteristics of what dead bones look like). But due to the infected bone that was still inside my ankle socket, the split-thickness skin graft didn't take. The doctor told me even after a successful surgery and all the medication that this was not a guarantee that I wouldn't be dealing with this in the future and that I may have to live with this disease for the rest of my life.

After having undergone extensive medical treatment and surgeries for approximately three months (June 1978–September 1978) as an inpatient at Los Angeles County USC Medical Center, it was in September of 1978 that I was transferred to Los Angeles County Rancho Los Amigos National Rehabilitation Center in Downey, California, as an inpatient for an additional three months (September 1978–December 1978) where I received rehabilitation medicine and physical therapy to restore functional abilities and quality of life for my physical impairment and disability that resulted from significant weight loss due to anemia, the dislocation of my right talus, and the subsequent debilitating disease of Osteomyelitis, which also caused a large open wound and chronic drainage from my right ankle with the partial exposure of my talus bone and the atrophied muscles of my lower extremities in both legs.

Five Thousand Dollars ($5,000)!

During my stay as an inpatient at, and prior to my discharge from Rancho Los Amigos National Rehabilitation Center in Downey, California, I was informed by my lawyer who visited me in November of 1978 that he settled my insurance claim against the woman's insurance company. According to eyewitness accounts at the scene of the accident, and the unfavorable California Highway Patrol/CHP collision report, it was determined that she was the cause of the accident. After a short negotiation, my attorney and her insurance company agreed that she was liable for failing to yield while making an unsafe left turn at the intersection. Furthermore, she was found 100 percent liable for my resulting injuries, pain, and suffering, and the medical bills I incurred at both Los Angeles County USC Medical Center and Rancho Los Amigos National Rehabilitation Center for diagnostics, surgeries, medical treatments, rehabilitation, and physical therapy.

When I first interviewed with my attorney who came highly recommended by a female friend, I was told that the driver had only a minimum liability insurance policy which classified her as under-insured. In other words, her insurance policy was insufficient and would only cover a small portion of my medical bills and pain and suffering, which exceeded $100,000, although my attorney suggested that I could sue for her house and personal assets; but I vehemently declined out of compassion and empathy for her who had shown compassion for me as I lay agonizing in the street moments after the accident. So her insurance company went ahead and settled with my attorney for the policy limit of $15,000 and each party entitled to receive payment received an equal distribution of one-third of the policy limit; that is, in spite of my dreadful circumstances, I felt some comfort when I received $5,000 cash which was a considerable sum of money in 1978, and my attorney received $5,000 for legal services rendered, and Los Angeles County USC Medical Center received $5,000 for medical services rendered. The $15,000 insurance payout was completed in exchange for my signature on the release which released the woman from further liability regarding my injuries, pain and suffering, legal fees, and medical bills.

I Thought I Was Falling in Love with My Nurse's Aide, Cheryl

While I was a patient at Rancho Los Amigos, I found myself strongly attracted to my nurse's aide whose name was Cheryl. And the attraction seemed to be mutual. But Cheryl soon realized she could have been heading for a problem. At the beginning of our relationship, she knew it was unethical to enter into any type of romantic relationship with me and that such a relationship could have led to a charge of professional misconduct and even losing her job. But she didn't care about the rules because she would often tell me, "I can't help myself." According to hospital rules, while caring for me, Cheryl was expected at all times to remain within the boundaries of a professional therapeutic relationship.

While the nurse-patient relationship blossomed between Cheryl and myself, it also became an unequal one. Because being a nurse's aide put Cheryl in a position of power while as her patient, I was put in a dependent, vulnerable position. She also had a lot of sensitive personal information about me while, in contrast, I knew very little about her as a person. The main things that concerned me about our relationship was how it was affecting Cheryl's professional judgment. I also felt that since I was vulnerable, our romantic relationship could cause me more harm than good emotionally and physically. However, all of our concerns regarding proper conduct for nurse-patient relationships rapidly evaporated as Cheryl and myself gradually overindulged in sensual pleasures with each other.

After a while, the most important thing I asked myself was whether or not the romantic emotions I felt for Cheryl was the real thing and not just part of the nurse-patient dynamic. I understood that it wasn't uncommon for a patient such as myself to become emotionally attached to my nurse or caregiver. As you know, this was a difficult time for me when I had unfulfilled emotional needs. And then along comes nurse Cheryl, compassionate and caring, who met those needs, and I fell for her. It was comforting to know that our relationship was becoming one based on mutual respect and understanding.

Cheryl, in turn, also had emotional needs. She had been overworked, stressed out, with little time to form meaningful relationships outside of her working life. I found out that when health care providers are burnt out, they are more likely to develop romantic feelings toward a patient. It was true. When I reached out to Cheryl by showing kindness and interest in her as a person, and she, in turn, fell for me. From the start, I believe we were just flirting with each other, but soon our romance became something more than that.

In December 1978, just days before Christmas, I was discharged from Rancho Los Amigos Rehabilitation Center on crutches. At this point in time, I had spent approximately six months in the Los Angeles County Health Care System where I had received all kinds of medical treatment and rehabilitation therapy for the injuries I sustained and for the chronic complications of Osteomyelitis. All of the pain and suffering I endured and would continue to endure for years to come was a consequence of the motorcycle accident which occurred earlier that year in June of 1978. But my feelings and those of Cheryl's had went from merely a crush to the real thing, and this left us with the possibility of starting a personal relationship after I was discharged.

Because of Cheryl's position of power in the health care setting, she left it to me to make the first move in which I did by asking for her telephone number. From her own romantic pursuits, Cheryl knew that I was really interested in continuing our relationship when I contacted her shortly after returning home to my normal life. From then on, Cheryl and I dated almost a half a year. During this time, we flew to Las Vegas, Nevada, where we spent a weekend of nonstop amusement. However, it was shortly after the Vegas trip when our heart lights went out and the romantic interlude between us came to an abrupt end; and then we departed ways never to see each other again. Eventually, I got over the pain of missing Cheryl, and by faith in God and hope in Jesus, I moved on as a newly disabled person walking down the narrow path of life with the aid of a cane and antiquated ankle shoe brace and analgesic medications.

The Agony I Suffered Seemed Like Eternity

Every doctor (most of them practiced at USC Medical Center), with the exception of Dr. Rieder (who practiced at LA Orthopedic Hospital), I had ever seen (and there were many) boasted a lot of "Maybes" and "It's very complicated" and "We're not sure it is all gone," leaving me with a deflated spirit and a feeling of hopelessness that led to great pangs of sadness and deep depression. I mean, what could I do? This was completely out of my control, and here were those so-called "experts" doing a lot of shrugging and shaking of the head, giving me no straight answers whatsoever and leaving me throwing my hands up and with an overall dead feeling inside. I was an athlete. I played all kinds of sports, activities, and I swam, danced, and more…

My foot was vital to me. The idea of my quality of life changing or even being altered somewhat was a feverish denial which led to much denial. When I noticed the familiar signs in 1978, I felt my soul had been cut in half. I had every nightmarish thought parading through my mind you could imagine. I thought to myself, *This is it. I am going to lose my foot.* It was pure unadulterated dread. I was looking forward to attending college, enjoying my life, and *bam!* There it was! The all too familiar pus-filled abscess or boil on my ankle. My world came to a screeching halt.

The first thing I did after all of the initial horror and shock dwindled was return to the leading Orthopedic Surgeon, Dr. Green, at LA County USC Medical Center who did the procedure several months earlier in June 1978. He ran some blood tests, took a culture from the abscess, and ordered an MRI. Everything came out positive. The MRI revealed the presence of Osteomyelitis. The doctor said to me, "It's a large abscess worthy of great concern."

I felt momentarily stunned that this was happening to me. The abscess persisted. The drainage was continual. Then I saw the Chief Orthopedic Surgeon, Dr. Patzakis, who was Dr. Green's boss, and he offered me no reprieve. He informed me that the Osteomyelitis doesn't always reveal itself in scans, tests, and cultures (which was confirmed by Dr. Rieder). He said that this was something the medical field hadn't found a cure for and that I "may" have to accept the fact that Osteomyelitis would be a constant in my life forever.

I felt absolute devastation. And even though this Chief Orthopedic Surgeon, Dr. Patzakis, wasn't any more hopeful than his lead Orthopedic Surgeon, Dr. Green, I went ahead with the split-thickness skin graft surgery to save my right foot from amputation. While I slipped into feelings of hopelessness and despair, I thought I had no other option. Supposedly, the surgery was a two-fold successful and unsuccessful one. On the one hand, most of the infected bone from my right ankle had been removed; however, on the other hand, the split-thickness skin graft didn't take, and my right foot was left with the problem of a large, gaping, deep open wound, which exposed the left side of my talus (ankle bone).

At this juncture, I was bitterly disappointed and very discouraged after Dr. Green informed me about the outcome of the surgery. He said the right ankle, unfortunately, didn't look good because of the large open sore and infected bone that remained, and it was indeed horrendous. This first surgical campaign to save my foot was a terrible fiasco.

After many side effects from the medication, which later resulted in me acquiring Clostridium difficile, otherwise known as C diff, a major gastrointestinal virus, I was lost at sea at that point. I felt about as hopeless as could be fathomed. I had resigned myself to the fate that every doctor had prescribed to me. I knew then that I would be living with Osteomyelitis for the rest of my life, if it didn't kill me at first or make me lose my foot. All my doctors at the time scratched their heads, offering me nothing more than the words, "I told you so." Nobody could talk to me. I was mad, I was frustrated, but most of all, I felt lifeless, done for. I didn't sleep at all. My mind constantly hovered over all the year's past events, and the surgeries and all the questions, frustrations, and "what ifs" blazed through my head with ceaseless repetition.

33

Hope Was on the Horizon (My Final Battle Against Osteomyelitis)

As I was moving forward, Los Angeles County USC Medical Center required me to return to the outpatient clinic time and time again for the next two years (1979–1980). This is where I would receive continuous bone debridement, drainage, and occasionally, skin and tissue grafting treatments for my chronic Osteomyelitis. For me, the future looked pretty grim because at some of my outpatient visits the treating Orthopedic Surgeon recommended amputation of my right foot as an alternative medical procedure to rid me of the Osteomyelitis; and not only did I face the prospect of limb removal but also loss of my life. It was during one of my visits at the outpatient clinic in late 1980 when my future soulmate, Stacie, accompanied me. After she witnessed the mayhem I had often encountered with the doctors at the clinic (especially when they suggested amputation of my foot), she said, "I don't know you very well, but because I care about you, I strongly urge you to go get a second opinion elsewhere."

By then, I had been receiving Medicare Health Insurance Benefits from the Social Security Administration, which entitled me to all medical services from any hospital or healthcare professional of my choice, including pharmacy services. Meanwhile, my little sister, Leslie, who was doing RN training at Los Angeles Orthopedic Hospital, recommended that I seek a second medical opinion from them; and so I did.

Leslie encouraged me that Los Angeles Orthopedic Hospital provided outstanding care for patients with musculoskeletal disorders, and I later found out that the hospital was dedicated to Osteomyelitis and that the treatment seemed very different than what Los Angeles County USC Medical Center had provided to me, although I will admit that I was very skeptical because my confidence in the world of doctors and medicine at this juncture had been completely desecrated. After praying and some encouragement from my girlfriend, Stacie, I finally got into my VW Super Beetle and drove to the downtown area of Los Angeles at Hope Street and Adams Boulevard where the Orthopedic Hospital was located. That was when I met Dr. John Rieder, an old-fashioned Orthopedic Surgeon who believed in not giving up (preservation of life and limb), and he changed my life forever.

When he took one look at the X-rays and MRI and discussed what he saw, it was startling to hear what he had to say. He saw exactly where the infection was, where the dead bone was that needed to be removed, and he didn't advocate IV antibiotics or anything else.

Dr. Rieder was confident and composed and took time to explain everything to me. He even gave me a percentage number for success outcome. He spoke of a method that just seemed to make sense, a method that included applying antibiotics directly to the source, rather than a systemic application, i.e., IV antibiotics. I saw him for a full hour, and I felt that in that hour, I was illuminated to my condition more than I was for the previous years of doctors, scans, hospital stays, outpatient clinics, and surgeries combined. After my interview with Dr. Rieder, I found that he was the foremost surgeon for musculoskeletal bone infection at Los Angeles Orthopedic Hospital and perhaps in the entire nation. I also found that he had written numerous publications specifically regarding treatment and application for Osteomyelitis and even pioneered a classification system for assessing different types of Osteomyelitis that was used by many doctors and had become an industry standard.

Fast-forward eight years later during the winter of 1986, just before I underwent my twelfth and final surgery in the battle against Osteomyelitis, I came in contact with some of Dr. Rieder's former patients who were still inpatients at Orthopedic Hospital, and they all had similar stories to mine (most of them had severe cases of bone infection, facing prospects of limb removal and loss of life) and they absolutely raved about Dr. John Rieder being the one doctor in their world that cured them from this mysterious and dreadful bone disease. I even met one patient who told me of how she went to more than two dozen different orthopedic doctors and didn't feel better until she had surgery with Dr. Rieder.

My eyes perked up, and my heart felt less heavy. I felt deep in my bones that I had finally found my doctor, and that this was the orthopedic specialist I needed who was a godsend to me. The thing that distinguished Dr. Rieder from all other doctors was that he was first and foremost a researcher. He had worked with cancer, researching bone tumors and removal, and his medical specialty was bone infection, specifically Osteomyelitis. So unlike most Orthopedic doctors, who worked on multiple cases every day, performing more than seven surgeries a day, on innumerable fractures, limbs and bones, Dr. Rieder's case load was specific, and he usually executed not more than one surgery a day; very rarely would he ever do more than one.

Another aspect that was great about Dr. Rieder was that he was straightforward. In the initial visit, and every subsequent visit after that, he never wavered, teetered, or went back on an assessment or evaluation. He was precise, methodical, and explained exactly what he was going to do and how he was going to do it. I liked that. It was refreshing relief to hear a doctor who was sure of what he was doing. Dr. Rieder oozed self-confidence and didn't shy away from making emphatic statements. He told me precisely the success rate and handed me a percentage point, and I was sold right there and then.

Since the final surgery that ended my battle with a victory over Osteomyelitis in 1986, I have had no flare ups but only occasional swelling and minor discomfort, which has continued to this day. And given the difficult nature of the circumstances, my right foot has never felt better. After that victorious and miraculous day, I felt like I had put to rest a long-time foe (twelve battles of surgeries in an eight-year war against Osteomyelitis), and I felt like my life had been handed back to me on a golden platter. I couldn't have been happier with the result. I'm blessed by God in the Spirit through faith, enjoying good health as all is going well with me, even as my soul is getting along well too.

In summary, I sustained an open fracture of the talus, a compound fracture to the hill bone in my right foot as a result of a motorcycle accident in June 1978. It was a very serious injury that turned my life upside down, so serious and complicated with a mysterious and horrendous bone infection (Osteomyelitis) that the orthopedic surgeons at Los Angeles County and USC Medical Center (where I faithfully laid in a hospital bed for three months, June–September 1978; both of my legs were plastered in a full-leg cast connected together with a metal rod to facilitate a split-thickness skin graft) recommended amputation of my right foot just above the ankle.

Man! In silence throughout this entire ordeal, I prayed and wept continuously for the Lord's promise of mercy.

> My grace is sufficient for you, for My strength is made perfect in weakness. (2 Corinthians 12:9 NKJV)

The Lord's never-ending promise of mercy has brought me abundant life, and after eight years and twelve surgeries later to this day, I still have the limited use of my right foot—no prothesis. Although I walk with a limp and I'm not able to run anymore, I am alive and well, and I can still walk and dance. For my life as it is, I give all the glory to him, Jesus Christ.

Also, I thank God for the care I received from Dr. John Rieder, a brilliant, old-fashioned orthopedic specialist who gave me hope in his belief of never giving up.

My Life as I Knew It Was Changed Forever Here on Earth

Adjusting to my life with a new disability wasn't ever easy, but thank God there were ways to help myself cope with limitations, overcome challenges, and build a rewarding life.

Disability defined: a physical or mental condition that limits a person's movements, senses, or activities.

My disability defined: I sustained a complete open dislocation of the talus as a consequence of a traumatic motorcycle accident. The talus was completely disconnected from my foot ("missing talus") and loosely connected to some soft tissue. As a result of my injury, I suffered for many years with a long-term bone infection (Osteomyelitis), which caused wound healing problems; also, I sustained serious bone tissue decay and collapse (Avascular necrosis of the talus), and I still suffer with occasional minor swelling and pain of the right ankle and permanent limitation of motion at the right ankle and subtalar joints.

Development of arthrosis (limited motion in the surrounding joints) has caused me to have long-term pain and disability; consequently, I am unable to run, hop, stand on my toes or sometimes maintain my balance while standing upright. The muscle thickness graft which was surgically taken from my left calf muscle (the donor site) to save my right foot from amputation resulted in atrophy and severe disfigurement of both my left calf and right foot. Psychologically, the scarring and disfigurement of my legs and right foot has significantly compounded, changed, and limited my activities and quality of life because I can never again wear shorts in public nor swim trunks for beach swimming, lake swimming, pool swimming, and scuba diving.

My PTSD

PTSD is short for post-traumatic stress disorder. PTSD is "a psychological reaction occurring after experiencing a highly stressing event (such as wartime combat, physical violence, or a natural disaster) that is usually characterized by depression, anxiety, flashbacks, recurrent nightmares, and avoidance of reminders of the event." After having experienced this shocking, scary, and dangerous motorcycle accident, which resulted in a compound fracture to my right ankle followed with the likelihood of amputation or removal of my right foot that hovered over me during those eight years (1978–1986) of pain, suffering, despair, and uncertainty; in consequence, I became vulnerable to and developed post-traumatic stress disorder (PTSD).

Making the adjustment to life with a new disability was a very difficult transition. Prior to my motorcycle accident, I tended to take my health for granted until it was gone. Then, the all too easy temptation to obsess over what I had lost began to attack me. But while I couldn't go back in time to healthier me or wish away my limitations, I did change the way I thought about and coped with my disability. I was still in control of my life! And I believed there were many ways I could improve my independence, sense of empowerment, and outlook. When I had to face difficult situations, disappointments, and tough times growing up, I remember my grandmother, Needie, who always encouraged me by saying, "Davion, rise above your circumstances and put mind over matter." Therefore, despite my disability, I understood it was entirely possible to overcome the challenges I faced while I enjoyed a full and fulfilling life.

It goes without saying that most of us expect to live long, healthy lives. So when I was hit by this disabling injury, it triggered a range of unsettling emotions and fears in me. I wondered how I'd be able to work, find or keep a relationship, or even be happy again. But while living with my new disability wasn't easy, it neither was a tragedy. And I wasn't alone. Millions of people had traveled that road before me (the CDC estimates that one in five Americans are disabled) and found ways to not just survive but thrive. I did too.

Learning to accept my disability was incredibly difficult, but I forced myself to come to terms with the fact that I was physically disabled, although acceptance felt like giving in—throwing in the towel on life and my future. But I also understood that if I refused to accept the reality of my limitations, this refusal or denial would keep me stuck and there wouldn't be any progress. It would prevent me from moving forward, making the changes I needed to make, and finding new goals.

Before I began my newly disabled journey and accepted my disability, I first needed to give myself time to mourn. I had suffered a major loss. And it wasn't just the loss of my healthy, unlimited body, but it was the loss of some of my employment plans for the future. Shortly after my discharge from the Navy and prior to my motorcycle accident, I had applied for and successfully passed a series of civil service examinations in which I was placed on the top of each of their waiting list because of my high examination scores and Veteran's Employment Preference Points. The civil service employment opportunities were with the US Postal Service, Los Angeles County/City Fire Department, Los Angeles County Sheriff's Department, Los Angeles Police Department, Los Angeles County Probation Department, etcetera. Yes, indeed! I was greatly saddened by the loss of those job opportunities.

I tried not to ignore or suppress my feelings. Naturally, it's only human that I wanted to avoid my pain. But just like you don't get over an injury by ignoring it, I knew I couldn't work through my grief without allowing myself to feel it and actively deal with it. So I often allowed myself on the onset and throughout my ordeal to fully experience my feelings. And I frequently did this without judgment.

I went through a roller coaster of emotions from anger and sadness to disbelief, although it was my understanding that this was perfectly normal. And like a roller coaster, the experience was unpredictable and full of ups and downs. But I just trusted that with time, the lows would become less intense, and I would begin to find my new normal. Best of all, when I needed it, I found my comfort and emotional support in 2 Corinthians 12:9–10 NKJV of the Bible where it is written:

> And He said to me, "My grace is sufficient for you, for My strength is made perfect in weakness." Therefore most gladly I will rather boast in my infirmities, that the power of Christ may rest upon me. Therefore I take pleasure in infirmities, in reproaches, in needs, in persecutions, in distresses, for Christ's sake. For when I am weak, then I am strong.

I didn't put on happy faces. Learning to live with my disability wasn't easy. I had many bad days, which didn't mean I wasn't brave or strong. And I resisted the pretense that I was okay when I wasn't, which didn't help me or anyone else, least of all my family and friends. So I usually let the people I trusted in on how I really felt. It certainly helped both them and me. Coming to terms with my new reality made it healthy for me to grieve the life I had lost, but I also realized that it wasn't healthy for me to continue looking back and wishing for a return to my pre-disability "normal." As tough as it was, I gradually let go of the past and accepted where I was.

I was happy, even with my broken right foot and severe disfigurement. It didn't seem like it then, but the truth is that I was able to rebuild a happy, meaningful life for myself by my faith in Jesus Christ. Even though I walk with a limp, can't run, nor wear shorts in public anymore, I'm nevertheless joyful and thankful to God for his continuous blessings, who had mercy on me and who spared my life. I'm also just as thankful to the Holy Spirit who helped me search out inspiring stories of people with disabilities who were thriving and living lives they loved. I'm blessed to have learned from others who had gone before me and their successes, which helped me stay motivated during those tough times.

In the beginning of my ordeal, I decided I wasn't going to dwell on what I could no longer do. My Godly wisdom helped me steer clear of spending lots of time thinking about the things my disability had taken from me. This also helped me avoid the surefire recipe of depression. Instead, I mourned my losses and put those issues aside, then continuously moved on. Faith helped me focus on what I could do and what I hoped to do in the future. This gave me something to look forward to.

What also helped me during those tough times in my life was learning as much as possible about my disability. While obsessing over negative medical information was counterproductive, I found it more important to understand what I was facing. Throughout my ordeal, I consistently and persistently asked the doctors who were medically treating or caring for me during my visits, "What was my diagnosis? What were the typical progression or common complications?" Knowing what was going on with my body and what I could expect helped me to prepare myself and adjust to it more quickly.

As I moved forward not accepting the calamities of my life to break me, I found ways to minimize my disability's impact on my life. It was self-evident that my disability had already changed my life in big ways. And it wouldn't help me to live in denial about that. I had limitations that made things more difficult. But with my commitment, creativity, and a willingness to do things differently, I reduced the impact that my disability was having on my life.

Jesus Christ is my High Priest and Advocate, but here on earth, I had to become my own advocate. With the help of the Holy Spirit, I have been my own best advocate as I have negotiated the challenges of life with a disability, including when I was a college student, when I worked, and in the health care system. Knowledge is power, so I've educated myself about my rights and the resources available to me. As I took charge at the onset of my disability, I began to feel less helpless and less dependent. Since then, I've gained total spiritual and financial independence and I feel greatly empowered.

I took advantage of the things I could do. While I wasn't able to change my disability, I could and I did reduce its impact on my daily life by seeking out and embracing adaptive technologies and tools that were available. In the beginning of my recovery during 1978–1979, I needed and I used wheelchairs, crutches, canes, and an antiquated artificial shoe brace device for my broken right foot which was provided to me by a Certified Orthotist of Los Angeles County USC Medical Center. The ankle brace gave my right ankle more support so that I was less likely to twist, roll, or even reinjure it. Afterward, and throughout the years to this day, I've depended vitally on the VA Healthcare System's Orthotic and Prosthetic services at Loma Linda, California, which has provided me with Rocker Bottom Orthopedic Shoes for the care of my foot, and most importantly, the shoes have helped me to maximize support and stability while I walk and stand.

During my quarterly visits at the VA Podiatry Clinic, I've also received ongoing healthcare services and maintenance for my badly injured right foot. Currently, I am living in northeast Tennessee where I continue to receive these same vital services from the James H. Quillen VA Health Care System at Mountain Home, Tennessee. All of these adaptive technologies and tools I've needed and used since the onset of my disability has helped to make my life easier. However, during this journey of faith, I've had to let go of shame and any embarrassment or fear of stigma because I realized I'm not defined by the aides I use.

Acting out of hope, I patiently set for myself realistic goals. My disability forced me to learn new skills and strategies. I also had to relearn simple things I used to take for granted like learning to walk again without limping. It was a frustrating process, and I found it only natural that I wanted to rush things and get back to functioning as quickly as possible. But it was more important, however, that I stayed realistic. So I avoided the pitfall of setting overly aggressive goals which could have actually led to setbacks and discouragement. "Davion, you'll bounce back" or "Davion, be patient with yourself. Rome wasn't built in a day," my mother used to say. And so every small step I took forward counted. Eventually, and more often than not, I would get to where I needed to be. Hooray!

Throughout my journey, I have asked for (and accepted) help and support. While struggling with my disability, many times, I had felt completely misunderstood and alone. On those occasions, I was almost always tempted to withdraw from others and isolate myself. But instead of withdrawing, I stayed connected to them. And it made a world of difference in my mood and outlook.

Regarding interpersonal relations, I found it necessary to nurture the important relationships in my life. Then, more than ever before, staying connected was important. Spending time with my family and friends helped me stay positive, healthy, and hopeful. Sometimes, I needed a shoulder to cry on or someone to vent to, and who better than my mom and my grandmother, Needie, who both were always there for me. But I didn't discount the importance of setting aside my disability from time to time and simply having fun.

I considered even joining a disability support group until I met the love of my life and soulmate, Stacie, who happened to be a Special Education Teacher for the mild to moderate special education student. She's exactly what I needed for my support as I continued on my journey as a newly physical disabled twenty-four-year-old young man. Stacie's large family and friends also warmly welcomed me into their lives with understanding, compassion, love, and support. This was good enough for me. But still, I believed that for many of those who were not as fortunate as myself to have had the support of a girlfriend or boyfriend as I was blessed to have, then one of the best ways to combat their loneliness and isolation was to participate in a support group for people dealing with similar challenges.

I understood that by participating in these groups, you quickly realize you're not alone. They say just that realization goes a long way. And you benefit from the collective wisdom of the group. However, knowing that if I ever needed it, the support of a group would have been a great place to share my struggles, solutions, and encouragement.

I also understood that accepting help didn't make me weak. In fact, it made me stronger, especially if my refusal to seek out needed assistance would have delayed my progress or made me worse, either physically or emotionally. So when I sought help, I let go of the fear that asking for support would inspire pity. I allowed the people who cared about me to pitch in. Not only did I benefit, but it made them feel better too!

In the beginning, while I was in the hospital at Los Angeles County USC Medical Center (August 1978), I didn't at all consider talking to anyone in the mental health profession until the hospital provided me with that service. I recall that I was restricted to my hospital bed one sunny morning with both legs encased in a long leg-plastered cast (from above my ankles to my thighs) when this young and pretty social worker, who was also a psychologist, came to visit me at my bedside. She was very helpful to talk to about what I was going through which made a huge difference. It was at a crucial time because my loved ones weren't providing me with any support in that way, so talking to this lovely psychologist was a godsend. She helped me process the changes I was facing, work through my grief, and reframed my outlook in a more positive, realistic way. Moreover, and most significantly, she helped me qualify for and subsequently I was awarded Social Security Disability Benefits and Medicare Health Benefits!

For many people who are newly disabled, finding things to do that give them meaning and purpose can be a daunting task. As I know too well, my disability had temporarily taken away many aspects of my identity, leaving me questioning who I was, what my value was, and where I fit in society. It was easy feeling useless and empty, especially when I became aware of the fact that I couldn't do the same work or activities as I had done before. But blessedly, there were three important things dear to me that I knew would make me feel good about myself. I had felt a yearning for making my confirmation in the Catholic Church, receiving my GI Bill educational benefits to attend college, and earning my college degrees.

The three foregoing things I listed in the previous paragraph gave me a renewed sense of meaning and purpose. One year and eight months after my motorcycle accident, I was freed from sin on the twenty-ninth day of February 1980 when I received the Holy Sacrament of Confirmation in Saint Eugene Church. I believed on that day, God sent his Holy Spirit upon me to be my helper and guide. He gave me the spirit of wisdom and understanding, the spirit of right judgment and courage, the spirit of knowledge and love, the spirit of reverence in his Service. With God's ultimate peace in my heart, I received the seal of the Holy Spirit, the gift of the Father.

Three years after my motorcycle accident, Los Angeles City College congratulated me on completing my studies for my college degree. The Los Angeles Community College District Board of Trustees on the recommendation of the Los Angeles City College Faculty conferred upon me the degree of associate in arts. My college degree was given to me at Los Angeles, California, on the twenty-first day of June 1981. Six and a half years later, after my motorcycle accident, the Trustees of the California State University on recommendation of the faculty of California State University, Los Angeles, conferred upon me the degree of bachelor of science in business administration with the rights and privileges pertaining thereto. My college degree was given to me on the eighth day of December 1984. And eighteen years after my motorcycle accident, I was congratulated on completing my studies for my University of Phoenix degree. The University of Phoenix, upon the recommendation of the faculty, conferred on me the degree of master of business administration with all the rights, honors, and privileges thereunto appertaining. In witness whereof, the seal of the university and the signature as authorized by the board of directors, University of Phoenix, are hereunto affixed this thirty-first day of March, 1996. With humility and praise, I gave the glory of my educational achievements to the Lord who, in turn, shared his deserving glory with me.

34

I Met the Love of My Life Inside the Speakeasy Social Club

Two years after my traumatic motorcycle accident, I met the love of my life inside the Speakeasy Social Club, which was then a popular nightclub at Hollywood, California. We met on a Friday night, July 5, 1980. Soon after we became acquainted, I realized that our meeting was providentially arranged by God. To my delight, I had found a girlfriend in whom I also found the best friend I had always desired. I thank Christ for revealing her to me. My faith in him blessed me with the one thing I had longed for but never had until forty years ago, and it was love for this woman.

For most of my life, I had hoped to meet a beautiful young woman, fall in love, and get married. Along the way, I had been preparing myself for this to happen by fearing God, attaining understanding, and developing good character. My desire was to be desired by a beautiful young woman. The more I grew in God's Word and my faith in Jesus, the more I received that blessing, the blessing of being enough. I also had hoped for a beautiful young woman who was seeking to fall in love with me as well.

I felt gratitude, not just toward the important people in my life and for my increasingly good health and blessings. But I regained my self-esteem, and I began to thank myself for being me, which was most important. I appreciated myself more, valued myself more, and this brought about the realization that I deserved nothing but the best. And that's how I found her, the best friend, the best girlfriend I could've asked for. Her name is Stacie. The first time I saw her, she was standing next to the counter at the bar inside the social club, and she was wearing a pretty red, white, and blue dress with a pattern of sailboats. She attracted me with her pleasant look and beautifully arranged long shag hairstyle. However, as I walked toward her, I observed from her facial expression that she was disappointed as I was in the entire dating scene. So to cheer her up, I made a contrarily corny statement, complimenting her, and I said, "You have a nice smile."

That made her smile, and she said to me, "You sure are cute!"

Our friendly exchange broke the ice for the both of us, and we hit it off.

When I met her, I had just completed two semesters of study at Los Angeles City College, and I was enrolled in the summer school session where I was taking a Western Civilizations course. On the other hand, Stacie's status was much more impressive than mine because she had completed her studies in the prior year at California State University Los Angeles and received the degree of bachelor of arts in liberal studies. She also had just completed her training for and received her California Special Education Teaching Life Credential and Multiple Subjects Teaching Life Credential. Additionally, she had already signed a contract with Pomona Unified School District to teach elementary school, special education, first-grade through sixth-grade during the 1980 to 1981 school year. Wow. She amazed me to have accomplished so much at the young age of twenty-three.

Stacie has become such a tremendous part of my life now that I actually call myself blessed. Before her, I had never been in a mature and loving relationship with a female. Although I had come close and had girls who fancied me and had girls who I fancied, none of them made the cut. For the most part, I struggled with my fear of loss, shyness, and not being enough for the girls I liked. Nevertheless, it seems like most girls have been attracted to me since my childhood. This difficulty of mine with girls happened before I really understood and applied God's Word. Thus, I resisted, avoided, and departed from making this mistake with Stacie.

The first time I met her, I knew she was it. I just had this crazy feeling, an intense feeling that I couldn't seem to shake off. I was meeting her for the first time, but there was also something very familiar about her. She initiated the conversation, she flirted in that forward but subtle way that I found attractive, especially when she said to me, "You sure are cute!" She smiled, then I asked her for her telephone number. Her womanly charm won over my fear and doubt, and I found myself trusting her enough to accept her offer to meet again at her parents' home for Mexican food while perhaps watching a scheduled episode of SNL on television. That's all it took.

Looking back now, I had always hoped for a friendship between me and my "perfect partner." It is that friendship that I found with Stacie. She's literally the personified version of all my dreams. She has been an extremely positive influence in my life, again a trait I had hoped for in my dream girl. She encourages me, supports me in every one of my decisions, and pushes me to my best potential, both personally and professionally.

This is what my faith in Jesus Christ manifested for me, my best friend, my girlfriend, and now my wife. And I give him the glory. Stacie is flawed, just like every other human being, but the one thing I love about her is her ability to look past my flaws. It is because of her that every single love song ever written makes absolute sense to me. I don't think I've stopped smiling since the day I met her, and I don't think that now I ever will. Out of all the wonderful things life has given me, she takes number one position. She reinstated my belief in love and passion.

Our Friendship Soon Blossomed into a Deepening Romance

While I was living with my mother at Inglewood, California, I began dating Stacie from Pasadena, California, on July 6, 1980. She's the beauty I met the night before inside the Speakeasy Social Club at Hollywood, California. After a few dates, our friendship soon blossomed into a deepening romance. This overjoyed me because up to the time that we met, I had longed for an exciting, meaningful, and mature friendship with an attractive woman. Thus, our friendship had been the beginning of a deepening romantic relationship.

I knew when I first met Stacie that we were both attracted to one another and we both were available for dating. We became good friends. There was lots of laughter between us, and the banter helped with the days away from each other go faster until we were together again. I missed her like crazy. During the week, we had long nightly conversations on the telephone. She and I had so much in common but didn't always see eye to eye, which made for some good great debates and revelations.

At some point along the way, Stacie and I grew closer, and our friendship grew stronger. Four years into knowing each other, we had been intimate until we decided to become chaste for religious reasons. Shortly afterward, we were engaged. It was a mind-blowing moment when this woman who I already loved and respected became my lover; and we fell in love. But true friendship was the bedrock of our love, and ultimately, it was what sustained us.

Friendship was the solid foundation for our successful romantic relationship. After the giddy rush of chemicals that flooded our bodies during our "new love" subsided to more normal levels, friendship was our anchor. When we faced difficulties as a couple, the respect and trust of our friendship helped carry us through it. I constantly thought about what our friendship meant to us. With Stacie, our relationship included, most importantly, a common bond that we shared as members of the Roman Catholic religion (a denomination of the Christian faith), and we both grew up in similar Catholic families. We attended Sunday Mass together on a regular basis.

Just as my mother had done, Stacie completed twelve years of Catholic school, which was icing on the cake for me and our relationship. She attended Catholic schools from grades one through eight at Sacred Heart in Altadena, California, and grades nine through twelve at Saint Andrews, an all-girl Catholic high school in Pasadena, California. This is where we would ultimately receive the Sacrament of Marriage (or Holy Matrimony) in the adjoining church building.

Her Catholic childhood memories were filled with songs, prayers, religious lessons, countless true stories about God, Jesus, the Holy Spirit; and when it was time for her First Holy Communion, she remembers having to have learned the Ten Commandments, the Sacraments, etcetera.

Stacie's high school was located right next to the adjoining church where she remembers having to have gone once a week during schooldays or, at times, every day.

I had my epiphany experience of belief in God when at seven, I made my First Confession and subsequently my First Holy Communion. My epiphany experience in God kept me on the narrow path of righteousness as I attended Catholic schools from grades one through three: first-grade at Holy Spirit Catholic School, second-grade through third-grade at Saint Agatha School, including public schools, and beyond. The Catholic parishes and schools Stacie and I attended as children of God were all part of the Roman Catholic Archdiocese of Los Angeles, California. While devout Catholics, we learned and believed that the Roman Catholic Religion was the true religion. Catholicism also played a significant role in helping me remain chaste and drug-free through high school.

Even though our lists of "best things ever" were not identical, we had shared interests or common ground between us from favorite restaurants to movies. I recall that we went on our first date as a double date with her older sister, Trena, and her husband, Frank Spurlock, who drove a nice-looking BMW. When in early July 1980, soon after Stacie and I had first met at the Speakeasy, we saw the hit movie in Hollywood, California, called *The Blue Lagoon*. The setting was in the Victorian period. Two children, Brooke Shields and Christopher Atkins, were shipwrecked on a tropical island in the South Pacific. With no adults to guide them, the two made a simple life together, unaware that sexual maturity would eventually intervene. The movie was as enjoyable as we had expected. The entertainment was followed by a tasty fried chicken and fried catfish soul food meal in which we finished it with a delicious hot peach cobbler a la mode. The name of the restaurant, South Town, was located on Gower Street just north of Sunset Boulevard and south of Hollywood Boulevard in Hollywood, California. Although we had double-dated with her sister and brother-in-law, our first date was superb.

It felt good when we were together. I thought about the happy hours just "being" with her. Going to the beach, relaxing at the park, strolling through the shops at the mall on a Saturday afternoon, or just going for a walk at the Pasadena Rose Bowl and Country Club together. Having had a friend like her made me happy. But she made me feel especially happy when I got to spend time with her.

The ability and desire to share my secrets, fears, hopes, and dreams with Stacie was the real test. She passed with flying colors. Her wisdom and understanding allowed me to blab all the deep stuff and the hopeful stuff and the scary stuff to her because she proved herself to be a true friend. We were very closely connected in our trust for each other. This relationship between us was, by definition, a friendship indeed. We felt safe with one another. And so were our secrets.

We supported one another through thick and thin. As friends, she had my back, and I had her back. This was a good thing for our loving relationship. Tell it like it is. Kindly. That's what we counted on our friendship for. We also understood that if there was even a sliver of dishonesty between us, there was a problem. We admired and respected each other, which made for good friend status. The equilibrium we established in our playing field was comforting to both of us. The mutual respect between us allowed us to operate as equals. And the bond of our friendship secured the loyalty which successfully navigated our romance as well.

Consistent and meaningful conversations brought momentum to our relationship. The respect, honesty, trust, and the ability we both had in sharing our common interests all meant that there was nothing superficial about our new friendship. Fun-time was being silly together and giggling like fools while we told stories and joked with one another. This included watching *Saturday Night Live* (SNL) and dumb movies on television and eating tacos during my visits at her house in Pasadena. But we also had deep, long talks about things that mattered profoundly to both of us. Those connecting conversations were (ultimately) more sustaining than physical intimacy (but after our nuptial, physical intimacy was really important!).

So all of the above was true of our friendship, and we both understood then that there was no better foundation for our romance or our truly successful love relationship than our true friendship. I'm forever thankful to God for all the benefits of friendship I received from him. Because the honeymoon stage in our relationship was fleeting, we had the stability of our friendship to sustain us into our future. Not only did we love each other, but we liked each other too, which was huge. And we knew this going in. By God's grace, we also shunned what many couples go through in a new relationship; that is, when "new" love/lust get in the way early on, they may not learn until too late that they really didn't like each other.

Sexual attraction wasn't enough for our meaningful long-term relationship. It was very important, but without the connection of emotional intimacy and the ability to form a true attachment, physical intimacy was ultimately unfulfilling. Being that our relationship was already established on a basis of compatibility, lots of stuff got worked out because we both were simpatico. Love is not necessarily "logical," but our friendship was in place, and this made our love relationship more grounded and stable, and we were given the ability to address any issue(s) that arose with rationality (well, at least some). Thus, we resolved many issues that affected us because we placed a high value on our relationship.

When a romantic relationship is new, without the foundation of friendship, it is vulnerable because issues arise and couples don't always have the motivation to do what is needed. Thinking about it, I wasn't always in agreement with my family or friends, but I valued the relationships enough to be open to their point of view and learned from that knowledge or compromise for the greater good. I thought no less of them just because I disagreed because we had respect for one another. Having had this outlook in romance, my relationship with Stacie weathered more of the challenges that came our way.

I went into this with a lot of the information I needed. I knew her likes, dislikes, family, work ethic, life goals, relationship goals, sense of humor, etc. It was a definite leg up! And I had already built up the trust and habits of honesty and authenticity that are at the heart of all great relation'ships. I also already knew we could play together and really enjoy shared experiences. These were bonus points, for sure!

As true friends, we enjoyed an interdependent relationship based on mutual desire, shared values, and love. As our love deepened, the rewards became ever greater. Sometimes friendship is just friendship. And that's great too. We can all use as many loyal good friends as we can get. But, as with Stacie and me, it was the beginning of a deepening romance that grew and flourished.

The Holy Sacrament of Confirmation

While I was recovering from my injuries, which resulted from a motorcycle accident in June 1978, I chose Catholicism as my preferred religion, thus confirming the decision my mother made when I was baptized along with my brother, Rene, and my sister, Leslie. This process took approximately six months in a weekly class to complete. So on the twenty-ninth day of February in the year of our Lord and Savior 1980, just four months before I met Stacie, I received The Holy Sacrament of Confirmation; and as a newly confirmed Catholic, I was presented to the congregation at the Easter Vigil Mass on Sunday, April 6, 1980, at St. Eugene Church:

> The All-Powerful God, Father of our Lord Jesus Christ, by water and the Holy Spirit freed me from sin. He sent His Holy Spirit upon me to be my Helper and Guide. He gave me the Spirit of Wisdom and Understanding, the Spirit of Right Judgment and Courage, the Spirit of Knowledge and Love, the Spirit of Reverence in His Service. From that day forward, I received and will always have the seal of the Holy Spirit, the Gift of the Father and His peace is with me right now.

35

HONORABLE DISCHARGE CERTIFICATE UNITED STATES NAVY

On the twenty-ninth day of September 1980, I was awarded an Honorable Discharge, the highest discharge certificate a military member can receive. It reads:

> Honorable Discharge from the Armed Forces of the United States of America. This is to certify that DAVION MAURICE WOODMAN was Honorably Discharged from the United States Navy on the 29th day of SEPTEMBER 1980. This certificate is awarded as a testimonial of Honest and Faithful Service.

And from my heart, I will forever give the LORD all the honor, glory, and praise for this noble and patriotic accomplishment.

Preparing to Tie the Knot: Our Catholic Engagement

As a Catholic couple, our Catholic engagement period was a time to deepen faith, especially our personal and interpersonal spirituality (Preparation for the Sacrament of Marriage). According to the Los Angeles Catholic dioceses, we were required to complete a formal marriage preparation program for this purpose. The early days of our engagement were a wonderful, giddy time filled with a seemingly endless number of opportunities. For my fiancée, Stacie, there was the gown to choose, flower selections to make, and many friends to tell of the wonderful news. As a Catholic bride, she chose to be married in the tradition of her church, the Roman Catholic Church; those first weeks were also the beginning of a beautiful rite of passage which extended far beyond the wedding ceremony itself.

When I proposed to Stacie at the beginning of our engagement in July 1983, the decision to marry in the Catholic tradition was made. Our Catholic engagement lasted a full year. Beyond this, we met with our priest as soon as possible and discussed with him our wedding plans and the religious preparations we needed to make. Marriage rites differed slightly from church to church, and our priest was able to help us take our first steps toward a Catholic wedding. According to tradition, Catholic couples are married in the bride's home church, which was Saint Andrews Church in Pasadena, California, although this certainly was not a rule cast in stone.

During our engagement, our priest guided us through several preparatory steps. First, he insisted that my fiancée and me not live together. It was a minor step to take because she lived with her parents in Pasadena, California, and I lived with my mother in Inglewood, California. This stipulation had proven to be a major stumbling block for some couples. However, we considered the wonderful opportunity this situation presented.

Living apart during those final months of our engagement allowed us both to approach our wedding from a position of interdependence. When we did reunite in our new home, we had truly embarked upon a new beginning with each other. Additionally, both Stacie and myself needed to take part in a Pre-Cana Conference. This wedding preparation course was a weekly class, during which we had the opportunity to explore our understanding of marriage and the commitment we were about to make. The Pre-Cana Conference was moderated by married couples and delved into many aspects of marriage from spirituality and commitment to financial matters. The Pre-Cana conference made certain that we were entering into our marriage with realistic expectations and a firm commitment to each other.

To have our marriage sanctified or recognized by the Catholic Church, my fiancée and I completed all of the above-mentioned requirements. At that time, we realized in a world in which the preparation for a wedding can be short as the time it takes to travel to Las Vegas, our Catholic engagement was a refreshing step back to a more patient era. The commitment to the success of our marriage was shared by the local religious community. And each stage of the engagement process was geared toward ensuring that our wedding itself was a beautiful, meaningful, once-in-a-lifetime experience. As a result of this process, our engagement was exactly what we had hoped for.

Our Catholic Wedding: Stacie and Davion July 28, 1984

After dating for four years, we were united in marriage on Saturday, July 28, 1984 at 10:00 a.m. My bride was Stacie Ann Mickens, and the groom, of course, was myself, Davion Maurice Woodman. Our Catholic wedding was officiated by Reverend Daniel Fox; and the ceremony was held at my bride's beautiful Saint

Andrews Catholic Church in Pasadena, California. The matron of honor was my bride's oldest and only sister, Trena Spurlock, and the best man was my younger brother, Vernon "Sputdoll" Woodman. Bridesmaids were my bride's friends: Judy Wong, Cindy Warlick, Patrice Traylor, her cousin, Jamille Kenion, and my younger and only sister, Leslie Woodman. Groomsmen were my younger brothers, Rene Woodman, Richard L. Carey, Marcus Carey, and my bride's cousin, Harrison "Buddy" Bailey. The usher was our mutual friend, Michael Farmer; flower girls were my niece, Desiree Woodman, my bride's cousin, Kristal Jacques, my bride's niece, and my godchild, Franqui Spurlock; ring bearer was my bride's cousin, Robert Spurlock Jr.; soloists were Jenny Gonzales, Christina Gonzales, and Thelma Diaz; organist was Marlene Puccinilli; and our photographer was Joel Bogeberg.

History of St. Andrews Church
Established in 1927

> St. Andrews Church, an architectural masterpiece built in 1927, was the inspiration of Monsignor John McCarthy and architect Ross Montgomery. The Romanesque church tower and facade are replicated from Santa Maria in

Cosmedin, a church dedicated in 1123 and situated in Rome on the left bank of the Tiber River. The interior of the church is a replica of the Basilica of Santa Sabina dating to the early days of Christianity in Rome. In that church, situated on the Aventine Hill, marbles from many lands enhanced the columns. At St. Andrew's, the Corinthian-capped scagliola columns are the work of Italian artisans of the 20th century. The altar and baldachin are structured of white Carrara marble, and the mural above, depicting the legend of St. Andrew, was painted by Carlo Wostry, a Venetian master descended of Italian mural painters of the Renaissance. St. Andrews Church is recognized as an extraordinary replica of Romanesque architecture and is listed on the National Register of Historic Places.

Considered one of the seven sacraments or channels to God's grace, our wedding ceremony was a serious affair in the Catholic Church full of deep spirituality and rich symbolism. The ceremony began with an opening prayer by our priest, Father Daniel Fox, naming us and asking for God's blessing on our wedding day. My bride's sister, Trena, read several biblical passages which were selected by us and preapproved by the priest. The opening prayer and biblical readings were then followed by a short sermon about marriage given by the same priest. Afterward, the entire congregation stood as we took our vows, declaring our commitment to each other. The actual vows we spoke to each other were:

"I, Davion Maurice Woodman, take you, Stace Ann Mickens, to be my wife."

"And I, Stacie Ann Mickens, take you, Davion Maurice Woodman, to be my husband. I promise to be true to you in good times, in sickness and in health. I will love and honor you all the days of my life."

The priest then blessed us, joined our hands together, and asked us both, "Do you take Stacie Ann Mickens as your lawful wife? And do you take Davion Maurice Woodman as your lawful husband, to have and to hold, from this day forward, for better or for worse, for richer or for poorer, in sickness and in health, to love and cherish until death do you part?"

After we both joyfully responded, "I do," to the vows, the best man, my brother, Vernon, gave the bride's ring to the priest who blessed it and handed it to me to place on her finger. Then, the matron of honor, Stacie's sister, Trena, handed my ring to the priest, who blessed it and handed it to the bride to place on my finger. Then each of us said, "I take this ring as a sign of my love and faithfulness in the name of the Father, the Son, and the Holy Spirit."

The Catholic ceremony included Mass; accordingly, Father Fox asked for the "sign of peace," in which everyone shook hands with their neighbors. Then Holy Communion followed. Finally, Father Fox recited a concluding prayer and nuptial blessing asking for strength and protection for both of us.

After Our Wedding Ceremony, the Best Was Yet to Be

After the completion of our marriage ceremony, the wedding reception party where we received our family and friends for the first time as a married couple was nestled in the picturesque arroyo next to Pasadena, California's famed Rose Bowl, Brookside Golf Club. The country club's panoramic view gave our special occasion an air of distinction. On that cheerful wedding day with sore cheek muscles from smiling for hours, we both began a brand-new life together. Friends and family gave their gifts and best wishes to a joyful me and my blissful wife. But the greatest gift of all was the gift that we received from heaven above; it was love forever, ending never, our everlasting love.

Since that wonderful day, we have shared life's joy and pleasure; we have had plenty of this, it's true. But looking back, love was the real treasure for my new bride and me. Life has handed us challenges as it does to one and all, but our love has held us steady and it has not let us fall. Our wedding day was full of joy; tomorrow, we couldn't see. But one thing was for sure for the both of us: The best was yet to be.

We Had the Ultimate San Francisco Honeymoon

It was during the following weekend after our wedding, August 3–5, 1984, when we had the ultimate San Francisco honeymoon, traveling along California's scenic Pacific coastline rail on Amtrak's Coast Starlight from Los Angeles' Union Station to Oakland's Jack London Square where we hopped on a bus to the city of San Francisco. The Amtrak trip from LA to Oakland took a little more than eleven hours. Like many newlyweds, we dreamed of escaping to an exotic overseas locale for our honeymoon, but planning such a trip was as stressful as the planning of our wedding. Instead, we ventured to the magical city of San Francisco (no passport required!) and spent our first vacay as a married duo exploring all that the Bay Area's crown jewel had to offer.

With its wealth of scenic locations, top-notch restaurants, and numerous places to explore, San Francisco, the endless charming City by the Bay, brimmed with honeymoon potential. For a rustic romantic retreat with a world's away feeling (which was still within driving distance of the heart of the city), we stayed in our bridal suite at my wife's cousin Buddy's Victorian-style home in Oakland, California. He also was one of our groomsmen.

At our bridal suite, my lovely bride and myself took in sweeping views of the Golden Gate Bridge, unwound in the spa, and toasted our newlywed status with a candlelit bubble bath, rose petals on the bed, and a big bottle of champagne. Additionally, we were within walking distance from San Francisco's Nob Hill neighborhood where its historic cable cars conveniently stopped to whisk us away to explore the city's main attractions.

The next morning, on Saturday, August 4, my bride and I decided to explore San Francisco on foot, so we put on our walking shoes, caught the cable car to San Francisco, where we began roaming around Golden Gate Park's lush gardens and marveled over the exotic blooms at the Conservatory of Flowers. Then we checked out the touristy sea lion-filled Pier 39 at Fisherman's Wharf and hopped a ferry to Alcatraz Island where we took a haunting tour of the former prison. We followed that adventure with a stroll under the picturesque lanterns in San Francisco's vibrant Chinatown and browsed the shops for souvenirs. After that stroll, and craving some serious retail therapy, we shopped until we literally dropped at Union Square. Then, needing a little downtime, I chilled out alongside my love with a picnic in front of the iconic Painted Ladies Victorian Home.

It goes without saying that the iconic Golden Gate Bridge and one of the "Seven Wonders of the Modern World" was a major San Francisco attraction we couldn't miss. So we checked, biking across the big beautiful bridge off our bucket list, regrettably because of the excitement and awe of it all, we forgot to take tons of pictures in the process. But next on the agenda, my bride and I explored the city's impressive collection of museums. We toured the architecturally stunning de Young museum and the Legion of Honor, which was filled with beautiful ancient art. Then we visited the interactive Exploratorium. We also toured an aquarium, planetarium, natural history museum, and four-story rainforest inside the wondrous California Academy of Sciences.

When we were on our honeymoon, San Francisco was arguably one of the best food cities. Arriving on Friday evening and hungry as a bear, we dug into some hot clam chowder and oysters at Hog Island. The next day, we visited the bustling Ferry Building, a true food lover's paradise. For a romantic newlywed dinner, that evening we dined at the exquisite Paris-style bistro, Café Jacqueline, and I shared one of their signature souffle's with my new partner. Afterward, we enjoyed watching the classic movie, *Beverly Hills Cop*, starring Eddie Murphy at Foreign Cinema. My bride and me ended our honeymoon in San Francisco with a stop at the cult-favorite Mr. Holmes Bakehouse where we indulged guilt-free in a mouthwatering cruffin which was a deliciously fluffy muffin-meets-croissant pastry. It was yummy!

Our return trip home on Sunday, August 5, to Pasadena, California, as passengers on the Amtrak train, was too slow, uncomfortable, and tiresome. We both agreed that flying home on the return trip on a more faster and powerful passenger jet would have been the best mode of transportation. For we probably would have gained nine hours in the air instead of losing nine hours on the rails. However, my bride and I eventually arrived home safe and sound. And we praised the Lord's name.

I Had Quit Smoking!

After eighteen years of smoking cigarettes, on March 28, 1986, I successfully completed The Schick Smoking Control Program and had graduated with honors, for I had quit smoking! The Schick Centers for the Control of Smoking in Pasadena, California, awarded me the "Certificate of Achievement." Since quitting thirty-four years ago, I haven't smoked one cigarette to this day. And I praise the Lord's name.

36

OUR FIRST HOME IN PASADENA, CALIFORNIA: 1987–1992

After getting married, earning my college degree in business administration and renting the house that we lived in for three years, it finally happened in the summer of 1987 when I proudly used my well-deserved VA Home Loan to purchase our first home in Pasadena, California. Homeownership gave us both a stake in our new neighborhood's long-term stability, and it was our first significant investment as a married couple. After soon realizing the tremendous benefits of owning our home, we were delighted. In addition to the obvious benefits of home ownership, such as building our credit, stable monthly payments, opportunity to build equity, cheaper than renting overtime, tax advantages, and freedom to make changes to the property.

The first major benefit of owning our new home was the substantial amount of equity we received from the property as a gift from my new father-in-law, Thomas Mickens. As co-owner of this free and clear, quaint, two-bedroom, one-bathroom, 850-square foot house on one acre of land, Thomas spoke from his heart. "I want to give you guys a great start." And he sold the house to us for just $50,000, which was 45 percent or a little less than half of the property's appraised value of $110,000! Stacie and I both were over the moon and grateful to her dad for his kindness and generosity. After all, owning our home was so much more than just having a place to live!

> Pasadena is a city in California, northeast of downtown Los Angeles. In the center, Old Pasadena is a shopping and dining district known for its Victorian and art deco buildings. The strikingly modern Norton Simon Museum houses notable European and Asian art, plus a sculpture garden. The Rose Bowl is a sports stadium known for hosting the Rose Bowl Game, an annual college football clash usually held on January 1.

> Pasadena is also known as the City of Roses, Pasadena is most famous for its New Year's Day Rose Parade and Rose Bowl Game. Pasadena also boasts the world-renowned California Institute of Technology, whose alumni and faculty have garnered 32 Nobel Prizes.

The home in Pasadena, California, was also our son and only child, Davion Jr.'s first home (he was the first child to ever live there) after he was born on December 5, 1987. My young and new family lived in it until we moved to our newly constructed home in Ontario, California, on February 10, 1992. When our son was born, my wife, Stacie, had been working a little more than seven years as a Special Education Teacher with the Pomona Unified School District.

Meanwhile, I had been receiving monthly Social Security Disability Benefits, Medicare Health Benefits, and the GI Bill while I attended college full-time at Los Angeles City College and California State University, Los Angeles. Just under three years after earning my college degrees (associate in arts and bachelor of science) nine years after my devastating motorcycle accident and five months before the birth of my son, Davion Jr., I became gainfully employed. With the help of my wife's good friend, Marie, God blessed me with a federal job in the US Department of the Treasury/Internal Revenue Service as an Internal Revenue Agent on July 15, 1987.

Newlywed and My In-Laws

As a newlywed, I began my marriage on good terms with my wife's parents which has contributed to an enjoyable and long-lasting marriage to date. Yet, my wife's relationship with my parents was nonexistent. I bonded with my in-laws because I genuinely liked them, and they were kind, compassionate, and God-fearing people. My wife got the message that "her family was important to me because she was important to me." I wanted to feel closer to them because I wanted to be closer to her, and Stacie loved this.

Because both of my parents divorced when I was young and the dysfunction that existed between my mother and stepfather, I can only write about how my relationship with Stacie's parents has positively impacted our marriage. Stacie's mom and dad, Thomas and Frankie, were married for over fifty-seven years before Thomas's passing more than thirteen years ago. Thomas was the first man in my life who treated me like a beloved son and a friend; likewise, I was fond of him and loved him like a son who loves his dad. He reminded me of the song, "Color Him Father," released by funk and soul group The Winstons in 1969 when I was thirteen years old in the seventh grade at Monroe Junior High School in Inglewood, California, and it reached number two on the R and B charts. Parts of the lyrics to this song perfectly describe how I felt about my father-in-law, Thomas:

> Think I'll color this man father
> I think I'll color him love
> Said I'm gonna color him father
> I think I'll color the man love, yes, I will.
> —Source: LyricFind

We experienced many good times together like fathers and sons do, especially when we watched HBO's PPV Heavyweight Boxing Matches throughout the 1980s, which included heavyweight boxing champions Muhammad Ali, Larry Holmes, Michael Spinks, Evander Holyfield, Mike Tyson, Jerry Cooney, and George Foreman among many. With both of my wife's parents, we liked going to musical and dramatic stage plays, movies, Disneyland, and we enjoyed eating at high-quality restaurants of all cuisines. Frankie is now widowed, and Stacie continues to enjoy her company as she talks to her on the telephone weekly; we plan to visit her on our next trip to Pasadena, California, as we now live in a small town in Northeast Tennessee.

I reflect on the good memory that I had when I first met my mother-in-law, Frankie; she did what no other girlfriend's mother ever did for me. She always asked me to stay the night at their home because I lived too far to drive to my home late at night. The distance in driving time from Pasadena to Inglewood, California, was fifty-one-minutes on the southbound Harbor Freeway, so I gratefully accepted her warm invitation and hospitality.

Since the beginning of our marriage, I've had a fairly healthy relationship with my wife's parents, particularly with my late father-in-law, Thomas. Horror stories about monstrous mother in-laws, bigoted father in-laws and clueless sister or brother in-laws abound in pop culture. You can see in-laws at their worst in *The In-Laws* (1979 and 2003), *Hush* (1998), *Monster-in-Law* (2005), *Mother Knows Best* (1997), and *The Governor's Wife* (2008). Plus, nearly every week, someone is writing to a newspaper advice columnist about in-law trouble. With all this evidence that in-laws are bad news, I had contrarily a beneficial and rewarding connection with mine.

Put simply, I love my in-laws. For I didn't forget God's Second Greatest Commandment that "I love my neighbor as myself for love of you." As a believer in God's Word, I was also called to love my in-laws, no matter what. This didn't mean I ignored bad behavior, but it did mean that my first thought of them was love. And for these reasons, I've strived to practice being a loving son-in-law as well.

Loving my in-laws has meant praying for them too. Whether or not my in-laws were believers, in which they are, God called on me to pray for my new family. However, I understood that I had to be vigilant and not fall into the trap of praying like the Pharisee in Luke 18:11 ("Thank God I'm not like that sinner!"). When I find myself only praying that God cure other people of their faults, I will also pray that God work in my heart to help me see them like he does. I say a prayer of thanksgiving before I go to sleep each night, thanking God for all the benefits I have received from him on that day. I also pray for light to see what sins I have committed and the grace to be truly sorry for them, remembering that I need grace too and that sometimes, I'm part of the problem!

I have a thankful heart. I've appreciated my in-laws as a blessing from God. Because, after all, these are the people who have loved my wife and my son as much as I have. I'm grateful for this. And I have looked for other traits for which to be thankful versus looking for traits that I thought could have benefited from change.

I've respected my wife's parents for who they are. They are people of Godly wisdom and good character, although they haven't been perfect, but neither have I. Everyone has faults, but everyone has been made in God's image. This doesn't mean I've agreed with them on everything, but I treated them as I wanted to be treated. The Golden Rule isn't just for kids but for everyone, including me.

The essence of me, I am a very sensitive person. While growing up, I recall my mom telling me on occasions that I was too sensitive. Sensitive people like myself tend to take almost everything personal. As I've grown in the Christian faith throughout my life, I've come to realize and understand that actions and words spoken by others is not always personal. I've kept this understanding in my mind and heart over the years, which has helped me with my interpersonal relationship with my in-laws, particularly my mother-in-law. By faith, I successfully avoided developing very prickly skin when it came to interactions with them and filtering everything they say as a critique of me.

After I married, I decided ahead of time that nothing my in-laws can say was necessarily a direct attack on me. At times, it has helped me in my interactions with them when I give them the benefit of the doubt. Occasionally, I was much too quick to assume the worst or assign the wrong motive to something said or done by them. So I made it a habit to look at each interaction from the best angle and overlooked as much of the little stuff—those annoying habits or expressions—as I could (and hoped that they would do the same for me).

I have enjoyed my in-law's traditions as I married into a family whose traditions were very similar, yet different to my own. They celebrated all of the major holidays, especially Thanksgiving, Christmas, Easter, Memorial Day, and Fourth of July the same way my family had done; and for several years with my wife's family, I attended the midnight Christmas service at St. Elizabeth Catholic Church in Altadena, California. So it was easy for me to fit into my new family and celebrate with them. Most importantly, we shared the same Roman Catholic heritage and African American culture. However, my wife benefited greatly from having had a traditional family with both parents (mother and father) in a home that was filled with love and unity; whereas I myself came from a broken fatherless home due to my parent's divorce.

I asked my father-in-law, Thomas, lots of questions about his unique heritage; he was born and raised as a Roman Catholic in Key West, Florida, where he was the youngest child of three brothers and one sister and a descendant of Cuban (father) and Jamaican (mother) parents. Thomas came to Pasadena, California, with his older sister in 1946 when he was eighteen years old, and he spoke only Spanish at that time. From him, I learned many interesting things about his tropical island birthplace (While Thomas was a child in Key West, Florida, he befriended the famous author, Ernest Hemmingway, and would visit the writer from time to time at his beautiful Spanish Colonial house. On November 24, 1968, Hemmingway's house was designated a US National Historic Landmark.) and his Cuban and Jamaican culture. Knowing some of my in-law's background stories provided me with new insight into the persons they were and brought fresh understanding to our relationship.

Generally, there's no right way. This was especially important to keep in mind when I tackled holidays and other things that had been done a certain way in my family. Some people insist that their way is the only way, but I had a healthy relationship with my in-laws because I was able to appreciate their various points of view when it came to celebrations and traditions. This was crucial when we had our son,

Davion Jr. My wife's mother, Frankie, and my mother, Marlene, both graciously told us that they were fine with our spending Christmas morning in our own home by ourselves rather than at our childhood homes with them. That gift of understanding, how important it was for a new family to establish our own holiday traditions, was very precious to us and one we plan to pass on when our son marries.

Thomas and Frankie got it. Stacie married me, and this was all they needed to know to extend their love and good wishes. They might have chosen differently, but they understood indeed that it wasn't their choice to make. Their efforts of being gracious and loving provided our marriage with a life of mutual love and affection. They also were delighted in knowing that I would be the father of their grandchildren or might have already been the father of their grandson.

As their son-in-law, I didn't forget that my in-laws were the ones who raised the woman I love. I may not have agreed with everything they did, but I was appreciative of the fact that they had a large part in the person I married. Having had a healthy relationship with my in-laws took effort, but the payoff was worth it. After all, they are the grandparents of my son and the parents of my wife. Praise the Lord, Jesus Christ.

A Prayer to Saint Joseph the Worker for Employment

> God our Father and our Creator, You, bestow on us gifts and talents to develop and use in accord with Your will. Grant to me, through the intercession of St. Joseph the worker, as model and guide, employment and work, that I may, with dignity, provide for those who depend on me for care and support. Grant me the opportunities to use my energy and my talents and abilities for the good of all, and the glory of Your name. Grant this through Christ our Lord. Amen.

Working for the Internal Revenue Service/IRS: 1987–1989

On July 15, 1987, while we were still settling into our newly purchased home and after nine years of struggling and recovering from my devastating disability and graduating from college just three years earlier at California State University Los Angeles and after God our Father granted to me employment through the intercession of St. Joseph the worker, I became employed for the first time with the US Department of the Treasury/Internal Revenue Service at its Los Angeles District Headquarters Office, Examination Division, 300 N. Los Angeles Street, Los Angeles, California. After I was hired and received my orientation at the former Parker Center headquarters for the Los Angeles Police Department in downtown LA, I went on to train successfully for the position of Internal Revenue Agent at the paygrade GS-05 and a starting salary of $15,622 in Monterey Park, California; and then I was permanently reassigned to the IRS District Office, Examination Division in Glendale, California, where within one year on July 15, 1988, I received a career promotion from Internal Revenue Agent GS-05 to Internal Revenue Agent GS-07 with a $3,104 increase in salary of $18,726.

Working for the IRS was a great career opportunity to financially help support my new family life. Having had a college degree in business administration under my belt, I qualified for an upper-level position as an Internal Revenue Agent. The job description of Internal Revenue Agent required me to collect unpaid tax bills, examine complicated tax returns for businesses and negotiate payment options.

Working for the Internal Revenue Service had meant stability, competitive pay, and ample opportunity for promotion. At that time, I thought with the changing job market, its many benefits coupled with the prestige of working for the federal government (US Department of the Treasury) could go a long way toward helping me build a lifelong career I would have been proud of. It was cool to begin a career working for the Internal Revenue Service then because the agency was full of middle-aged employees nearing retirement age, and so the IRS needed some young blood like myself to help it collect taxes and keep our country afloat. However, after a little more than two years of government service with the IRS and terribly disappointed, I had to submit my resignation to the agency. This happened in response to its employment discrimination practices based on either my disability, race, or other reasons unbeknownst to me.

The Premature Birth of Our Son, Davion Jr., December 5, 1987

My wife, Stacie, was diagnosed with toxemia very late in her pregnancy. Instead of attending her baby shower, she was put into the Huntington Memorial Hospital in Pasadena, California, on December 4, 1987, just eight weeks before her due date of January 20, 1988, and ended up with an emergency c-section. The emergency c-section (cesarean section) resulted in the premature birth of our son, Davion Jr., on December 5, 1987. However, the surgical operation saved their lives. Afterward, the pediatrician who performed the emergency c-section entered the waiting room where I had been sitting on pins and needles, eagerly awaiting to hear the news about my wife and newborn child. Upon entering the waiting room, he announced my name as Mr. Woodman and introduced himself to me as Dr. Jordan.

He told me not to worry, my wife and son were both resting comfortably. The doctor also said that he was encouraged and relieved when he heard my four-pound seven-ounce infant son "screaming at the top of his lungs" at birth. Then he ended our conversation, I thanked him, we shook hands, and before he departed from the waiting room, he said to me, "Your son is tiny, but he's mighty!" A condition called persistent pulmonary hypertension (PPHN) occurs when premature babies with PPHN cannot breathe properly because they have high blood pressure in their lungs. But thank God, at my son's birth, in response to his first minutes of breathing air, the blood vessels in his lungs were relaxed and allowed blood to flow through them. Therefore, he was able to breath normally and without difficulty.

Our baby stayed in the hospital, and then he was released just after two days of observation on December 7, 1987.

Toxemia is a serious medical condition that usually affects women after 20 weeks of pregnancy. Also known as preeclampsia or pregnancy induced hypertension (PIH), toxemia is characterized by sudden elevated blood pressure and the presence of excess protein in the urine. If toxemia is left undiagnosed and untreated, the continuous increase in blood pressure can lead to deadly complications for both mother and baby. In fact, toxemia and other diseases associated with high blood pressure are leading causes of maternal and infant mortality worldwide.

Cesarean section or c-section is a surgical operation for delivering a child by cutting through the wall of the mother's abdomen.

My Spiritual Journey Toward *Christlikeness*

After the birth of my son, Davion Jr., I decided that I needed to become more Christlike. My spiritual journey toward Christlikeness started in 1988 when I began faithfully praying to God, reading, and meditating daily and nightly. As I pondered over these things, which are written in the Holy Bible, the heart of my understanding opened, and the Spirit of the Lord indwelled me. These works and belief persist to this day. As a believer, becoming more like Christ is a yearning that I've had most of my spiritual and religious life, and it is encouraging to know that God has the same desire for me. The Bible says that God "predetermined [believers] to be conformed to the likeness of His Son" (Romans 8:29). Making me Christlike is God's work, and I believe he will see it through to the end (Philippians 1:6).

I remain steadfast and true to my belief that God will transform me and all believers into Christlikeness. However, this hasn't meant I've done nothing for this miracle to manifest itself in me because it is written that faith without works is dead (James 2:14–26). Instead, the process commands me as believer in the Word of God to submit myself fully to the power of the Holy Spirit.

Becoming more Christlike has required of me to continuously work within the divine power of my faith, thereby giving of myself, a human sacrifice to the Almighty God.

Embracing the mind and character of Christ has meant my total surrender to God. It is written in Romans 12:1–2 that worship involves a total self-dedication to God. When we offer our bodies as "living sacrifices," our minds are renewed and transformed. When Jesus said, "Follow Me," Levi left his money tables immediately (Mark 2:14); so do I myself freely surrender all I have for the sake of following the Lord. As John the Baptist said, "He must be greater; I must become less" (John 3:30), so I've focused more and more on Jesus and his glory, losing myself in his will.

My amazing journey to becoming more Christlike has been the result of freedom from sin. Since Jesus lived a sinless life, the more I consider myself "dead to sin" (Romans 6:11) and living a life of purity; the more like Jesus I become. As I offer myself to God, sin is no longer my master, and I am more clearly identified with Christ (Romans 6:1–14). Jesus invites me every moment of my life to follow him, and I have his example of obedience (John 15:10), sacrificial love (John 15:12–13), and patient suffering (1 Peter 2:19–23). I also have the example of the apostles who modeled Christ (1 Corinthians 11:1).

When it comes to restraining sin in my life, I have divine help by praising the Lord for the Word of God (Psalm 119:11), the intercession of Christ (Romans 8:34; Hebrews 7:25), and the power of the Holy Spirit who indwells me (Romans 8:24; Galatians 5:16)!

My spiritual journey toward Christlikeness is the result of my Christian growth. When I was first saved, I was immature in Godly wisdom, understanding and knowledge, and inexperienced in grace and love. But then I grew. In each of these things, my charge is to become stronger and more Christlike.

Grow in the grace and knowledge of our Lord and Savior Jesus Christ. (2 Peter 3:18)

May the Lord make your love increase and overflow for each other and for everyone else. (1 Thessalonians 3:12)

Right now, at this moment, as I'm working on my Christian autobiography this twenty-first day of February 2020, it is a cold (37 degrees) and sunny afternoon in Northeast Tennessee where God is also working in me, blessing me, and the gift of writing among many gifts that he gives me.

We, who with unveiled faces all reflect the Lord's glory, are being transformed into His Likeness with ever-increasing glory, which comes from the Lord. (2 Corinthians 3:18)

One day, however, the process will be complete.

When He appears, we shall be like Him, for we shall see Him as He is. (1 John 3:2)

The promise of being fully Christlike in the future is in itself motivation for me becoming more Christlike now.

Everyone who has this hope in Him purifies himself, just as He is pure. (1 John 3:3)

37

My Son's Holy
Sacrament of Baptism

My son, Davion Maurice Woodman Jr., was baptized in the Church of St. Andrew's Church on April 30, 1988, at Pasadena, California, by Reverend Kevin Kostelnik. It was the same Catholic church where his mother and I had married more than three years earlier. This was a new experience for us because Davion Jr. was our first and only child whom we dedicated to God. At his baptism, I remember thinking, *This is indeed a very special occasion.* It meant that after his baptism, he would become a child of God. And I cherished that moment as I stood praising the Lord. The sponsors were my younger brother, Vernon Marcell "Sputdoll" Woodman, and my sister-in-law, Trena Mickens Spurlock.

The Catechism has rather powerful language to describe this spiritual event. Baptism is a sacrament in which the grace of justification is conferred. The gift of faith is given gratuitously by God through no proceeding merit on our part. Through Christ by the power of the Holy Spirit on the water, the baptized are "born of water and the Spirit" (John 3:5). We die to this sin and are given new life in Christ (Romans 6:3–6). Sins are washed clean through faith in Christ and by his merit. All sin is forgiven (Acts 2:38), including personal sin and original sin, that sinful nature into which we are born. We are made to belong to the body of Christ. For babies, baptism means original sin is washed clean and they are imprinted with God's gift of faith with the mark of those who belong to Christ.

We can ask for God's grace of faith for our child, wash clean the stain of original sin, promise to bring him up in the faith, and graft him into the body of Christ with this simple sacrament. Why would anyone not want to give these things to their child? So without reservation, I made the sign of the cross on my son's forehead. I affirmed the faith and promised to bring him up in it. I asked the priest to baptize him. And I watched as he washed in the name of the Father, the Son, and the Holy Spirit, made into a new creature and a little man of God.

I Worked as a Special Claims Representative at Farmers Insurance Group of Companies: 1989–2001

After leaving the US Treasury Department/IRS in 1989, and eleven years after my traumatic motorcycle accident, I soon found good and gainful employment as a Claims Representative at Farmers Insurance Group where I was successfully employed for nearly twelve years. The employment interview, hiring, orientation, and training all took place at Farmer's Regional Office in Simi Valley, California. It was a good company with excellent income and fringe benefits, including a company car, profit-sharing, 100 percent employer pension contributions and career opportunities, which were far superior to my former employer at the IRS. In the beginning, I liked working there. The management was very considerate of my daily life, and their motto was work to live, not live to work, and it was a flexible caring workplace. Claims was a fast-paced environment where I had to remain focused and diligent to complete my assigned workload within forty hours. The flexible work hours and benefits left me time for personal development and networking.

It was a great place with nice work areas and up-to-date facilities. The Branch Claims Office (BCO 69) where I worked for more than nine years handling automobile liability claims was located at 5461 East Telegraph Road in the City of Commerce, California. It was a very busy branch claims office. But needing more office space nine years later, our team moved to a larger branch claims office on Imperial Highway near Santa Gertrudes Avenue in La Mirada, California. Some coworkers had referred to our commerce office as the "armpit of the region" because of its location and the communities it served such as East LA, Compton, Watts, and South Central, Los Angeles, California. Working in a branch claims office was a very fast-paced environment with telephones ringing off the hook. Mondays and the day after a holiday were usually the busiest.

As a Field Claims Representative, I spent very little time in the office as did my coworkers because we were either too busy out in the field in our company cars, investigating accident claims or representing Farmers Insurance Company as witnesses to subrogation claims in civil court or representing our policyholders in mediation/arbitration disputes at Arbitration Forums, Inc.

The staff was friendly and helpful, and the managers cared about us. They always seemed anxious to provide me with as much education and tools as I needed to do a good job. Job training was ongoing and insightful. Overall, it was a culture that encouraged learning and advancement. So I took advantage of the opportunities and rapidly got promoted up the ladder from humble entry level Office Claims Representative to Field Claims Representative with company car to Senior Claims Representative, and finally, Special Claims Representative with more responsibilities and salary increases respectively.

Consequently, I learned a new profession at Farmers on the liability side of the insurance business, which improved my own personal resume and brand. This was a huge benefit as I was ambitious and aspired to move into management.

To increase my career opportunities and leadership potential at Farmers Insurance Group, I took advantage of their tuition paid program and earned my accredited master of business administration degree at the University of Phoenix on March 31, 1996. The MBA degree prepared me for advancement in my chosen career as a Liability Claims Manager with Farmers Insurance. The MBA curriculum was embedded in leadership development, organizational growth, and operations management. At that time, my in-demand MBA degree was perfect for a future as an executive and business leader at Farmers. And I had a yearning to foster my entrepreneurial spirit and become a critical thinker and decision-maker grounded in a Christian worldview. This future promotion within the organization would have made me a more well-rounded individual with a plethora of information to pass on to others.

However, the management at Farmers had other plans that were contrary to my ambitious plans. Farmers company culture became vastly different from the way it had been the first ten years to the point where change was done for the sake of change, audits were unfairly harsh, and they were looking for ways to get rid of people, especially those employees who were deserving of promotions and those ultimately retiring from the company and receiving company pensions. Additionally, management was getting worse with discrimination, nepotism, and lack of diversity in the workplace. It was apparent to me that the company was creatively cutting labor costs and pension costs by systematically terminating or forcing a large number of employees to resign for various reasons.

The main issue that was used to justify a termination or forced resignation was poor performance. This was an issue used unfairly by management against employees time and time again, and it was an issue that was very difficult to defend. In view of this dreadful trend at Farmers, I soon understood my plans for advancement into management were probably a 99.5 percent uncertainty. Therefore, within three months of 9/11, I submitted my resignation to the Branch Claims Manager of Farmers Insurance Group at La Mirada, California, and resigned my position as Special Claims Representative in June 2001; this action happened just shy of twelve years employment with the insurance company.

A quick recap of my typical day at Farmers Branch Claims Office consisted of reviewing new claims, returning voicemails to customers, drafting disclaimers and releases for bodily injuries and property damage, reviewing medical bills and estimates with management. I learned to diffuse volatile situations, explain complicated insurance processes with customers for understanding and customer service. I also learned negotiation skills with regards to settling bodily injury claims. Again, management was helpful and informative, many times working alongside me to resolve various issues. The most difficult part of working at Farmers was the frustration of wanting to assist all customers and failing to provide a favorable outcome for all parties due to policy limits or insurance guidelines.

The most enjoyable and satisfactory part of working for Farmers was the collaboration among coworkers and the various competitions and awards that motivated us.

Subsequently, after my resignation from Farmers Insurance Group in June 2001, I continued to work in the insurance industry as a claims representative. For several more years, I handled substandard (high risk) and standard automobile insurance claims for The General Insurance Company in Orange County, California; Sterling Insurance Company in Huntington Beach, California; and Mercury Insurance Company in Brea, California, respectively. I worked for each of these insurance companies in a relatively short duration throughout those years. But they gave me consistent employment and work, which helped provide for my family who depended on me for care and financial support. I finally departed from working in the insurance industry in 2005.

Raising Our Only Child

When my son was four years old, we decided to leave Pasadena, California, and move to Ontario, California. It happened in February 1992 where we purchased a newly built, single-story, 1,800-square-foot Lewis track home. This was the second time that I used my VA Home Loan to purchase a house. At that time, we talked about having at least two children—a girl and a boy—but decided to have only one child instead. And he brought great joy to our family.

Ontario is a city located in southwestern San Bernardino County, California, thirty-five miles east of downtown Los Angeles and twenty-three miles west of downtown San Bernardino, the county seat. Located in the western part of the Inland Empire metropolitan area, it lies just east of Los Angeles County and is part of the Greater Los Angeles Area. As of the 2010 Census, the city had a population of 163,924, up from 158,007 at the 2000 census.

A recent cover story by *Time Magazine* indicated that one in five American families are choosing to have only one child. This is a shift in previous decades where larger families were the trend. There are a lot of negative stereotypes that get attached to an only child, such as spoiled and selfish as well as positive labels, such as mature and independent. Regardless of research, every child is different and behaves and develops in his or her own way, regardless of how many siblings, if any, are in the house.

We decided to raise our only child, Davion Jr., by encouraging socialization and cooperation. When he was old enough, we enrolled him in day care, preschool, and after-school activities while we lived in Pasadena, California. We consistently and persistently encouraged this type of socialization for our son, even after we moved to Ontario, California, where he attended Cookie Land Preschool, kindergarten at Ranch View Elementary School, and first, second, and third grades at First Baptist Christian School in Pomona, California. Socializing and cooperating with others began to pay off because as he grew and interacted with other kids, Davion Jr., learned how to share and empathize with other kids, as well as standup for himself. By the time he was four or five years of age, we presented options to him for group activities and sports.

The first thing he did was join a soccer team with AYSO. Then he took karate and swimming lessons. He played T-ball and basketball, then we signed him up for the YMCA, and finally, he joined the Cub Scouts when he was eight years old. By joining sports activities and group activities rather than playing alone made it better for our only child to feel like he was part of a group. My wife and I also encouraged close relationships early. Even though Davion Jr. didn't have siblings, he became close with his cousins, neighbors, and good friends who provided the same type of bond. For recreation, especially during the summer vacations, we regularly went camping with our friends who had a bunch of kids that our son bonded with as well, and he had a blast!

Also, we realized that we had to preserve adult-only time. As an only child, Davion Jr., often felt like one of the adults because there were no other kids around. Consequently, we found it important to establish boundaries of adult and child time. When my wife and I had adult evenings out, we left our son with friends, relatives, and babysitters. Although we still had family time throughout the week, we made a conscious effort to teach our son that he could not always expect to be included in what we did and where we went.

Similarly, we spent quality time teaching our son to pay attention to others. This helped him understand how to help others and consider their needs. Also, we made clear to him that as his parents, we make the decisions. It wasn't uncommon for him as an only child to dictate meal plans or shopping preferences, so on those occasions, we reminded him that we are the adults who needed to make the adult decisions. On the other hand, we encouraged his input but maintained our decision-making power. For example, if he wanted hotdogs for dinner but we had already decided on meatloaf, then we explained that we were cooking meatloaf but allowed him to pick between broccoli or corn as the side dish.

Likewise, it was important that we taught Davion responsibility. When you have three or four kids, you might divide up chores so that the dishes get done and toys get picked up. With our only one son in the house, the mess was smaller (pieces of Lego), but we still held him accountable for cleaning it up. Truly, when it came to providing support, we reminded ourselves that we were his parents, not his friend. Parents of an only child might slip into the role of confidante more easily than the parents of multiple children. Therefore, we allowed our son to form adult relationships. We didn't feel threatened or disappointed when Davion turned to other adults for advice, support, or help. This was normal and similar to a kid with siblings going to them for help instead of their parents.

Finally, we kept up with Davion's developmental stages by introducing him early on to the concept of God in Christianity who is the eternal being who created and preserves all things, and we taught him such things as shoelace tying, bike-riding, the basic rules of etiquette, swimming, and other milestones at the same pace of his peers.

38

My Mother Died on Labor Day

My mother died of natural causes on Labor Day, September 5, 1995. She was only fifty-nine years old. It was several months from her diagnosis of sclerosis of the liver to when I got a call late Monday morning on Labor Day. The next-door neighbor's daughter, Sharon Taylor, said, "Marlene died, and she had been alone in her bedroom." My first thought as I sat on the edge of my bed was, "I should have been there." And then I stood up, walked inside my bedroom closet, sat down on the floor, and wept with my eight-year-old son, Davion Jr., who was sitting on the floor next to me. After I stopped weeping and still sitting down on the closet floor, I began wondering perhaps she died during the period of time between midnight and dawn or midnight and midmorning. However, only God knew exactly what time my mother died.

I had just seen my mother three days prior at our family home in Inglewood, California. It was on Friday, Labor Day weekend, when I brought her a tasty barbeque dinner from Woody's Restaurant. While we ate our hot barbeque meal and talked to one another as we sat at the kitchen counter, I couldn't help but notice how frail and sick she looked, and this concerned me; I was deeply hurt. Then moved with compassion, I embraced her and said, "You were a good mother." I said this because I didn't know how much time she had left to be with me.

During those months, I had made the trip back and forth several times weekly to Inglewood where my mother dwelled in the comfort of her home on West 79th Street. Whether she was intoxicated or sober, she had lost none of her cognitive abilities, so we talked as we often did about everything, including our family, the good old days when I was a child growing up in Los Angeles and Inglewood, the Hollywood movie classics and movie stars where we spent countless hours over the years watching television together, the Catholic church and religion, politics of the day, and what was coming. Though she was under a doctor's care and taking the prescription medication (Phenobarbital) used to control the chronic seizures she had been having, my mom refused treatment for her alcoholism. In her final days, she told me she was "ready to go and be with the Lord, and see her big brother, Vernon Jr., and grandmother, Mama Dear, again." It was apparent to me that she had been ready for this for many years, but she never abandoned her religious belief in Catholicism nor her Christian faith.

While mother was alive, I felt compelled to deal with her terminal illness (sclerosis of the liver), the social stigma of her alcoholism, and her eventual death by obedience to God's first commandment to honor her. What did it mean for me to honor my mother during this difficult time in my life, especially while she was being despised, devalued, rejected and excluded by family, friends and foe alike? Partly, it meant speaking well of her and politely to her. It also meant acting in a way that showed her courtesy and respect (but not to obey her if this meant disobedience to God). It meant following her teaching and example of putting God first. I understood that my mother had a special place in God's sight. During those emotional times, when I found it difficult to get along with her, I was still commanded to honor her, even now in her death.

Mom's prognosis changed from "days" to "weeks," so I felt comfortable going home for the weekend. I planned on coming back Labor Day, Monday, of the following week, which turned out to be the day she died. While at my home in Ontario, California, I talked multiple times, day and night with my wife, Stacie, about my mother's grave condition, and she always comforted me to ease the grief, making me feel better when I was sad. When the phone rang late that Monday morning, I didn't know who it was, but I knew it was wasn't good. In the coming days, however, I learned from my brother, Rene, when he found my mother, she was lying on her back with eyes closed and hands clasped (appeared to have been praying as the Catholic that she was), just moments before she took her last breath and yielded her Spirit to God (Jesus Christ) in heaven. Who knows about these things? Who understands the final acts of the dying? Is there anything more painful than for a parent to leave their child for any reason, particularly by dying?

Even so, I was blessed by God with these final loving words from my mother who said to me that Friday afternoon before Labor Day, "Davion, you were always comforting to me." I had known for a while that she certainly would die because she had battled alcoholism (a progressive disease) since I was a kid; and in the recent months leading up to her death, she had been diagnosed with sclerosis of the liver. Actually, though, I believe my mom died of a broken heart caused by the emotional losses and premature deaths of her beloved late brother, Vernon Jr., sixteen, and grandmother, Mama Dear, sixty-two, many years before. It had only been a matter of time until I had to face the heartbreaking reality of losing her at the young age of fifty-nine.

Back then, I realized she would not be there to ever see me be a loving husband, an outstanding father and role model to my only son, Davion Jr. She also would not see her grandson grow up and get married nor would she ever get the opportunity to be a great-grandmother to her three beautiful granddaughters. Neither would she be around to celebrate thirty-five years of marriage to my wife, Stacie, and she wouldn't be there to help me get through the difficult times, disappointments, and issues of life. I think of her every single day.

Through the heartbreak, change, and devastation, I have resolved some key issues of life in Christ whose carried me (and he still carries me) along my continuous journey to recovery and healing. And I am reminded with help from the Holy Spirit of Solomon's general observations (the Word in the Bible) that there is an appointed time for everything. And there is a time for every event under heaven:

1. A time to give birth and a time to die; A time to plant and a time to uproot what is planted.
2. A time to kill and a time to heal; A time to tear down and a time to build up.
3. A time to weep and a time to laugh; A time to mourn and a time to dance.
4. A time to throw stones and a time to gather stones; A time to embrace and a time to shun embracing.
5. A time to search and a time to give up as lost; A time to keep and a time to throw away.
6. A time to tear apart and a time to sew together; A time to be silent and a time to speak.
7. A time to love and a time to hate; A time for war and a time for peace.
8. What profit is there to the worker from that which he toils?
9. I have seen the task which God has given the sons of men with which to occupy themselves.

—Ecclesiastes 3:1–10 NASB

My beloved mother's funeral sermon was delivered by Father Walsh, pastor of St. Eugene Catholic Church. There was standing room only because her memorial service was so well-attended by her family and friends that all of the chairs in Angelus Funeral Home in Los Angeles were occupied, leaving only flooring for other attendees to stand. Her internment was at Holy Cross Cemetery in Culver City, California. Many people attended her funeral where her body was laid to rest. But my mother's soul was with Jesus Christ in Heaven.

I will always love and miss you!

If you look down from Heaven and see me, Mom, I hope you're proud of what I've done in my life...

I do it in honor of you. I will always love and miss you!

How I Honor My Dishonorable Father and Cruel Stepfather

After mom's death and her funeral, I had a rude awakening concerning both my father and stepfather. Twenty-four Father's Day have come and gone, and many sons and daughters have had wonderful times celebrating their dads. Others have felt sad, disappointed, and overwhelmed with memories of an awful childhood. I myself was betrayed, abandoned, denied, emotionally battered, treated with indifference and cruelty by both of them. I've suffered horrendously from their evil deeds. After years of turmoil, torment, and treachery, I finally have eternal peace and joy in Christ.

God hates how they both neglected and verbally abused me; and to this day, they are still selfish and uncaring. When evil thrashes my soul, my natural tendency is to become overwhelmed by it. While I was a kid growing up, I often felt shame and bitterness toward the dysfunction of my family caused by my father's abandonment and my stepfather's cruelty. When this happened, the struggles I faced and the spiritual battles I fought were much bigger than what I did on Father's Day. Every day was a battle for my mental, emotional, and spiritual health. The Apostle Paul describes it this way: "Our struggle is not against flesh and blood, but against the rulers, against the authorities, against the powers of this dark world and against the spiritual forces of evil in the heavenly realms" (Ephesians 6:12).

Paul writes that we do not fight battle with darkness with human weapons, but rather with spiritual ones (2 Corinthians 10:4–5), and he tells us how to win. He writes, "Do not be overcome with evil, but overcome evil with good" (Romans 12:21).

Because of what happened to me during childhood, I was especially vulnerable (emotionally, mentally, psychologically, and spiritually) to being overcome by evil. However, I learned to be vigilant by understanding the Word of God and avoided resembling the very things that I once abhorred. The only way I kept this poison from turning me into someone evil was to fight it back with good. Doing good did not necessarily overcome my father and stepfather (or any other evil person), but I overcame the evil done to me as I walked in the truth, light, love, and goodness of God.

Also, this meant that I didn't have to, and I never had a close or personal relationship with them. Nonetheless, they both harmed me and never asked me for forgiveness nor were they ever sorry or changed. Over time, I found out that it wasn't wise or safe to try to have a relationship with them anyway. And God didn't ask me to. But I overcame their evil against me when I applied the biblical antidote of doing good.

Despite their evil ways, I love my father and my stepfather, and I have always treated them with respect. Whenever they needed something from me, I gave it to them. When my father was in Kaiser Hospital for back surgeries, and when my stepfather was in Kaiser Hospital for the gout, I visited them both. As a son and stepson, I did what I was able to do to minister to their particular needs. My stepfather also played the role of groom's father in my wedding. Throughout the years, I invited them to my home for holiday celebrations and special occasions as well. I was kind to them, not because they deserved it; they didn't. I did it because I didn't want their evil to overcome God's goodness in me.

God calls me to love and to do good to even my enemies. When I've been injured by evil, I thought it was crucial that I didn't allow myself to be defined by what happened to me (victim) but rather by what God is doing in me and through me now. I have also overcome evil with good by making sure I worked through the lies that I've believed (or have been told) about myself so that Satan does not have a louder voice in my head than God's Spirit does. And as God has given me strength and courage, there was a time, several years ago, when I wrote my father a detailed handwritten letter about the many wrongs he did to my mother (She said to me one time, "He messed me up."), myself, and my siblings, and what he continues to do and fails to do, inviting him unsuccessfully to repent.

God's commandment tells me to honor my father. He doesn't qualify this by saying, only if my father is a good parent. But what does it mean to honor? When the Apostle Paul defended himself before the Sanhedrin, Ananias, the high priest, ordered that Paul be slapped across the mouth (abuse of power). Paul reacted to this abuse by calling Ananias a hypocrite and telling him that God would strike him. When Paul was informed that he had insulted the high priest, Paul immediately felt remorse because he knew God had said, "You must not speak evil of any of your rulers." Paul didn't stop defending himself, but he showed respect for the position of high priest, even though Ananias was corrupt (Acts 23:1–9).

I pray and ask God daily, "How can I honor my father for his position, not the way he carries out his position?" But right now, the only safe thing I continue to do is pray for my father and ask God to show him the evil of his ways. As I pray for my father, I'm careful not to be too hard on myself because I can't do anything else yet. So I just work on the larger battle while willing to overcome evil with good. As I obey in this area, God shows me how I can specifically honor my father, and he gives me the right and safe moments to do so.

The Home in Chino Hills, California

Several months after my mother's funeral, we sold our home in Ontario and moved to Chino Hills, California, in February 1996. Chino Hills is where we bought a beautiful 2,100-square-foot two-story Lennar single family home. Living there provided us with a sparse suburban feel, and most of the residents owned their own homes. There were a lot of restaurants, coffee shops, and parks. Many families and young professionals, like my family, lived in Chino Hills, and the residents tended to lean liberal and were Roman Catholic. We attended the local church at St. Paul the Apostle Catholic Church where we worshipped and fellowshipped every Sunday. The public schools in Chino Hills where our son attended Eagle Canyon Elementary School (fourth to sixth grade), Townsend Middle School (seventh to eighth grade) and Chino Hills High School (ninth to twelfth grade) were highly rated.

Chino Hills, California, also is where my son played all of his sports, and he was a good athlete. When he was eight years old, he began playing Chino Pop Warner football. The third year that my son played Pop Warner, I was chosen to be his football team's coach and equipment manager. And then the next few years afterward, Davion Jr. played Junior All-American Football at Community Park in Chino Hills. He also played Little League Baseball at the same park as well as NJB Basketball for St. Paul the Apostle Catholic Church and AAU travel basketball. My wife and I spent countless hours of enjoyment watching him practice for each sport and play the positions on his teams against their rivals.

The fond memories of our son's childhood sports are a timeless treasure, and during those years, he received numerous accolades, awards, and trophies for baseball, basketball, football, and soccer. Soon we hope to convert or transfer his many years of recorded sports playing from 8mm tape to DVD. Davion Jr. went on to play great basketball at Townsend Middle School under the coaching of my junior high school classmate, Stanley Stewart. Then at Chino Hills High School, he played junior varsity basketball and football; and he played varsity football for the Huskies when he earned his first varsity letter and jacket in the tenth grade.

My Beloved Grandmother, Needie (May 1996)

> Needie, your life was
> full of loving deeds,
> forever thoughtful of
> our special needs.

Today and tomorrow,
my whole life through,
I will always love and
cherish you.

Dedicated to God

Davion Jr. had just completed the third grade at First Baptist Christian School in Pomona, California, when we settled in Chino Hills. In every possible way, I continued dedicating my son to God as I always had done, which showed that I recognized him as a gift from God, and I was dedicating myself to being a godly example to him too. I understood that this dedication didn't secure salvation, but rather, it was a symbolic moment of entrusting my child's life to God's will. The Word (Bible) told me that my child was a gift and a reward from the Lord. The Bible verses and prayer for my son have assisted me in reflecting on God's Word and remembering his promises as I've dedicated my precious gift back to God in prayer.

I have faithfully and continuously asked God to bless my son with a healthy, productive, and godly life. When I pray for my son, I remember Scripture passages spoken by Jesus in Matthew 19:13–15: "Let the little children come to me and do not hinder them, for to such belongs the kingdom of heaven."

I pray that my son answers Jesus's call to come to him, that his thoughts will be pure, and that he will give himself to the Lord's work. As much as I love my son, Christ and our heavenly Father love him even more. Bless us, Lord, and all the gifts you give us.

39

My Son's First Holy Communion

It was on the second day of May in the year of our Lord and Savior 1998 in the Church of St. Denis in Diamond Bar, California, when my son, Davion Woodman Jr., received for the first time the most sacred Body and Blood of Our Lord Jesus Christ by the pastor Rev. Msgr. James J. Loughnane. The Body of Christ. Amen. After my son's First Holy Communion, we celebrated this blessed special occasion with our family, including his grandparents, Thomas and Frankie, and families of the other children who received their communion for the first time. And I praised the Lord Jesus Christ.

Moving Forward in Christ; A Christian Prayer
Dear Heavenly Father,

Thank You for this treasured son of mine. What a profound blessing he is to me! Although You have entrusted this child to me as a gift, I know he belongs to You. Like Abram offered his son, Isaac, to You, I dedicate my son to You, Lord. I recognize that he is always in Your care.

Help me as a father, Lord, with my weaknesses and imperfections. Rather than worry, help me to remember that my son is secure in Your mighty hands. Your love is perfect, Lord, so I can trust that Your love and concern for my son is even greater than mine. I know that You will protect my child.

Give me strength and Godly wisdom to raise my son after Your Holy Word. Please, supply supernaturally what I lack. Keep my child walking on the path that leads to eternal life. Help him to overcome the temptations of this world and the sin that would easily entangle him.

Dear God, send Your Holy Spirit daily to lead, guide and counsel my son. Always assist him to grow in wisdom and stature, in grace and knowledge, in kindness, compassion, and love. May he serve You faithfully, with his whole heart devoted to You all the days of his life. May he discover the joy of Your presence through a daily relationship with Your Son, Jesus Christ.

Help me never to hold on too tightly to this child, nor neglect my responsibilities before You as a parent. I promise to do everything in my power to raise my child according to the precepts in Your holy Word. I look forward with great anticipation to the day this child decides on his own to follow You.

Help me to be an example to my child, and to teach and train him in God's Word. Give me wisdom to discipline my son according to Your ways. May I never stop praying for this gift You've entrusted to me. Lord, let my commitment to raise this child for the glory of Your name cause his life to forever testify of Your faithfulness.

In the name of Jesus, I pray.

Amen.

Broken Chain: My Beloved Father-in-Law, Thomas (July 2006)

> We little knew that morning that
> God was going to call your name.
> In life we loved you dearly,
> in death we do the same.
>
> It broke our hearts to lose you,
> you did not go alone;
> for part of us went with you,
> the day God called you home.

You left us peaceful memories,
your love is still our guide;
and though we cannot see you,
you are always at our side.

Our family chain is broken,
and nothing seems the same;
but as God calls us one by one,
the chain will link again.

St. Paul the Apostle Catholic Church: Prison Outreach Ministry (2006)

In 2006, I got involved in the prison outreach program with St. Paul the Apostle Catholic Church. There has always been a great need behind bars but also great opportunity to see the Gospel transform lives. Getting involved with St. Paul's prison outreach program at Heman Stark's California Youth Training School (YTS) in Chino, California, was one of the most effective ways as a disciple of Jesus Christ that I was able to directly impact the life of an incarcerated seventeen-year-old boy. He was serving a long-term prison sentence after being convicted of felony kidnapping and rape of a fifteen-year-old girl. I started my prison outreach ministry by becoming his spiritual mentor and sharing the Gospel or the Good News with him.

This kid who was a ward (because he was a juvenile) of California's Youth Authority and had come from a fragmented or dysfunctional family, and as his mentor, I started providing a positive relationship in his life. I believe God created us with the need to know and be known as well as to have relationships that foster our spiritual growth, hold us accountable, and encourage us to press toward healthy goals. As his spiritual mentor, I'd like to think that I was a loving friend to this young lost soul who was locked up in prison. While demonstrating Christlike living, I offered him accountability and honest feedback. But he didn't respond to my outreach as well as I had hoped. During my first visit with him at the youth facility, he told me that he was only seeing me to get out of lockup.

For several months in 2006, I visited my mentee at the youth facility with the goal of building a positive relationship with him. I didn't try to fix him or change him. As his spiritual mentor, my intention was to be wise and loving toward him while establishing appropriate boundaries that didn't encourage passiveness, dependency, or manipulating me for gain. Unfortunately, the last time I went to see him, his correctional officer informed me that he refused to see me and he didn't want to see anymore. This hurt my feelings at first because I believed we had made a lot of progress, and I wondered why he did this. Then I understood that it is very easy to forget that no human being can instigate change in another's life. So being comforted by the Holy Spirit, I believed in my heart I had planted good seed in this young man's heart with my encouragement and prayers but knowing the truth that only God is the one who is responsible for true life change.

Facebook: Sharing the Good News, the Gospel of Jesus Christ (2013–2020)

By the grace of God, social media gave me (a middle-aged Christian man) more ways to further the work of the Lord and share the Gospel. After I joined Facebook in February 2013, I wondered what I was going to share on my posts. Then I remembered how many times I heard in the Gospel and throughout my Christian life as a disciple of Christ how important it is to share the Gospel. The prophets taught "every member a missionary." In the scriptures, the Lord declares that everyone should have the opportunity to hear the Gospel. Jesus left the disciples with these last words of instruction referred to as the Great Commission: They were under His authority; they were to make more disciples; they were to baptize and teach these new disciples to obey Christ; Christ would be with them always.

Whereas in previous missions, Jesus had sent his disciples only to the Jews (Matthew 10:5–6 NKJV), their mission from now on would be worldwide. Jesus is Lord of the earth, and he died for the sins of people from all nations. We are to go—whether it is on social media, next door, or to another country—and make disciples. It is not an option but a command to all who call Jesus "Lord." We are not all evangelists in the formal sense, but we have all received gifts that we can use to help fulfill the Great Commission. As we obey, we have comfort in the knowledge that Jesus is always with us (Matthew 28:18–20 NKJV).

For seven years, while I was on social media, the Lord gave me the divine opportunity each day to reach out to nonbelievers through Facebook and faithfully share the Gospel. I was very enthusiastic and eager about sharing the gospel on Facebook because I had done it in other settings most of my Christian adult life. Furthermore, not only did I do this because Jesus *commanded* me to, but also, I wanted to! Having the fantastic news of the Gospel, I *wanted* to share it with my fellow Christians, family, friends, and the world alike. And I'd venture to say the Good News is the most important news of all!

Prodigal Son Turns to Drugs; the Battle with My Son's Addiction

"I'm scared and I'm sorry, Dad," Davion Jr. said to me when I leaned over and hugged him as he laid on his back in the hospital bed with an IV drip in the vein of his left arm. And suddenly, he began weeping and said to me, "I'm scared and I need help!"

Then I held his hand and responded to his dramatic plea for help with a prayer for healing:

> Lord, You invite all who are burdened to come to You. Allow Your healing hand to heal my son. Touch his soul with Your compassion for others. Touch his heart with Your courage and infinite love for all. Touch his mind with Your wisdom, that his mouth may always proclaim Your praise.
>
> Teach him to reach out to You in his need, and help him to lead others to You by his example.
>
> Most loving Heart of Jesus, bring him health in body and spirit that he may serve You with all his strength.
>
> Touch gently this life which You have created, now and forever. Amen.

My twenty-nine-year-old son, Davion Jr., wept as I prayed for him in his Arrowhead Hospital bed in San Bernardino County, California. After praying and witnessing him struggle in agony due to a near fatal injury, I was overcome with emotions of compassion, empathy, relief, and fear. Davion's fight with addiction started when he was in middle school. He began experimenting with drugs like marijuana. His continued use of marijuana included cigarettes, alcohol, and other addictive narcotics, which he began abusing in his senior year in high school.

Davion used to play every team sport he could (soccer, baseball, basketball, and football). From elementary school to high school, we were constantly running from activity to activity, and he loved it. He wasn't afraid to try and do things, even if he wasn't good at it—he just wanted to have fun and would get out there and do his best. During his senior year in high school, he noticed that his coaches weren't letting him play much on his junior varsity basketball and varsity football teams. I knew it bothered him, and he went from a kid who loved being with his friends and playing basketball or football for the love of it to becoming attracted to and distracted by girls and the things of the world.

It was heartbreaking to watch, and it wasn't long before he stopped playing everything and didn't want to join any teams, despite the fact all his friends played. He just wanted to quit sports. But it wasn't until years later when I discovered my son's internal battles with insecurities and anxieties which drove his need to use drugs during social gatherings.

After Davion graduated from high school, he married his high school sweetheart, Liz, and she gave birth to my beautiful granddaughter, Larissa Marlene, on September 6, 2006. Shortly after Larissa's birth, in February 2007, they moved away to live with Liz's family in Johnson City, Tennessee. Once Davion settled in Tennessee, he discovered opioids, which inevitably led him and our family to rock bottom. My wife and I both felt betrayed.

When Davion returned home over three years later after his divorce from Liz, I noticed he was skinnier, his hair was long and disheveled, he was easily irritable and not interested in spending time with our family. As Davion moved further and further away from the person he once was, my wife and I grew more and more concerned. We often found ourselves praying together to the Holy Spirit for guidance, wisdom, and rejoicing in his consolation; and we asked this through Christ our Lord. Hopefully, we thought, this was all just a phase he would soon grow out of.

As time went on, my son became unrecognizable to us, and my wife and I were in denial. Watching him struggle and reflecting on what his addiction was doing to our family, it was in those moments when I often felt helpless. Occasionally, I even treated Davion's addiction as if I caused it.

For years, I lived under the "This cannot happen to my son" that physically and emotionally affected me. As a father and a parent, it was difficult to come to terms with the fact that my adult child had a serious problem. My wife and I foolishly chose to believe Davion's lies and sent him thousands of dollars when he was away living in Tennessee in his own apartment—money he used to fund his addiction. While my wife and I were not to blame for our son's choices and his flawed behavior, we were guilty of enabling him and allowing denial to cloud our judgment.

After years of self-destruction, incarcerations, probation, and numerous trips to rehab, my son inevitably hit rock-bottom, which was caused by near fatal injuries he sustained from multiple stab wounds to his torso by the hands of a knife-wielding maniacal drug addict; consequently, by the divine intervention of God's mercy, he survived this violent and brutal attack on his life. Having had enough, Davion Jr. was able to admit he needed professional help.

After more than one week in the hospital for the treatment of his stab wounds followed by three months as an outpatient at Inland Valley Recovery Center in Upland, California, Davion Jr. was able to turn his life around, and my family was able to start our long and difficult journey toward a happier and healthier process. It was difficult for his mother to accept the fact that our son needed to go to rehab. Perhaps the most rude awakening part of the experience was when she visited him in the ICU at Arrowhead Hospital where he was being treated for his life-threatening injuries. There, he had a drainage tube inserted in his collapsed right lung to drain the rapid buildup of fluid and an IV drip in the vein of his left arm, which was used to administer antibiotics for the prevention of an infection, hydrate and boost his energy levels, and release the unwanted toxins in his body.

After visiting him at the hospital, his mother later told me she was forced to see our son and his addiction in its truest light. In that moment in the ICU, there was no more denying that our son had a real problem.

Accepting that our son was a drug addict and helping him get treatment at Inland Valley Recovery Center was half the battle. For years, my wife and I hid behind denial and enablement. It took time, but finally we realized that we had to admit he had a drug problem and we had to stop enabling him. In fact, the only thing that we needed to do instead of denial and enablement was to help our son through faith and by the grace of God. Once we admitted that Davion was a drug addict and alcoholic, we stopped enabling him and sought refuge among family members, friends, and a faithful Christian prayer group at Calvary Chapel who were supportive of our situation, including Alcoholics Anonymous.

The Father Waits with Open Arms

From my study of this story (the Prodigal Son) and several Bible commentaries, the father is considered to be God. There is no condemnation for the son, no criticism, but just patient love. One day, the son realizes his folly and decides to return to his father and work as a servant since he believes he has sinned. Was the father waiting with a rod, a stick, all his servants to teach him a lesson? No, love, God is always waiting to receive his children with open arms, and that is the turning point in anyone's experience when after having committed wrong; he feels the Father's love and is not afraid but responds to the love that is waiting patiently.

In the case of the Prodigal Son, he was received with open arms. A banquet was prepared upon his return. I, too, had let my heart be moved with compassion, not pity, with love that transformed and redeemed my son, love that called my son (the Prodigal) home. It's the right of every child of God to feel loved.

After freeing myself from the bondage of denial, I was finally able to focus on my professional career as a California Real Estate Broker (which was a challenge at age sixty-one), my own health, and most importantly, my family's healing process. To this day, and by the mercy of God, I am happy to report Davion Jr., who's now thirty-two-years-old, has been sober for more than three years. He's involved with our local Christian church, Calvary Church, working in a prayer group. He worked full-time at Frontier Treatment Facility, and he is now working full-time at AO Smith, a global water heater manufacturing company, and continues to work on his recovery every day here in Johnson City, Tennessee. It is my hope that by sharing this story, I am able to help other families find the strength they need to seek help and support for a family member struggling with addiction.

Our New Retirement Home in Small Town, Northeast Tennessee: A Blessing of Deliverance

Before my wife retired from Pomona Unified School District (PUSD) on June 3, 2016, after thirty-seven years of teaching Special Education, we had considered moving from Southern California to Tennessee to improve our quality of life and live close to our granddaughters, Larissa and Maliyah. On February 16, 2018, we arrived in our cars after a three-day trip from Ontario, California (2,100 miles), to our newly built retirement home in a small town near Johnson City, Tennessee (a fast-growing town in the extreme northeastern corner of Tennessee). Since our relocation and continued settling, this has been a blessing of deliverance because the beautiful rustic area where we live has become popular for retirement with its low-cost living and its friendly, welcoming people. Johnson City is near Kingsport and Jonesborough and only about sixty miles north of the City of Asheville, North Carolina. So far, we've enjoyed plenty of great recreation in the area and the nearby mountains.

I like the more relaxed style of living, and I appreciate the friendly nature of the people who live in Tennessee. However, Tennessee is a conservative state and it has taken a liberal like myself from Southern California a little adjusting. The state works hard to attract retirees. People from other states all across the nation have settled here for its lower cost retirement. East Tennessee State University is in our town with over 13,000 students. Al Capone was said to have had bootleg liquor operations in Johnson City. Manufacturing (the industry in which my son is gainfully employed), construction, and education fuel the economy. Even though my wife is a California-retired teacher (STRS), her passion is still in the classroom, teaching young students. Currently, she is a substitute teacher for Johnson City School District.

The small Northeastern Tennessee town where I live is located below West Virginia and to the west of North Carolina. It is near the Blue Ridge Mountains. Bluegrass music is big in Johnson City. The Big Plum Festival is a major annual arts and musical festival. East Tennessee State adds to our local culture. Johnson City serves as a regional medical center for northeast Tennessee and southwest Virginia, along with parts of western North Carolina and Kentucky. Although there are two major hospital systems in the Tri-Cities, only one—Mountain States Health Alliance—has a presence in Johnson City. Additionally, the James H. Quillen VA Medical Center where I am an enrollee, located in the Mountain Home community in Johnson City's southside, serves veterans like myself in our four-state region. The VA center is closely involved with the ETSU College of Medicine.

The State of Tennessee offers a rich culture, natural beauty, and a low cost of living. Unlike California, Tennessee doesn't have a state income tax. Since living in this state, we've received an additional $250 per month in income. This is the amount not taken out of our retirement check for state income taxes, and we haven't owed any state income taxes at tax time. Tennessee is a great place for music lovers such as myself. As a lover of jazz, blues, rock, and some country, I have found Tennessee's music scene and music history thrilling. There are plenty of small live venues, plus legendary spots like Grand Ole Opry. I have yet to visit Loretta Lynn's ranch and Sun Studio or walk in the footsteps of B.B. King and Aretha Franklin.

Tennessee whiskey is in a category of its own. Tennessee whiskey is an industry term that refers to whiskey made according to a specific method. The most famous example of Tennessee whiskey? Jack Daniels. Jack Daniels—or "Jack" as locals call it—is big in Tennessee. On my bucket list, I plan to visit the Jack distillery and take a tour.

Festivals and fairs are big in Tennessee. I plan to go to all of them. Festivals, including the ever-popular Bonnaroo, are a big part of life in Tennessee. I like both small local fairs or big events like the CMA Music Festival. Tennessee is a place that has something for everyone.

Since we've lived in Tennessee, our family has visited Dollywood twice. And we've taken my granddaughters with us both times. We hope to visit the amazing Graceland soon. We have always been fans of music legends Dolly Parton and Elvis Presley. I plan to take our next road trip to Graceland and/or take our guests there when they visit us in our new Tennessee home.

The National Civil Rights Museum in Tennessee is an interesting place where I hope to visit soon. I want to learn more about the Civil Rights Movement and its greats. My home here in Tennessee is a good place where I can dive into that history. Memphis is home to the National Civil Rights Museum and an Underground Railroad museum. Nashville was the site of famous sit-ins during the Civil Rights Movement.

Near the top of my bucket list, I plan to visit the Great Smoky Mountains National Park because mountains, forests, waterfalls, and wildflowers appeal to me. So I think I'll love Great Smoky Mountains National Park. When we visit the park, we'll probably stay in a nice hotel in a nearby town. Or perhaps, if given ideal weather conditions, opt for camping or cabins inside the boundaries of the park.

I enjoy eating good-tasting Southern cuisine that reminds me when I was a kid of Mama Dear's Texas-style made from scratch homecooked meals. It's my African American culture. And just the same, I like eating Tennessee BBQ, which generally means dry-rubbed ribs. Tennessee barbeque is slow-cooked and succulent. It can be "wet" or "dry," but a spicy dry rub is the classic Tennessee barbeque option. Since I've lived here, I haven't missed out on Tennessee barbeque.

Fall colors in Tennessee are stunning. Fall colors are not only worth seeing in New England states like Maine and Vermont but also here in Tennessee. Tennessee trees put on a stunning display every fall. Unlike some other Southern states and my home state of California, Tennessee really experiences all four seasons, including a beautiful autumn. And of course, we enjoy the snow during the Christmas season.

Bottom line, Moving to Tennessee was a great opportunity to bring me close to my granddaughters and steep me in history and culture while I've enjoyed a low cost of living. The state has a lot more to offer new transplants like my family and myself, whatever our interests.

40

PRAYER OF THANKSGIVING

O my God, I thank you for all the benefits which I have received from You to this day. All generations have called me blessed because You have done great things for me, and "Blessed is the man who fears the Lord" (Psalms 112:1). Especially since my devastating motorcycle accident back in June 1978, You, have blessed me with my life in Jesus Christ, You, have restored my health, mended my bones, cleansed and closed my wounds, and brought me to recovery, healing and restoration. Lord, You, continue to bless me and all the gifts you give me. Through Christ our Lord, You, have granted me employment and work, so that I was able to provide for my family who depended on me for care and support. You granted me, and continue to grant me the opportunities to use my energy and my talents and abilities for the good of all, and the glory of Your name.

God our Father and our Creator, during rehabilitation for my wounds and broken bone, and continuous recovery, You, have consistently and faithfully restored me to a condition of good spiritual and physical health, ability to work, and the like. You have bestowed on me the following accolades, accomplishments, gifts, talents and benefits to develop and use in accord with Your will:

- Former recipient of Social Security Disability Benefits (1978–1988)
- Former recipient of Medicare Benefits/Social Security Administration (1979–1988)

- Former recipient of the GI Education Bill for college (1980–1984)
- Received the Holy Sacrament of Confirmation (February 29th 1980)
- Recipient of the Certificate of Achievement by the College Scholarship Service of the College Board for recognition in the 1981 Talent Roster for Distinguished Academic Performance at Los Angeles City College, a two-year college (January 1981)
- Received the Degree of Associates in Arts (June 30, 1981)
- Received the Degree of Bachelor of Science in Business Administration (December 8, 1984)
- Received the Degree of Master of Business Administration (March 31, 1996)
- Successfully passed the California Basic Educational Skills Test/CBEST (June 20, 1998)
- Successfully passed the California Real Estate Broker Examination (May 2006)
- Successfully passed the National Mortgage Licensing System/NMLS Examination (2011)
- Currently possess a California Real Estate Broker License which is valid through 04/05/2020
- Formerly possessed a California Emergency 30–Day Substitute Teaching Permit (2007–2011)
- Formerly possessed a National Mortgage Licensing System/NMLS License (2011–2013)
- Recipient of the Farmers Insurance Group, Inc. Employees' Lump Sum Pension Distribution (November 22, 2012)
- Formerly employed as an Internal Revenue Agent with the US Department of the Treasury/Internal Revenue Service (1987–1989)
- Formerly employed as a Special Claims Representative with Farmers Insurance Group, Inc., (1989–2001)
- Formerly employed as a Substitute Teacher with Pomona Unified School District (2007–2011)

- Formerly in business as a Broker Associate with New Source Lending Mortgage Brokerage (2011–2013)
- Early retirement (57 years old) from employment (November 22, 2012)
- Formerly self–employed as a successful California Real Estate Broker (2006–2017)
- Formerly self–employed as a successful California Mortgage Broker (2006–2013)
- Formerly employed as an Armed Security Officer with Inter-Con Security Systems (2016–2017)
- Current recipient of Social Security Retirement Benefits since November 22, 2017
- Currently a VA Healthcare Enrollee with the VA US Department of Veterans Affairs
- Recently used my VA Home Loan benefit to purchase a newly built retirement home in small town, Washington County, Northeast Tennessee (February 12, 2018)
- Completed the word–processed manuscript for my autobiography (March 22, 2020)

CONCLUSION

Within a few months after relocating and becoming a resident in the beautiful state of Tennessee, I had an epiphany moment of faith by simply forsaking all and taking Christ. This epiphany moment of faith has significantly changed my religious life. For I now live as a maverick Christian, which is incidentally attributed to my ever-increasing faith in Christ alone. While I've been a spiritual being most of my life, I have at all times believed in God's awesome Word and all that he has taught because he said it, and his Word is absolutely true. As a maverick Christian, I maintain the right as a believer in Jesus to freely understand the Holy Bible for myself, and I'm not part of a denomination, but I am now part of an unbranded movement of believers in Jesus Christ, led by the Holy Bible as God's Word, and led by the Holy Spirit. Therefore, I follow the Lord Jesus Christ exclusively, and I'm not bound by creed and the controls of religious institutions, and when and where I gather with other Christians in homes, church buildings, or other locations, we follow our great Shepherd, the Lord Jesus Christ.

> When all has been heard, the end of the matter is: fear God [worship Him with awe-filled reverence, knowing that He is almighty God] and keep His commandments, for this applies to every person. (Ecclesiastes 12:1, Amplified Bible)

FAVORITE QUOTE

Living one day at a time; enjoying one moment at a time; accepting hardships as the pathway to peace; taking as he did, this sinful world as it is, not as I would have it; trusting that he will make all things right if I surrender to his will; that I may be reasonably happy in this life and supremely happy with him forever in the next. Amen.

ABOUT THE AUTHOR

Trust in God, No Matter What

Davion Maurice Woodman, Sr. has been among the most blessed of men in his generation, known for his life example of a righteous, sincere, and sensitive man who has suffered. He has gone through the highest "highs" and the lowest "lows" in his life by enjoying; then as a child, losing his father to incarceration, and the rest of his family members to death, mental illness, alcoholism, dysfunction; and later, as a young adult, losing his own health to a traumatic motorcycle accident.

Amid his suffering, Davion has desperately forsaken all and has remained faithfully steadfast in the redeeming power of God. After all his painful experiences, his eyes have opened to know God. By repentance and prayer, his relationship with God has been renewed time and time again, and he has restored his health in body and spirit that he may serve God with all his strength. Through his life, he has learned about God's sovereignty over his suffering. Life for him has meant a journey of knowing the Lord and trusting him in every moment, especially the darkest ones.

CPSIA information can be obtained
at www.ICGtesting.com
Printed in the USA
LVHW020552240321
682296LV00008BA/57

9 781098 065294